The Two-Party Trap

ALSO BY STEVEN VERRIER
AND FROM MCFARLAND

*George Gordienko:
Canadian Wrestler, Artist and Renaissance Man* (2022)

*Gene Kiniski:
Canadian Wrestling Legend* (2019)

*Professional Wrestling in the Pacific Northwest:
A History, 1883 to the Present* (2017)

The Two-Party Trap

*Recipe for Dysfunction
in American Politics*

STEVEN VERRIER

McFarland & Company, Inc., Publishers
Jefferson, North Carolina

ISBN (print) 978-1-4766-8945-6
ISBN (ebook) 978-1-4766-4703-6

Library of Congress and British Library
cataloguing data are available

Library of Congress Control Number 2022033871

© 2022 Steven Verrier. All rights reserved

No part of this book may be reproduced or transmitted in any form or by any means, electronic or mechanical, including photocopying or recording, or by any information storage and retrieval system, without permission in writing from the publisher.

Front cover images © 2022 Shutterstock

Printed in the United States of America

*McFarland & Company, Inc., Publishers
Box 611, Jefferson, North Carolina 28640
www.mcfarlandpub.com*

Dedicated to all who are committed
to returning American democracy
to its true owners—the people

Table of Contents

Preface	1
Introduction: How Did It Come to This?	3
1. Bouncing on the Rails	7
2. The Gingrich Effect	13
3. "Independents" and "Democracy"	19
4. The Electoral College	23
5. Microcosm of the Nation: Spotlight on Washington State (Part 1)	28
6. Microcosm of the Nation: Spotlight on Washington State (Part 2)	39
7. A Brief Historical Survey of the U.S. Congress	50
8. States, Municipalities, and Counties	57
9. Lay of the Land, 2018 (Alabama–Montana)	65
10. Lay of the Land, 2018 (Nebraska–Wyoming and DC)	76
11. Coming Out of the 2018 Midterms (Pacific Coast, Western Interior, Midwest, and Southwest)	90
12. Coming Out of the 2018 Midterms (Northeast, Mid-Atlantic, Appalachia, and Southeast)	100
13. Playing a Field of Two	108
14. Stacking the Deck	115
15. Missed Opportunity: The Kavanaugh Hearing	127
16. Three Walls	138
17. Spinning the Mueller Report	143

18.	Justin Amash: A Bold Statement	148
19.	July–September 2019: Embarrassing Developments	152
20.	Impeachment and Acquittal: A Foregone Conclusion	161
21.	Covid-19: Division Trumps Unity	173
22.	Law and Disorder	177
23.	Flipping (and Flopping) the High Court	180
24.	The Year 2020 In Review: A Step Back	183
25.	A Sad Ending	189

Epilogue: Let It Go — 196
Bibliography — 199
Index — 217

Preface

The dividing line between Republicans and Democrats has widened considerably in recent times, as illustrated during the July 2018 televised House Judiciary Committee hearing into alleged anti–Trump behavior by FBI agent Peter Strzok. Views on whether Strzok had betrayed his agency and nation seemed to hinge entirely on party affiliations in what a *Guardian* headline labeled as "Washington's partisan dysfunction." A *Vanity Fair* headline went a little further: "The Peter Strzok Hearing was a WWE-Style Bipartisan Beatdown." Not far into the story, writer Tina Nguyen declared, "In fact, if there was any difference between the Strzok hearing and a wrestling match, it was that the Republicans and Democrats on the committee were actually out for blood."

Nguyen's comment seems to capture not only the spirit of a bitter 2018 House committee hearing but the nature of American politics in general during the current era. In recent times American politics seems to have borrowed, more liberally than conservatively, from the wrestling world, and there are probably times that a strong case could be made to move local, state, or federal political bodies from the usual seats of government to the nearest arena. But perhaps even more convincing to many commentators and observers is the argument—put forth regularly in recent years—that Americans are fed up with the current nature of politics and are ready to separate themselves entirely from the antagonistic two-party system that has riven a country whose well-being has always depended on unity.

The truth is, though, that while millions of Americans are clearly fed up with present-day hyperpartisanship and a two-party system whose failings have become all too obvious, relatively few of the large bloc of voters identifying themselves as "independent"—often in the 30 to 40 percent range, according to recent polls—actually end up casting their ballots for alternative candidates. The vast majority fall back to their major-party preference, in effect holding their noses and voting either (D) or (R) … again and again and again.

What follows in this book is an account of why anything but a two-party stranglehold in the United States seems a dim prospect anytime soon. *The Two-Party Trap* traces the utter domination of the "major parties"—even extending to "nonpartisan" political offices, including judgeships, across the nation through the 2018 midterms, the 2020 elections, and to the present day—and illustrates how, before the advent of the "modern" Republican Party in 1854 and the 168-year era of Democratic-GOP domination that has ensued since then, the early decades of American nationhood were dominated in a similar manner by pairs of "major parties" of the day.

Two-Party examines all levels of government, pointing out how the two-party system—with the two "players" themselves writing most of the rules—has extended its influence in places many Americans thought were off-limits. Every part of the country, including the author's Washington State, is examined in a manner sizing up the sad state of American politics in the current era and showing how the two-party system is largely to blame.

But rather than presenting a specific blueprint for change, as other books—ill-advisedly, given the results—have sought to do, this book aims simply at helping "independent" voters (and others) see the big picture, painted over a period now approaching a quarter of a millennium, and take the leap toward voting their consciences and transforming that big picture to something more inclusive, less corrupt, and more democratic. In other words, this book, drawing on a wide variety of sources, seeks to further inform the electorate by painting a clear and detailed picture of political duopoly from the early days of American nationhood to the current era. There's no paint-by-numbers guide here to producing an alternative picture for the present or future, and there's no easy solution to what is presented in this book as a problem of serious proportions.

Yet one thing seems certain: Any solutions there *are* out there need to start with a well-informed electorate.

Introduction:
How Did It Come to This?

While nearly everyone seems to agree that partisanship in American politics has gotten out of control in recent decades and especially in recent years, it would be fair to say partisanship and partisan bickering have barely skipped a beat in 23 decades since electors selected George Washington as the first American president in a show of unanimity that wouldn't last for long.

The administration of President Washington faced the barbs of an emerging free press over the course of his two terms in office. As with every president since Washington, any semblance of a rosy "honeymoon" period after inauguration would give way to the realities of regional concerns, polarized views, and, at times, personal attacks when the strength of arguments didn't seem to be enough. In a June 26, 1796, letter to Alexander Hamilton, Washington, discussing why he was unlikely to seek a third term as president, wrote that he was "disinclined to be longer buffeted in the public prints by a set of infamous scribblers" (National Archives).

Despite a spirit of relative goodwill when the first U.S. Congress certified Washington as the unanimously elected first president of the new republic, the seeds were in place from the beginning to ensure Washington and future presidents would get some serious buffeting not only from the press but from the Congress as well. While Washington refrained from belonging to a party during his political career—making no secret of his concerns about political parties—his alignment with the Federalist cause was public knowledge, and the designation of members of Congress as "Pro-Administration" or "Anti-Administration" ensured that the unanimity illustrated by Washington's selection by electors wouldn't hold for long in New York, the nation's capital at the time, or Philadelphia, the seat of government through most of the 1790s until the permanent move to Washington, D.C., in 1799.

As New York University history and education professor Jonathan

Zimmerman put it in a November 8, 2014, *Los Angeles Times* op-ed, "Tension between the chief executive and the upper body of Congress is baked into our national DNA." According to Zimmerman, just a few months after the Senate declared Washington "His Majesty, the President of the United States of America, and the Protector of the Same," the president's relationship with the Senate started to cool off, and "one senator wrote in his journal, 'The president wishes to tread on the necks of the Senate.'" By the same measure, President Washington wasn't without his detractors in the lower house of Congress as well, particularly among members of the Anti-Administration camp who were concerned about his Federalist leanings and what some saw as a readiness to bypass Congress when it came to making key decisions.

While Washington may have tried to stay above the fray when the Anti-Federalists morphed into the Democratic-Republican Party to go head-to-head with Alexander Hamilton and the Federalists, the prototype of the current two-party system was an undeniable presence before Washington got through his first term. Yet both parties asked him to remain in office for a second term—a term in which partisanship would be on the rise as "the divisions between the two political parties became defined," as Dennis Jamison wrote in the December 31, 2014, *Washington Times*. After a second term in which he took hits from the press and observed increasing bickering and gridlock in Philadelphia, Washington couldn't be persuaded to seek a third term. In Washington's Farewell Address, a long letter published in September 1796 as he neared the end of his second term, Washington warned Americans that political parties "serve to organize faction, to give it an artificial and extraordinary force; to put, in the place of the delegated will of the nation the will of a party...." He continued, "[T]hey are likely, in the course of time and things, to become potent engines, by which cunning, ambitious, and unprincipled men will be enabled to subvert the power of the people and to usurp for themselves the reins of government."

When Washington wrote those words, every seat in both houses of Congress was held by a Federalist or a Democratic-Republican—and that would remain the case for a generation, though the Federalist Party would largely run its course by the end of the War of 1812. Two-party dominance continued when the Democratic-Republicans splintered in the 1820s into the Democratic Party and the anti–Jacksonian National Republicans, who would largely form the basis of the Whig Party in the 1830s.

During the Democrat vs. National Republican and Democrat vs. Whig eras from the 1820s–1850s, while two-party domination was the general rule across the country and in the nation's capital, there was moderate representation in Congress by men who weren't aligned with the major parties of the day. The vast majority of that alternative representation was in the House of Representatives, whose members were elected by the public and reflected some of the regional divisions, movements, and concerns of an era in which the nation was moving in many directions at what seemed, at the time, a furious pace. Yet two-party control of Congress remained the rule, and only once during the Democratic/National Republican and Democratic/Whig eras did alternative officeholders represent 10 percent or more of all officeholders serving in the Congress.

Since the establishment of the "modern" Republican Party in 1854, the American two-party system has been embodied by two organizations with a combined age, as of the early 2020s, of over 360 years—and some would say those two elderly parties have remained strong for so long by representing citizens' best interests and providing Americans political stability and a standard of living and personal freedom normally second to none. In the 2000s, though, it seems clear that a substantial number of Americans have come to regard the two-party system more as a Trojan horse—or, worse, a chronic, debilitating disease it may be too late to treat.

To sum up how we've arrived at this point, almost since the dawn of nationhood in the United States, two dominant parties have essentially colluded to keep all hands but their own from getting or keeping a grip on the levers of power. Much more often than not, the public has gone along—at least while the wheels of government have turned at a normal pace and a decent semblance of democracy has been maintained. While outliers have crept into governmental institutions and legislative bodies—though never posing a long-term threat to the duopolistic powers of the day—the American electorate has nearly always looked to two dominant political parties to work out issues of concern and to lead the nation forward. But public confidence in the two-party system presupposes a measure of cooperation and at least minimal efficiency in state legislatures and, especially, the nation's capital—expectations that haven't always been met and, to many observers, seem out of reach or unreasonable in the present day.

1

Bouncing on the Rails

Periods of political gridlock or stalemate have tended to give a boost to the fortunes of alternative political movements, which have sometimes been able to capitalize for a time when voters and the mainstream press have seen through the inefficiency of the two-party system and been open to at least a temporary alternative. As 2018 Kansas independent gubernatorial candidate Greg Orman reported in his 2016 book, *A Declaration of Independents*, "Over a century ago, 'populist sentiment' helped bring down the curtain on the era of political stalemate that gripped America from the late 1800s to the end of the First World War. That reform happened because of the efforts of a Populist Party that arose out of the Democrats' grassroots and a Progressive Party that emerged from the ranks of disaffected Republicans. In other words, it happened because independent Americans ... made it happen" (Orman, 8).

"Independent" may be too strong a word to use in that instance because, while it was certainly some degree of independent-mindedness that caused large numbers of Americans to reconsider their allegiance to one or the other of the dominant political parties in the late 1800s and early 1900s—much along the lines of what has been taking place in the United States in more recent times—the period of relative Populist/Progressive success at the state and federal levels, like every other instance of third-party or independent success in opposition to the American two-party system, proved to be an aberration and not a transition to lasting change. In most cases, such moments of success throughout American history would perhaps better be identified as blips than aberrations. As far as the Populist/Progressive movement of the late nineteenth/early twentieth century was concerned, it did result in a wake-up call and minor resetting of the major-party "powers that be" in Washington, D.C., and some state capitals around the country, and Progressive efforts toward establishing income tax, worker protections, women's suffrage, and other developments Americans have since come to take for granted are remembered as a vital contribution to America's long-term sustainability and vitality and a shining example of American democracy as more than a tool or birthright of two major parties. Yet the Progressives, as a strong voice for change or a significant political force, would be sidelined by World War I, and electoral politics in the United States would soundly reestablish itself as essentially a two-horse race.

Orman credits the Populist/Progressive era—and the voters who stood behind it—with "[forcing] the two major parties to adapt," resulting in an "ensuing era of cooperation." As Orman points out, in the aftermath of the Populist/Progressive movement, Democrats and Republicans—all but deadlocked in earlier years—"produced constitutional amendments authorizing a federal income tax, direct election of U.S. senators, and women's suffrage [and] banded together to create the Federal Reserve, a system of national parks, and uniform standards for food safety" (Orman, 8).

Although partisanship, one-upmanship, and reluctance to compromise have been evident in American two-party politics at almost every stage of U.S. history, there is much to Orman's view that bipartisan cooperation has played a part in keeping the wheels of government moving—especially when the nation has faced uphill challenges. But as numerous commentators and countless citizens have observed over the past half-century or more, the partisan divide has been widening since a series of national crises and a cold war riveted the nation's attention during the first half of the twentieth century and for some years afterward.

The Vietnam War heightened divisions, helping create two camps in Washington, D.C., that seldom seemed to see reality through the same lens. Yet a Gallup poll conducted during the height of the war in 1968 determined that Democrats, Republicans, and "Independents" nationwide all saw U.S. involvement in the war in much the same way—as a mistake, in each case, by a 50-something to 40-something margin. Positions of elected officials in Washington, D.C., at the time were often nuanced and not entirely in conformity with what appeared to be the "party line." In other words, there was room for debate, even in a time of national crisis, and the general rule—though certainly broken with regularity—was that the debate would be conducted with some civility.

Another "broken rule"—or a series of them—occurred when Republican staffers broke into the Democratic Party's campaign headquarters in the Watergate Hotel on June 17, 1972, setting off a frenzied series of cover-ups, lies, and desperate attempts not to drop the reins of power. Republicans in Washington, D.C.—some fearful of Democratic policies and others simply fearful of losing their jobs—stood behind President Nixon, at least until that became a losing proposition. The public had lost trust in the president—at a time when that seemed to matter—and Nixon himself stepped down in August 1974, defending himself in the process but refraining from launching any verbal torpedoes at his opponents, perhaps out of fear they'd come back to get him.

Though President Ford's pardoning of Nixon chilled the air and widened the gulf in Washington, D.C., a small bridging of the partisan gap seemed to occur over the course of the half term Ford served as president. Despite partisan, political, and ideological differences separating the parties, Democrats in Washington generally saw Ford as a man of decent character—certainly, in that regard, an upgrade in comparison to the two men he replaced en route to becoming the first-ever and only unelected president of the United States, Vice President Agnew and President Nixon. Not surprisingly, the Democrats won big in 1974's elections, picking up seats almost across the board and significantly increasing their margin in the U.S. House of Representatives. While ensuing congressional investigations into illegal spying on Americans by the CIA and FBI, particularly during the Nixon years, caused plenty of partisan rancor and distrust, the Ford presidency was generally characterized by a business-first, semi-cooperative approach to dealing with pressing issues of the day. Among those issues were getting the last U.S. forces out of Vietnam, nursing an ailing economy, solving an energy crisis, and working to restore the morale of a nation that had suffered its first humiliating loss on an international stage and, in fairly recent memory, taken some jarring blows from within over the course of the Civil Rights movement, Vietnam, Watergate, and so on.

Despite efforts aimed at healing or reuniting the nation, Ford clearly had the deck stacked against him from the moment he stepped in as president. Reaching stalemate on numerous issues with a Democratic Congress, Ford never quite projected an image of effective leadership or seemed to convey the impression that he was likely to help lift the nation out of the doldrums.

Former California governor Ronald Reagan sensed as much and mounted a challenge to lift the 1976 Republican Party presidential nomination from Ford. Viewed by many Americans as a fresh voice without the taint of a Washington insider, Reagan, criticizing Ford and the Republican Party for a lack of conservative leadership, took the fight all the way to the Republican National Convention before falling just short of taking the nomination. Later in the convention Reagan would deliver a speech solidly endorsing Ford and the Republican Party platform and warning his fellow Republicans and "all of those millions of Democrats and independents who I know are looking for a cause around which to rally" about "the erosion of freedom that has taken place under Democratic rule in our country; the controls and restrictions of the vitality of the great free economy that we enjoy" (*The New York Times*, "Transcript…").

Reagan's message made a much stronger impression on the Republican Party establishment four years later, during the latter stages of the Jimmy Carter presidency. Carter had defeated Ford in a close election that a simple glance at a map might suggest showed an East–West Democratic–Republican split that didn't bode particularly well for national unity. During the Carter presidency, Democrats maintained the majority in both houses of Congress and in state governments across most of the country. In 1980, with many Americans blaming Carter for the very "crisis of confidence" he said was gripping the nation in July of 1979, the tables were turned as Republicans—riding Reagan's optimistic vision and his exhortation, delivered at the 1980 Republican National Convention, to "make America great again"—took back the Congress, made gains just about everywhere, and reclaimed the presidency in a landslide.

While the Reagan era in Washington was marked by lines drawn in the sand between the major parties when it came to ideologies and issues of the day, Reagan himself seemed far more at odds with the Democratic Party's shifting stance in recent decades than with the party itself. A Democrat during most his years as a Hollywood actor, Reagan was widely quoted as having said, regarding his departure from the Democrats and realignment with the Republicans, "I didn't leave the Democratic Party, the Democratic Party left me."

Buoyed by a strong Republican majority in both houses of Congress during his first term, Reagan didn't have much cause for worry about bipartisan relations as he was generally able to get key bills—mainly concerning tax cuts and increases in defense spending—passed by a wide margin. Although much of the nation had reservations about the direction in which things were going—and while things weren't always going so smoothly in the state governments—the general consensus was that at least things were getting done in Washington, D.C.

But having to deal with a Democratic Congress during his second term as president proved to be a more challenging proposition for Reagan. While Reagan reached compromise with Congress on taxation and immigration issues, "The 100th Congress," as the *Chicago Tribune* reported on August 2, 1987, "has turned into a mean-spirited, partisan trench warfare between the Democrats and President Reagan backed by his Republican allies. … The result of the sulfurous atmosphere has been a stalemate over issues such as arms control, defense spending, taxes and campaign financing" (Collin)—and it was driven in large part by the parties' polar views on Iran-Contra and the Democrats' perception of Reagan as a second-term

Republican ideologue who could simply be waited out until a Democratic president got elected in his place.

That didn't happen, of course, as some below-the-belt campaigning by Republicans and some blundering campaigning by the Democratic nominee himself cost former Massachusetts governor Michael Dukakis an election in 1988 that he might well have won. Many observers largely attributed Dukakis' loss—which turned out to be a semi-landslide—to a racially charged ad suggesting Dukakis' easy-on-crime stance had put innocent Bay Staters in danger while he was governor and would likely do the same to citizens nationwide if he were elected president. The beneficiary of the infamous Willie Horton ad, Republican nominee George H.W. Bush—second-in-command to Reagan for eight years more as a result of a marriage of convenience than true love—took office in 1989 as the Democratic Party retained the upper hand in Congress and in most levels of government around the country.

Democrats in Congress had wearied of seeing their agenda largely put on hold during the Reagan presidency and seemed more insistent, with Reagan out of the picture, on getting their way. As *Time* put it decades later, on December 1, 2018, "From the moment he took office, Bush walked a tightrope: doing deals with Democrats who controlled both chambers and hoping the right wing of his party would not object. For nearly two years, his balance was perfect; then the tightrope began to quiver" (Duffy).

Two years of working with Congress—often appearing to compromise his or his party's views without making a compelling public case for doing so—hadn't greatly endeared Bush to either end of the political spectrum. Never a communicator equipped to follow a Reagan in the political or public arena, Bush, to many, came across as a compromiser, a bit of a waffler, and a leader who seemed to value efficiency more than political doctrine or, some would say, principle. Reaching agreement with Congress on legislation regarding issues such as civil rights, environmental protection, and the protection of savings and loan institutions highlighted the perception of Bush as an efficient "general manager" who, after many years in the nation's capital, seemed to know how to get things done.

In foreign affairs Bush scored mixed reactions from both Democrats and Republicans—the former largely concerned about implications of American action in Panama and the Persian Gulf, and the latter wary of any form of appeasement as exemplified, probably most famously, in Bush's August 1991 "Chicken Kiev" speech to the Ukrainian Parliament in which the U.S. president was widely viewed as offering little or no encouragement to nations seeking to secede from the Soviet Union.

But the issue that played the biggest part in causing a rupture in the Republican Party—arming the party's ideological "right" with a sense of mission to take the reins of the Republican Party and the levers of leadership—was taxes. During the 1988 campaign Bush had borrowed a page from Clint Eastwood to deliver his famous "Read my lips: no new taxes" campaign promise—only to back off almost as soon as the votes were counted and it was clear he'd be partnering with a Democratic-dominated Congress. What made matters worse for Bush was his tendency to explain away his changing positions without really owning up to them—and the emerging ideological wing of the Republican Party would have none of that. According to a *Washington Post* headline on December 2, 2018, two days after Bush's death at age 94, "George H.W. Bush was the accidental catalyst that built the new Republican Party." The *Post* referred to "Bush's declaration of 'no new taxes,' which he made as he accepted the Republican nomination in 1988. The pledge was a bow to conservatives who always regarded him with suspicion, if not outright hostility. When he reneged on the promise, they exacted revenge" (Balz).

Bush's summer 1990 compromise agreement with the Democrats that "tax revenue increases" or "revenue enhancements" had to be included in the new national budget signaled, in the view of many, the beginning of the end of his presidency and the birth of the modern Republican Party (as opposed to the one birthed in 1854). Despite reaching almost unprecedented levels of public support months later in the aftermath of a resounding U.S. victory in the First Gulf War, Bush wouldn't be able to reverse the process that had begun when he backed off on a campaign promise that voters and, particularly, his own party had taken seriously. As the *Post* reported, "Twenty-one months later," following the height of Bush's popularity near the end of the First Gulf War, "he was driven from office by the voters. A transition inside the Republican Party that was already underway accelerated" (Balz).

2

The Gingrich Effect

Spearheading the early–1990s "transition" in the Republican Party was Georgia Congressman Newt Gingrich, a five-term veteran of the House of Representatives when George H.W. Bush won the presidency in 1988. Gingrich's 6th congressional district, just north of Atlanta, had been in Democratic hands for over a century when Gingrich got elected as the first Republican ever to represent the district after two failed attempts in 1974 and 1976. In getting elected in 1978, Gingrich was widely viewed as having run a nasty campaign, complete with the sort of labeling associated with more recent U.S. political campaigns, against Democratic opponent Virginia Shapard. Once in Congress, as *Mother Jones* reports, Gingrich "learned quickly that a back bencher in the minority party could distinguish himself and gain attention in Washington by employing extreme rhetoric. Ever in attack-mode, Gingrich swiftly moved up the ranks within the House GOP caucus" (Corn, "A Very Long List…").

While most of Gingrich's barbs during his early years in Congress, and throughout his career, were aimed at the "liberal" Democrats ("liberal" apparently being a four-letter word to many people without access to a good dictionary), he also spoke his mind about the state of his own party as he saw it. As recorded by PBS.org, in an Atlanta speech delivered to a gathering of the College Republicans during his 1978 campaign for Congress, Gingrich said, "Do you like the state of the Republican Party? Do you think you ought to respect [Tennessee senator] Bill Brock because he has done such a great job? Or Richard Nixon, or Gerald Ford, the only incumbent president since Herbert Hoover to lose an election? They have done a terrible job, a pathetic job. In my lifetime, literally in my lifetime, I was born in 1943, we have not had a competent national Republican leader. Not ever!" (PBS.org, "1978 Speech…").

During his first dozen years in Washington, Gingrich—though unafraid to voice his opinions in strong terms—generally managed to tone down his attacks on members of his own party, instead focusing the brunt of his verbal assaults on Democrats, who responded in kind, accusing

Gingrich of engaging in "skinhead politics" (Corn). But that changed with a force when George H.W. Bush made it clear he was prepared to renege on a campaign promise to the Republican Party's "conservative" base for the sake of getting things done with a Democratic Congress. As McKay Coppins put it in a November 2018 *Atlantic* retrospective identifying Gingrich as "The Man Who Broke Politics," Gingrich believed the Republicans were destined for failure "as long as they kept compromising with the Democrats out of some high-minded civic desire to keep congressional business humming along. His strategy was to blow up the bipartisan coalitions that were essential to legislating, and then seize on the resulting dysfunction to wage a populist crusade against the institution of Congress itself."

Also around the time he was at odds with Bush's and his fellow Republicans' willingness to work with Democrats in Washington, Gingrich, seeing blood, took over the leadership of GOPAC, established in the late 1970s "to cultivate promising young leaders within the Republican ranks and build a 'farm team' of candidates with the knowledge and drive to become a governing majority party," according to GOPAC's website in 2021. "With Newt Gingrich at the helm," the website continues, "GOPAC became the Republican Party's preeminent education and training center through countless campaign seminars, workbooks, audiotapes and years of grassroots organizing." Not included on that list was an infamous memo titled "Language: A Key Mechanism of Control," which listed dozens of key words Republican candidates in 1990 should use in campaign literature and speeches when discussing the Democrats. Among words listed in the memo—whose cover letter, according to *The Atlanta Journal-Constitution*, "encouraged candidates to 'speak like Newt'"—were "sick," "pathetic," "traitors," "corrupt," "disgrace," "lie," and "radical." Words used to illustrate Republicans and their campaigns, meanwhile, were to include "legacy," "crusade," "moral," "humane," "hard work," and the like. According to the *Journal-Constitution*, the memo advised the several thousand Republican candidates nationwide to whom it was sent, "The words and phrases are powerful. Read them. Memorize as many as possible" (Salzer).

More than anybody else from his era, Gingrich is "credited" with leading the charge to an ideologically and power-driven Republican Party and driving a wedge between the two major parties and their supporters. In a July 2016 *Atlantic* article titled "Why Democrats and Republicans Literally Speak Different Languages," Derek Thompson attributes the gulf separating the parties, in large part, to "the Republican takeover of Congress led by Newt Gingrich in 1994" (Thompson, quoting Gentzkow). As Thompson and others see it, Gingrich's unvarnished attacks on President Bill Clinton in the 1990s set the tone for Donald Trump's below-the-belt attacks on "Crooked Hillary" in 2016.

As Thompson explains, the two major parties "are now divided by a common language: Democrats discuss 'comprehensive health reform,' 'estate taxes,' 'undocumented workers,' and 'tax breaks for the wealthy,' while Republicans insist on a 'Washington takeover of health care,' 'death taxes,' 'illegal aliens,' and 'tax reform.'" Thompson and others agree that the rise of Gingrich (elected Speaker of the House in 1995) and like-minded Republicans in Congress in the 1990s set the tone for the present era and level of polarization and partisanship in which the major parties can barely speak to each other, let alone debate the issues in a meaningful way. A few Gingrich-inspired government shutdowns and a party-line vote on the Clinton impeachment highlighted the increasing separation between the Republican and Democratic parties; and while Gingrich himself wasn't immune to criticism from members of his own party, and stepped down as Speaker of the House after nearly four years shortly before resigning his House seat in January 1999 (two months after getting reelected by a 71 to 29 percent margin), consensus is that he was largely responsible for the hyperpartisanship with which Americans have become so familiar in the twenty-first century.

Much of the "credit" for the widening gulf in recent decades between the Republican and Democratic parties is attributed to former Georgia Congressman and Speaker of the House Newt Gingrich. Since Gingrich's rise to national prominence in the 1990s, many Washington Republicans have adopted his disdain for compromise (Biographical Directory of the United States Congress).

While partisanship and personal attacks have been present at all levels of U.S. politics from the earliest days, for the most part there was some sense that members of one major party ought to cooperate with members of the opposing major party for the good of the country. But, as Mark

Gerzon says in his 2016 call for bipartisan unity, *The Reunited States of America*, "During the Clinton-Bush-Obama administrations, what unites us—respect, dialogue, collaborative problem-solving, citizen empowerment, innovation—was relentlessly pushed to the margins of public life. Meanwhile, what divides us—blame, personal attacks, stereotypes, dark money—grabbed center stage" (Gerzon, introduction).

It seems clear that Gerzon's scenario has only intensified since he wrote those words.

Gerzon decries the major parties' "two competing, paralyzing narratives" or mutually exclusive views of the nation and the world that "consume almost all of the oxygen in the public square. Whatever the issue may be, the two competing armies polarize around it, even if that results in pitting neighbor against neighbor, employers against employees, family members against family members" (Gerzon, preface).

Disagreement, of course, isn't unhealthy in itself, and it provides grounds for healthy debate aimed at improving lives. But, as Gerzon explains, "When two people disagree about everything all the time, it's *hyper*partisanship. It's not a healthy disagreement. It's a toxic feud" (Gerzon, introduction).

Negative views about the opposing major party—and, nowadays, its supporters—often drive partisan voters' preferences more than feelings of optimism or trust toward the "preferred party" (or, often, the lesser of two evils). As Emory University's Alan I. Abramowitz and Steven Webster explain in their 2015 article "The Only Thing We Have to Fear Is the Other Party," "A growing number of Americans have been voting against the opposing party rather than for their own party. ... Supporters of each party have come to perceive supporters of the opposing party as very different from themselves in terms of their social characteristics, political beliefs, and values, and to hold strongly negative opinions of the opposing party's elected officials, candidates, and supporters. Negative perceptions of the opposing party are also reinforced by exposure to partisan news sources, which have proliferated in recent years."

According to Abramowitz and Webster, the national trend toward negative partisanship has intensified particularly since 2000 and has resulted in an increased tendency among voters toward "straight-ticket voting"—where voters generally refuse to look beyond their partisan boundaries. This fracturing of society and curtailment of political discourse was as evident, if not more so, during the George W. Bush and Obama administrations as it was during the highly contentious Bill Clinton years, when Clinton and his supporters were often painted in the most derogatory terms (though perhaps justifiably as far as some of Clinton's personal conduct was concerned). While Obama, John McCain, and others have demonstrated that "many Republicans and Democrats, as individuals, know how to play the role of partisan bridge builder, the locked-in partisan polarization of the two-party system turns the aisle between the parties into a chasm" (Gerzon, ch. 3).

It's not only in Washington, D.C., that such a chasm has been evident in recent times. In the escape-into-your-own-culture that has emerged in the United States during the last few decades and especially during the current century, it's become an increasingly viable option for people of all ages to stay largely within their comfort zones or "preference zones" for regular and extended periods of time. The local newspaper—showing increased bias as ownership of more and more papers has fallen into fewer and fewer hands—has become a thing of the past in the minds of an increasing number of people, and healthy debate of the issues from all sides often seems a lost art in the current culture. As popular media—many doubling as partisan mouthpieces—blare out their positions, hoping to drown out the other side, citizens often get on one bandwagon or the other and disengage from meaningful interaction with the opposing side. Even when a truce is called at work, at the club, or at home, it's likely based on an agreement to remain silent and simply to "agree to disagree." When that pact dissolves and one side tries to sway the other is often when things get out of hand.

The connection seems clear between the increased tendency in recent years to escape into personal comfort zones—whether through online forums and Facebook groups or through other media finding niches and avid choirs to preach to—and the dwindling sense that Americans ought to share some common views and knowledge if the nation is to remain vital, informed, and truly democratic. A generation ago, E.D. Hirsch, Jr., in his book *Cultural Literacy: What Every American Needs to Know*, made the case that there were "5,000 essential facts" that every American ought to know. The problem since the book came out in 1987, of course, is that modern views on diversity tend to brand any attempt to impose "required knowledge" on Americans as an exercise in arrogance or, worse, one more example of racial, economic, or cultural discrimination. Clearly, the trend in recent times has been toward relativity—i.e., along the lines of "all knowledge is equal" or "you go your way, I'll go mine"—or, as Robert Pondiscio put it in an April 2013 story in *The Atlantic*, "increasingly [living] inside our own information, entertainment, and cultural bubbles." He might as well have added "political."

But while it would be reasonable to expect that the fracturing of American society in recent times resulted in a proliferation of viable political parties representing bases of various sizes and interests, the record shows that has hardly been the case. Surprisingly or not, it's been precisely when more and more Americans seem to have gone in their own directions that the modern-day incarnation of the American political duopoly has dug in its heels and "risen" to new heights of dominance and control.

3

"Independents" and "Democracy"

Despite numerous reports in recent years that disenchantment with the major political parties may be a recipe for success for independent candidates who can present a compelling alternative to a disillusioned public, such sentiment doesn't take into account a key point raised in a 2016 Pew Research Institute report, written by Samantha Smith, titled "5 facts about America's political independents."

After going along with the general message cited in other sources—that "Independents outnumber either Democrats or Republicans" (according to Pew figures, in 2014, 32 percent of voters self-identified as Democrats, 23 percent as Republicans, and 39 percent as independents)—the Pew report went on to say that (in addition to those figures and, therefore, coming out of the 39 percent identified as independents) "[i]n 2014, 17 percent of the public leaned toward the Democratic Party while 16 percent leaned toward the GOP." That finding, at a minimum, suggested the vast majority of "independent" voters in the United States in 2014 weren't as independent as they claimed to be. The Pew report continued, "When the partisan leanings of independents were taken into account, 48 percent either identified as Democrats or leaned Democratic; 39 percent identified as Republican or leaned Republican." As far as the public at large was concerned, Pew reported that "just 6 percent declined to lean toward a party."

At least on the surface, the Pew report seems at odds with a poll sponsored by Unite America, a Colorado-based national organization founded in 2013 to support the rise of moderate independent candidates across the United States. According to Jim Brunner in the May 3, 2018, *Seattle Times*, a Unite America poll of 866 likely voters conducted in the early spring of 2018 "found 75 percent of voters said they are open to supporting independent candidates for the [Washington State] Legislature. In a hypothetical fall matchup, the poll found a generic independent candidate leading a generic Republican 43 to 24 percent, and leading a generic Democrat 35 percent to 27 percent." The poll apparently didn't address how that same generic independent candidate would face in a three-way primary when facing the generic candidates of both major parties, one of whom would likely be the incumbent.

Until 2008 Washington employed a "blanket primary" system in which voters cast ballots and the top finisher from each ballot-qualified party would advance to the general election. In 2008 Washington became the first state—with California becoming the second in 2011—to employ a top-two primary system, also known as a "jungle primary," whereby the top two finishers in a primary, regardless of party affiliation or non-affiliation, would advance to the general election.

Since candidates under the top-two system could express any party preference they wanted to, two candidates identifying with the same party could well end up going one-on-one in the general election. The flip side is that one of the major parties could come out of a primary without a candidate to run in the general election. Some observers argued there was a good possibility that if multiple candidates identifying with the same party in a top-two primary split the party vote too many ways, there might be fertile ground for a smaller-party or independent candidate to slip into the top two.

While Brunner reported the poll suggested a centrist independent candidate for the Washington Legislature might garner decent voter support "if only [such a candidate] could get past the state's top-two primary," plenty of independent candidates had in fact advanced beyond Washington's top-two primary since it was instituted in 2008. None, however, had come close to winning in a general election. Like Smith, Brunner hit on the reason independents had fallen short in general elections—and in primaries contested by candidates of both major parties. "The problem," he wrote, "is that voters are often reluctant to step out of the two-party box due to concerns about viability—60 percent of voters in the poll said they worried that voting for an independent 'might waste my vote or cause my least favorite candidate to get elected.'"

Distrust in the major parties appeared to be at or near an all-time high nationwide in the aftermath of the divisive 2016 federal election. Yet voters' distrust in recent years seems to have been directed primarily at one (or the other) of the major parties and its candidates but not at the two-party system in general. As a result, while the 2016 Pew study reported that most "independent" party leaners didn't "feel very warmly" about the parties they leaned toward, they tended to have stronger feelings—*negative* feelings—about the opposing major party. According to Smith, "Intense dislike of the opposing party has risen sharply among independents and others who lean toward a party. Today [in 2016] 44 percent of Republican and Democratic leaners say they have a very unfavorable impression of the opposing party, up from just 10 percent and 11 percent respectively in 1994."

The result is that many party-leaning "independent" voters are especially motivated to support the party they lean toward when that party faces opposition from the other major party, as is usually the case. Leaning "independents," while often feeling cold toward their preferred party's candidates, nonetheless lean in the direction they do for a reason—whether it's more along the lines of commitment to a shared ideology or simply a comfortable nominalism. As far as Washington State is concerned, recent legislative elections have demonstrated that leaning "independents" tend to default to the party they lean toward when candidates of the opposing major party are on the ballot. In other words, when both Democratic and Republican candidates are on the same ballot for a legislative seat, the majority of "independent" leaners tend to line up with the party faithful. Since relatively few truly independent voters are left over, independent or smaller-party candidates in a top-two primary routinely get squeezed out.

But despite the obvious acrimony, if not outright hatred, the two major parties have for each other, it's clear that each—despite an apparent inability to stomach much or most of what the other stands for—is far more accepting of the privileges the opposing major party enjoys. There are only two members—the Republican and Democratic parties—of an exclusive club, and for all practical purposes both are complicit in driving and perpetuating a duopolistic system that essentially kicks any meaningful alternative opposition to the curb. It could well be that this "collusion" is as worthy of a Robert Mueller–type investigation as the actual Mueller investigation that gripped the nation from 2017 to 2019—though the colluding political parties themselves, along with their special interests, would never let that happen.

At nearly every level of society, the gulf separating the two major parties from the outliers has been evident throughout much of American history but particularly so in recent times. Nationally, CNN and Fox News in many ways seem to present opposing views of key issues facing Americans and the politicians representing them, and each of those major news networks seems to be in the corner of one of the major parties while aiming its weaponry—usually blatantly—at the other major party's views and, often, at the character of some of its members. But even in the heat of battle, Fox News and CNN seldom seem to acknowledge that democracy in America is more than a game for two players—or even that it should be. Like the major parties themselves, the major news networks seem to buy into the duopoly view almost without question, and on that basis it can be argued that their views on American democracy are, ultimately, more similar than different. Despite their many obvious differences on the surface, CNN and Fox News seem to reflect values most Americans share with regard to what it means to be American. Without a doubt, one of those values is a belief in "democracy"—democracy rooted in a two-party system Americans have known all their lives and generally seem to accept without much question.

4

The Electoral College

Despite increased calls for new parties and improved opportunities for independent candidates across the United States, 2016 saw the nation's best-known independent politician shed his "independent" label in order to pursue the most powerful office in the world. That happened when independent U.S. Senator Bernie Sanders of Vermont ran for the Democratic Party's presidential nomination—though Sanders didn't actually join the Democratic Party—before bowing out to the ultimate partisan Democratic Party insider, Hillary Clinton. Whether Sanders was truly converted seems unlikely, since he remained an "independent" U.S. Senator after facing defeat at the hands of Clinton and her army of "superdelegates." Far more likely is that Sanders simply knew what many other voting-age citizens of the United States knew: that as long as the U.S. Electoral College continued to exist, the chance of anyone other than a Republican or a Democrat winning the presidency probably wasn't much greater than the chance of humans establishing a colony on the sun.

In short, the Electoral College system—in which the national popular vote is of no consequence—heavily favors candidates who win the popular vote in certain high-population states. The only states not using a winner-take-all system with regard to Electoral College voting are Maine and Nebraska, both with small populations. As a result, in theory, a candidate who finishes second in every state, even by a single vote, is likely to finish behind a candidate with virtually no support nationally who manages to win a single state—and, given the major-party mechanisms and advantages that have been in place nationwide for many decades, it's a daunting prospect for an independent/nonpartisan or alternative-party candidate to win the popular vote in even a single state, let alone in enough states to have a realistic shot at winning the presidency.

The best-known independent on the presidential ballot in recent decades, Texas billionaire Ross Perot, ran for the presidency in 1992 on a platform of keeping jobs in America and balancing the federal budget. Funded largely by millions of his own dollars, Perot, following a campaign marked by ups and downs and a period in which the campaign was suspended, won 19 percent of the national popular vote but not a single state or electoral vote. He followed up his 1992 performance by founding the Reform Party in 1995 and running as the party's candidate for president the following year. In 1996 Perot earned less than half the share of the national popular vote he'd earned in 1992 and, once again, no electoral votes.

In terms of electoral votes, the most successful third-party candidates of the twentieth century were major-party politicians who'd fallen out with their major parties and, presumably, taken some of their major-party supporters along to their new parties and affiliations. In 1912 former Republican president Theodore Roosevelt, who'd left office in 1909 after serving nearly two full terms and deciding not to run for another, voiced severe disapproval of the performance of his successor, fellow Republican William Howard Taft, and got into the race for the 1912 Republican presidential nomination. Roosevelt fell short of getting the nomination at the 1912 Republican National Convention, leaving behind a seriously divided party, and announced he'd run as the presidential candidate of the Progressive "Bull Moose" Party. As it turned out, loyalty to Roosevelt from previously stalwart Republicans was such that he outperformed Taft in the general election—though Roosevelt finished a distant second to Democratic candidate Woodrow Wilson, who won 40 of the 48 states at the time. Roosevelt captured 27 percent of the popular vote to Taft's 23 percent, carried six states to Taft's two, and won 88 electoral votes to Taft's eight.

In 1924, a dozen years after Roosevelt's strong third-party run for president, Robert La Follette, another well-established Republican, ran for president on the ticket of an updated version of the Progressive Party and won 17 percent of the national popular vote, along with the 13 electoral votes of his home state of Wisconsin.

Strom Thurmond and George Wallace were long-established southern Democratic Party politicians whose fallings-out with their party's national leadership and national base in many ways reflected thinking and events of the Civil War era. In 1948 Thurmond, running as a "States' Rights" candidate—specifically, supporting the rights of states to establish and maintain their own policies regarding segregation—didn't get on many states' presidential ballots but nonetheless won 39 electoral votes by carrying four southern states. In 1968 Wallace—long a Democrat both before and after his 1968 campaign for president—slightly bettered Thurmond's showing two decades earlier by riding his American Independent Party presidential nomination to victory in five southern states and an electoral vote count of 45.

In 1972 the fledgling Libertarian Party took one of the nation's 538 electoral votes when a single Virginia elector—one of 11 Virginia electors seemingly committed to declaring for Republican presidential candidate Richard Nixon, who swept Virginia along with 48 other states—cast his vote for Libertarian Party presidential nominee John Hospers, who earned fewer than 4,000 votes nationally and wasn't even on the ballot in Virginia (or 47 other states). The "faithless elector," Roger MacBride, had failed in a 1964 bid, running as a Goldwater Republican, to be the Republican Party nominee for governor of Vermont. In 1976, four years after casting his electoral vote for Hospers, MacBride himself would run for president as the Libertarian Party nominee, but while MacBride made the ballot in most states, he earned only 0.2 percent of the national popular vote. A few years later MacBride would rejoin the Republican Party.

While "faithless electors"—present throughout much of U.S. presidential election history—have come under fire over the years, there's nothing in the Constitution that forbids electors from exercising their free choice. Neither Article 2, which established the Electoral College system, nor the Twelfth Amendment, ratified in 1804, requires electors to vote in a manner reflecting voter choices in their states. The Twelfth Amendment sought to remedy the sort of situation that materialized in 1796—in the days before the popular vote really mattered in presidential elections—when presidential candidates John Adams and Thomas Jefferson finished one–two in the election and, by virtue of their one–two finish, were chosen by electors to be president and vice president despite the fact they'd been the nominees of different parties. One result of the ratification of the Twelfth Amendment was the establishment of the "presidential ticket" system, which survives to this day.

Alabama's George Wallace, a long-time segregationist and Democrat, ran for president as the American Independent Party nominee in 1968, winning in several Southern states. Wallace would later reestablish his ties with the Democratic Party and, about a decade after his third-party run for president, renounce his views on segregation (Library of Congress, U.S. News & World Report collection).

Ratification of the Twelfth Amendment followed the election of 1800, which saw electors deadlocked when Jefferson and running mate Aaron Burr—top finishers among a slate of candidates that also included John Adams and running mate Charles Pinkney—both failed to win a majority in the Electoral College. Because no candidate had won a majority of electoral votes, proceedings went to the House of Representatives, in accordance with Article 2, Section 1 of the Constitution; and following more than 30 indecisive ballots over the course of a week, the House declared Jefferson the president-elect and Burr the vice president-elect, as had been the intent of both candidates and their Democratic-Republican party all along. The Twelfth Amendment, apart from aiming to prevent rivals from having to serve together as president and vice president, also instituted separate electoral ballots for president and vice president, beginning with the election of 1804.

Debates over the effectiveness or fairness of the Electoral College system have persisted ever since the election in late 1788/early 1789 of George Washington—both the only president ever selected unanimously by electors and, at least officially, the only independent candidate ever elected president. While there have been some changes over the years in how U.S. elections are conducted and presidents are chosen, there's been no change in the requirement that presidential elections in which no candidate wins an outright majority of electoral votes get turned over to the House of Representatives. The Twelfth Amendment does, however, reduce the field of candidates for consideration by the U.S. House from the top five finishers to the top three.

As a result, it's not impossible that an election at least partly along the lines of the 1824 U.S. presidential election could play out in modern times. In 1824, the first year in which most electors were chosen by voters and not state legislatures, four strong candidates—all representing the Democratic-Republican Party—ran for president and won dozens of electoral votes. Leading the pack with 41 percent of the popular vote and 99 electoral votes was Tennessee's Andrew Jackson. John Quincy Adams of Massachusetts placed second, with 31 percent of the popular vote and 84 electoral votes. Joining Jackson and Quincy Adams in the House of Representatives runoff was Georgia's William Crawford, Treasury Secretary at the time, who edged out Speaker of the House Henry Clay by winning 41 electoral votes to Clay's 37. When the dust settled, the House selected Quincy Adams as president over Jackson, who'd led by a substantial margin in the popular vote and won a plurality of electoral votes while falling short of the 131 needed to clinch victory.

While the top finishers' matching party affiliation wouldn't be duplicated in the current age, there's still much in that 1824 scenario that could, at least in theory, apply to the present era.

4. The Electoral College

Aspects of 1824 seemed to resurface in an *Atlantic* article by Laurence H. Tribe and Thomas M. Rollins during the 1980 election season. In the article the authors pointed out that two U.S. presidential elections had been settled in the House of Representatives and several others had come close to getting turned over to the House. As for the 1980 presidential election, the authors wrote,

> [A] victory by independent candidate John Anderson in just a few states could throw the election into the House. If Anderson wins only the thirty-nine electoral votes of Massachusetts, New Jersey, and Connecticut—three states in which Ronald Reagan's polls have shown Anderson leading—Jimmy Carter could end up with 230 votes from the urban Northeast and part of the South, forty short of the 270 needed for a majority, and Reagan could take the rest—including the West and Midwest—for a total of 268 electoral votes, two votes short of the presidency.

That scenario didn't play out as Anderson failed to carry a single state and Reagan won in one of the biggest landslides in U.S. presidential election history. Yet Anderson, a 10-term Illinois Republican congressman going into the 1980 presidential election, did generate some discussion about the possibility that another U.S. presidential election—albeit the first in over a century and a half—would be decided in the House of Representatives.

Few people engaged in the discussion seemed to be under any illusion that Anderson stood to gain much if the election actually did go to the House. Just about everyone seemed to understand that any independent candidate lucky enough to squeak into a House runoff would almost certainly see his journey end there, as the House of Representatives—dominated in every way by the Republican and Democratic parties—wasn't a bit likely to settle on a president who wasn't an active member or trusted ally of a major party, particularly the party with the upper hand in the House at the time.

5

Microcosm of the Nation

Spotlight on Washington State
(Part 1)

In state-level elections—in the recent era as much as in past decades—while alternative candidates may not face such an obstacle as the Electoral College, they face numerous other challenges, as major-party candidates are generally advantaged at every point in a campaign. Of course, that doesn't mean everyone vying for a spot as a Democratic- or Republican-endorsed candidate has an automatic advantage, but once a major party decides which candidate best serves its interests, the playing field gets very challenging for a candidate choosing, more or less, to go it alone or to work with an alternative organization or party. And when both major parties throw their weight behind candidates in a race, the prospects of any other would-be contender in the race usually look bleak.

Against the backdrop of growing partisanship in Washington, D.C., and around the country, Washington State's 2016 legislative elections followed the pattern established in earlier years. One example is that, while over a third of Libertarians on the primary ballot advanced to the 2016 general election—none defeating both a Democratic and a Republican opponent to get there—all lost decisively to their major-party opponents in November.

Of 14 independent or nonpartisan state legislative candidates on the 2016 primary ballot, four advanced to the general election without having to face candidates from both major parties in the primary. But then, staying true to what was a 127-year Washington State tradition in 2016, all four lost in the general election.

Fast-Forward to 2018

In 2018 many people seemed convinced that someone other than a Democrat or Republican could get elected to the Washington State

Legislature for the first time in generations. Much of that hope was placed in Ann Diamond, a community physician in north-central Washington's large, rural Okanagan District 12, who'd filed as a candidate in the fall of 2017. While Diamond supported Obamacare and seemed to aim her strongest words at eight-term Republican incumbent Cary Condotta, her campaign website said, "Diamond is running as an independent because she says identifying with a party places an artificial separation between her and the community."

On December 7, 2017, Diamond submitted a C-4 report, covering the month of November 2017, to Washington Secretary of State Kim Wyman. The C-4—required of all candidates except mini-filers intending to keep total campaign spending under $5,000—is one of the forms on which a candidate in Washington records campaign or feeling-out contributions and expenditures. In her December 7, 2017, C-4 report, more than five months before the official filing of candidates for the 2018 primary, Diamond reported $25,105 in contributions raised to that point. She also reported $1,480 in expenditures, the majority to cover the costs of setting up her website. A smaller amount had been spent on renting a venue to get her name and campaign out to the public without delay.

In the early going, Diamond scored donations from in and out of state, the majority coming from individuals chipping in amounts ranging from $25 up to the legal maximum of $1,000. According to her website, "My campaign is financed by individual contributions only—no PAC, party, or special interest money." If small businesses were to be regarded as individuals, her statement was fair enough—though significant backing by one key PAC would be forthcoming. As John Stang would later report at Crosscut.com, "the Washington Independent[s] Political Action Committee ... has allocated $47,914 to boost [Diamond's] campaign"; and Washington Independents cofounder Chris Vance reports that the PAC ended up putting about $80,000 toward supporting Diamond's 2018 campaign for the legislature. According to Stang, Vance was highly impressed by Diamond's solid and early start to campaigning. As Vance puts it, "She raised $50,000 on her own before we even heard of her."

As far as Diamond's platform was concerned, she spelled out five priorities on her website, which flashed an invitation to "$ CONTRIBUTE." The first issue, as she spelled it out, was "Access to Affordable Health Care," and Diamond drew on her experience as a rural doctor to point out that there were people in her district who couldn't afford doctor visits or medications. On her website Diamond pledged to make an effort to reduce medication prices and prevent insurance companies from denying coverage for preexisting conditions.

Under the heading "Local Jobs for Local People," Diamond lumped together her commitment to policies aimed at providing skilled workers to rural businesses and policies providing training opportunities to young people hoping to take up skilled positions in the communities where they grew up. To that end she pledged investment in roads, schools, hospitals, Internet service, and affordable housing. Diamond's attention to improved schools and early education inside and outside her district resulted in an endorsement by the Washington Education Association.

Diamond's platform also addressed a couple of matters concerning the conduct and accountability of state legislators. Her website said, "We need to rebuild trust in government by holding elected officials to the highest standards of integrity." In particular, she cited the legislators' vote, during the early 2018 legislative session, to be exempted from the state Public Records Act. She also pledged "Responsible Use of Your Money" as she decried the influence of special interest groups on the major parties and the potential negative impact on communities when lawmakers fail to pass budgets "on time."

Diamond faced three opponents (and, only briefly, a fourth) in the primary campaign, all first-time candidates for the legislature. After Condotta announced, a few weeks before the official filing period, that he wouldn't seek reelection, two candidates identifying themselves as Republicans came forward to compete for the seat Condotta had held for eight terms. One, Jesse "JD" Greening, a U.S. Navy veteran with experience as a legislative assistant in Olympia, declared himself a mini-filer and pledged, in his Voters' Guide statement, to "bring knowledge of the legislative process, as well as the leadership I learned in the Navy, to Olympia to advocate for my District and its many needs." The second Republican opposing Diamond was Keith Goehner, a businessman and former teacher who had political experience at the county and school board levels, along with local Republican Party connections. Unlike Greening, Goehner didn't elect to be a mini-filer; and after registering his candidacy on May 18, 2018, Goehner got right down to the work of securing contributions from corporations, individuals, and PACs.

Although Vance reports that local and state Democrats agreed to step aside in order to clear Diamond's path to winning election over the Republicans, Diamond says she faced "active opposition ... and true anger" from the Democrats—anger, at least in part, because of her intent to challenge Republican domination in her district from outside, rather than from within, the Democratic Party. Recruited by both major parties to run in her district, Diamond says she declined the offers because she didn't want either party "to hijack what I felt was an independent run." She continues, "I find it interesting that in my region I have met plenty of candidates who have an (R) by their name ... not because of their party belief and not because of what they're working towards but because they believed it was the only way they could get elected."

One of Diamond's opponents in the primary race was Democrat C. Keiki Stacy Weigle, a transplant from California with a background in technology. According to her website, Weigle, who'd served for a few years as Vice Chair of Okanagan County Democrats, had over 40 years' experience as a human rights and civil rights activist. The statement of purpose on Weigle's website showed some overlapping with key parts of Diamond's platform, particularly concerning accessibility of healthcare; job creation, a living wage, and affordable housing; upgraded Internet service in her district with its geographic challenges and low population density; and commitment to improving prospects for young people raised in the district who wanted to remain there as adults. Weigle's campaign website also indicated that, while she and her family had lived in Okanagan County for just three years going into the 2018 campaign, she'd spent summers in the area when she was growing up.

With District 12 leaning heavily toward the Republican Party in recent times, there was some question of whether the stepping down of long-time Republican State Representative Condotta, combined with the likely vote-splitting of two first-time Republican candidates, might clear a path for someone other than a Republican to win the race. Although Weigle, with her Democratic Party credentials, may have seemed the likelier beneficiary, Diamond had already gone some distance with her campaign and had a sizable war chest by the time Weigle—like Greening, a mini-filer—registered her candidacy in May.

When the primary campaign was underway, Diamond pressed on in the manner she'd established while expecting to face a long-sitting incumbent until Condotta made his announcement in early May. She continued raising money and motoring around the district to appear at meet-and-greet events aimed at letting voters get a good glimpse of an independent who was dead set on taking the battle to whatever major-party opposition she was up against.

Diamond focused some of her spending during a busy primary campaign on print ads in the local newspapers, business cards, Facebook ads, signs and billboards, and fuel to get around to her meet-and-greet appearances as she brought her nonpartisan, grassroots-oriented message to mainly rural voters in the 12th district. She appeared at venues and events ranging from a pie shop to a parade and appeared to gain traction as a serious candidate to people who knew her more as a physician or activist and to others who hadn't known her at all until she announced her candidacy in late 2017 or, in many cases, until some months afterward. Diamond says, "I was a complete unknown in three of the four counties" in the 12th district. "I basically lived in the other three counties [during the campaign], and I knocked on doors all day long."

Outspending and out-appearing her opponents, Diamond nonetheless had her work cut out for her as she faced a statewide tradition of voters' sticking predominantly with the big parties and, in her district, overwhelming support for the Republicans. It perhaps worked to her advantage that one of her Republican opponents in the primary campaign, 28-year-old Greening, wasn't really hitting it off with voters and would probably gain greater notoriety a few months later due to allegations of cheating in a marathon and submitting a false time in an attempt to qualify for the Boston Marathon. The other Republican in the race, Goehner, was a four-term Chelan County Commissioner and a pear orchard owner in Dryden, Washington, with community roots and connections similar to Diamond's. On the surface, Goehner's message as a candidate seemed to have a similar for-the-people dynamic as Diamond's, particularly regarding the need to make healthcare more accessible. An interesting side note is that Goehner's nephew Chris Goehner was briefly in the same race as a candidate on the Democratic side during the early part of the campaign before stepping aside.

Weigle's campaign, meanwhile, didn't appear to resonate with many voters in the district who weren't already disposed toward supporting a candidate who identified herself as a Democrat. Although Weigle's profile on the Okanagan Democrats website informed readers that she'd marched decades earlier with Cesar Chavez, her relatively brief residency in the district, her message on behalf of a party that many voters in the 12th district had come to reject, and her mini-filer status with its limited resources seemed to keep her more near the edge of the campaign than near the center. While Weigle's (D) "branding" had the potential to pose serious challenges to an independent candidacy such as Diamond's, from early on it appeared the four-person race for state representative in District 12 would come down to Republican pear grower Goehner and independent doctor Ann Diamond—and if that scenario held true to form throughout the primary campaign and Diamond could manage a first- or second-place finish, she'd beat the odds and advance to the November general election.

Diamond says, "I felt I was [a strong] candidate. ... I had started early and had been in the race the whole time, so I was hopeful I would make it through the primary."

Right out of the gate in May, Keith Goehner spent the majority of his early contributions on management services from a company located in his district. Playing catch-up in the early stages, he also paid out a significant chunk of his contributions on a website, signs, and postal ads. Goehner pulled in plenty of cash from businesses, individuals, and PACS, but at no point did he catch up to Diamond when it came to fundraising. Yet, while Diamond outspent Goehner by a wide margin and often seemed to be the more visible and accessible candidate around the district, she probably had to do more catching up overall simply because of her decision to run as an independent and political outsider. Though her early start, grassroots appeal, and ability to attract contributions gave her some momentum going into the primary election, Diamond was well aware of what had happened to previous independent legislative candidates facing off in primaries against opponents representing, or seeking to represent, both major parties.

While history made her a decided underdog, she says, "Sometimes people like disruption. They like an underdog, and the fact I could say there hadn't been an independent since the very first [Washington] legislature [in 1889] caused people to pause, and I think it helped me."

After a final spurt of spending during the waning weeks of the primary campaign, when both Diamond and Goehner laid out money on print and radio ads and a new supply of yard signs, the results were announced on August 7: Diamond finished well behind Goehner, 45 percent to 30, but she finished ahead of Democrat Weigle and second Republican candidate Greening. That made Diamond the first independent in Washington since the top-two primary system was implemented in 2008 to advance to the general election after facing opponents from both major parties during the primary. Quoted by Stang, at Crosscut.com, following Diamond's successful primary showing, Chris Vance, referring to a common public perception of independent candidates, said, "So, by now, they know she isn't a kook." In the same article, Diamond added, "I won in my own county, so people don't think I'm a fringe candidate. Making it through a top-two primary should show I'm a viable candidate."

While Diamond was the only independent legislative candidate in Washington to make it through a primary while facing both Democratic and Republican opponents, she wasn't the only one to advance to the general election by finishing a race in the top two. Of the 29 independents, "independents," or nonpartisans who filed as candidates for the Washington State Legislature in 2018, there were six, other than Diamond, who managed to advance to the November general election. Five of the six had the good fortune of facing a single opponent in the primary.

One of those five was Pierre Malebranche, running for the State Senate in Washington's Legislative District 29, which covers most of Tacoma. Malebranche was an immigrant from Haiti whose U.S. Army service in the 1980s saw him stationed at Ft. Lewis, Washington, near Tacoma. After his discharge, Malebranche remained in Pierce County, Washington, working as a truck driver who, according to his bare-bones website, had "grown tired of politics as usual in Olympia." Pointing out that "[t]he incumbent is out of touch with his constituents," Malebranche pledged to lower property taxes, car tab costs, and crime rates in his district.

The incumbent on Malebranche's radar was Democratic political veteran Steve Conway, an academic and labor relations specialist who'd served in the state legislature without a break for a full quarter-century. District 29's state senator since 2011, Conway, in his Voters' Guide statement, touted the length of his tenure ("I have proudly served you as Senator and Representative since 1993") and his record of "[securing] state funding for many projects in our district." Conway also had a strong record of securing PAC and corporate contributions from in and out of state.

Malebranche, meanwhile, raised a few thousand dollars in what seemed to be portrayed as an everyman campaign waged by a naturalized citizen candidate standing up to a well-established Democratic incumbent—a Democratic incumbent the Republicans seemingly knew better than to waste any time or other resources opposing during the 2018 elections. After the primary, the Tacoma *News Tribune* referred to candidate Malebranche, "who's running as an independent," as "a Haitian immigrant, US Army veteran, and truck driver—a quintessentially hard working resident of the 29th."

Much of that may have been true, but a quick search of documents readily accessible via the Washington State Public Disclosure Commission (PDC) website revealed that Malebranche's claim of being an "independent" candidate in 2018's District 29 State Senate race was less than convincing. The PDC site shows Malebranche's first C-4 disclosure report was filed on June 8, 2018, to cover the period from May 15–31 of the same year. The C-4 provides a public record of a campaign's expenditures and contributions, and Malebranche's C-4 for the second half of May documented three expenditures: two, totaling about $44, for GoDaddy services related to Malebranche's website domain and email hosting and the cost of renting a post office box; and the $477.76 filing fee required of candidates running for the Washington Legislature (except those "without sufficient assets or income" [Washington Secretary of State website] who are granted a waiver and submit 477 signatures of registered voters in the district [to match the dollar amount of the filing fee]).

While those expenditures alone were unlikely to raise the eyebrow of anyone taking a moment to look into the finances of candidate Malebranche and the supporting committee he'd identified in his C-1 Candidate Registration form (which confirmed Malebranche's political party as "independent") as "Friends of Pierre," a glance at the "In Kind

Contributions" section (Schedule B) of Malebranche's C-4 covering May 15-31, 2018, reveals the identity of one of those "Friends of Pierre"—the only one listed as a contributor through the end of May and one that would chip in with contributions later in the race. The May contribution was for $477.76 and was declared to cover Malebranche's candidate filing fee, which it did to the penny. The contributor of Malebranche's fee to file as an "independent" candidate was identified as the "Senate Republican Campaign" based in Olympia. Later in the campaign, the same Senate Republican Campaign provided in-kind contributions of logo design and yard signs, according to C-4 reports submitted to the PDC by Malebranche or his campaign. On top of that, the Senate Republican Campaign Committee (SRCC) website listed the Legislative District 29 State Senate race as one of Washington State's "SRCC Races" in 2018 and showed 32 photos of candidates apparently backed by the SRCC—one of them Malebranche.

At any rate, Malebranche took 32 percent of the primary vote in his two-man race and advanced to the general election, still listed as an "independent," as would remain the case until November.

As far as other alternative candidates were concerned, a dozen Libertarians filed to run for the Washington State House or State Senate in 2018. Two Libertarians—despite registering as candidates months ahead of the filing deadline—dropped out of the primary campaign when facing opposition from more than one major-party candidate. The third Libertarian to drop out, District 49's Joshua Smith, would have faced a single candidate on the ballot, but that opponent was a Democratic incumbent, Monica Stonier, that Smith had virtually no chance of defeating. With plenty of corporate and PAC funding from in and out of the state, Stonier ran unopposed in a southern Washington district in which both state representative seats would be handed back to unopposed Democratic incumbents in 2018.

Of the other nine Libertarians who filed as candidates in legislative races, seven were mini-filers or might as well have been, given their level of contributions and expenditures. Five of those seven faced more than one opponent in the primary, with all five finishing well back and failing to advance to the general election. The other two, each facing only a single opponent, trailed their lone Democratic opponents 89 percent to 11 but advanced to the general election by virtue of their automatic top-two finishes.

The only other Libertarians who advanced in legislative contests also ran in two-candidate fields during the primary race but managed to raise more money. One was District 22 State House candidate Allen Acosta, who had experience as Regional Director of Washington's Libertarian Party and managed to raise several thousand dollars in mainly small donations.

In his Voters' Guide statement, Acosta said he could "integrate red district and blue district leaning solutions" and exhorted voters to "turn the 22nd purple." In the primary vote, Acosta trailed PAC-funded Democrat Beth Doglio 77 percent to 23. Matthew Dubin, meanwhile, had registered early as a Libertarian State House candidate in District 36, which was the only Washington legislative district that had a Libertarian running for each of its state legislative offices in 2018. Dubin raised a surprising total of about $60,000 before the primary election and spent over $50,000 of it in an effort to convey his message of empathy and inclusion. In the end, outspent by corporate- and PAC-funded Democratic incumbent Gael Tarleton, Dubin advanced from the primary to the general election with 13 percent of the vote.

Among the few other alternative candidates filing as state legislative candidates in Washington in 2018 was Keith Smith, a mini-filer who ran for state representative in Legislative District 32, which extends from North Seattle to suburban Lynnwood. On his C-1 Candidate Registration form, Smith identified his party preference as "Centrist," and his Voter's Guide statement followed up by indicating Smith "Prefers Centrist Party." As a result, some voters may have associated Smith with the Centrist Party founded by Californian John P. Reisman, whose website bio identified him as "a generalist by nature and inclination [whose] views are systems based, which allows for a widely scoped field of consideration." Reisman's bio contained a wide-ranging list of interests including economics, geopolitics, behavioral science, quantum physics, belief systems, and plenty more; and the bio credited Reisman with directing or producing several video or musical projects, with inventing the flight watch aviation timer, and with writing a book titled *Exposing the Climate Hoax: It's All About the Economy*.

Surprisingly, Smith—who reports he intended to identify himself as a small-*c* "centrist" and not as a member or ally of any Centrist party— earned the District 32, House Position 1 *Seattle Times* endorsement in its July 5, 2018, edition. The *Times* began its endorsement article by acknowledging, "Keith Smith, a Lynnwood grocery clerk and advocate for children and good governance, is a longshot candidate for the Legislature." But the *Times* went on to laud Smith's life experience and ability to overcome challenges. The article suggested the Democratic incumbent had served long enough, and it took a jab at Smith's Republican opponent for "[expressing] an unfortunate affinity for repugnant gadfly Milo Yiannopoulos." Despite the *Times* endorsement, Smith, who said he intended to caucus with the Democrats if elected, finished with six percent of the primary vote, well behind incumbent Cindy Ryu, at 72 percent, and trailing Republican Diodato Boucsieguez, at 21 percent. While it appears the endorsement didn't have much effect on the race, one may wonder whether the *Times* fell short in its reporting by not clarifying the exact nature of Smith's "Centrist/centrist" preference.

The 2018 primary campaign also saw the filing of a few "independent" candidates of the most dubious sort—i.e., those identifying themselves as "Independent Republican" or "Independent Democrat" in their runs for the Washington State Legislature. In District 29, Branden Durst registered as an "Independent Democrat" candidate for state representative in March. In 2016, running as a Democrat without the "independent" disclaimer, Durst had been ousted in the primary by fellow Democrat David Sawyer and "Independent Republican" Rick Thomas. But in 2018, not long after filing, Durst discontinued his candidacy and relocated to Idaho. Durst was born in Idaho and had served as a Democrat for two terms in the Idaho State House and for a year in the Idaho State Senate before resigning his seat in late 2013 and moving to Tacoma, Washington, according to ballotpedia.org, "to focus on his family, as he was splitting time between living in Boise and Seattle." Shortly after arriving back in Idaho in 2018, Durst jumped into another political race, falling short in a nonpartisan bid for a six-year trusteeship on the Boise School Board.

Running for the Washington Legislature in 2018 were two "Independent Republicans." In District 33 near Seattle, Kun Wang, a business owner and naturalized U.S. citizen, filed as a candidate for the State Senate out of concern, as expressed in his Voters' Guide statement, that "the American dream is threatened and is slipping away for so many." His statement expressed support for businesses as job creators and added, "High property taxes, job taxes, inflated car tabs and tolls are driving folks to the point they can't afford to live in our community." While Wang, running as a mini-filer, trailed PAC-funded, corporate-funded, three-term State House and three-term State Senate Democratic veteran Karen Keiser 68 percent to 25 in the August primary election, Wang—who wasn't acknowledged as a Republican candidate on the Washington Senate Republican Campaign Committee (SRCC) website—advanced to face Keiser in the general election as a result of outrunning the third candidate in the race, Libertarian Charles Schaefer.

One "Independent Republican" who was acknowledged by the SRCC—to the tune of a $5,000 contribution—was Savio Pham, a State Senate candidate in District 38 in Snohomish County north of Seattle. Like Wang a naturalized U.S. citizen and a newcomer to elective politics, Pham, in his Voters' Guide statement, made a similar reference to the American dream, saying, "[It] is now out of the reach of most of our Everett community. Between property tax hikes, home prices, tolls and car-tab fees, the current leadership forces families to make tough decisions while driving jobs out of the region." In his 38th district race, Pham faced Democratic incumbent John McCoy, a 16-year veteran of the legislature who, according to Pham in his Voters' Guide statement, "voted 'No' four times, rejecting $1 billion in property tax relief ... refused to fix dishonest car-tab valuations and voted to keep his files secret from the public. Plainly put, he's ignored our community and our voice to put the needs of his party and special interest[s] first." While Pham managed to edge out a second Democrat in his three-man primary race to face McCoy in the general election, Pham's message about party needs and special interests may have carried a little more credibility had he distanced himself from the Republican Party by some other means than standing behind a dubious "independent" disclaimer.

6

Microcosm of the Nation

Spotlight on Washington State
(Part 2)

Municipal, "Special Purpose," County, Judicial,
and State Executive Politics

Although legislative races in Washington State—as in the country at large—often reek of the bitter partisanship evident in federal election races, municipal elections in Washington, at least on the surface, are conducted as nonpartisan contests. Candidates in Washington's municipal elections—regardless of the size of the city, town, or village involved—don't declare party preferences or affiliations when seeking election, and elected municipal officials are considered nonpartisan as long as they remain in office.

While the nonpartisan requirement may seem to foster a level of cooperation not often evident in other political settings and political bodies, municipal politicking in Washington is hardly free of the troubles associated with red-and-blue power sharing and gridlock across the United States; and by no means does the requirement dictate that the majority of "nonpartisan" municipal candidates or elected officials don't share the major-party preferences, affiliations, or connections of their counterparts at the legislative level. That's especially true as far as Washington's larger cities are concerned.

Despite the restriction on municipal candidates in Washington declaring their party preferences, there's nothing restricting or preventing Republican and Democratic organizations from declaring *their* preferences with regard to candidates running for municipal office. Likewise, while candidates in all but the smallest municipalities are held to the same standard of financial affairs disclosure as candidates for the state legislature when it comes to reporting campaign contributions and expenditures, municipal candidates are also given similar latitude with regard to soliciting or accepting contributions. Like legislative candidates, Washington's municipal candidates can select, on the C-1 Candidate Registration form, either the mini-reporting option, indicating intent to raise and spend no more than $5,000 during the campaign, or the broader full-reporting option, which allows for unlimited campaign contributions as long as they fall within the same legal limits that apply to legislative candidates ($1,000 from any PAC or individual per election) and are properly reported.

And while municipal candidates in Washington may be nonpartisan in name, political party committees can legally contribute to their candidacies to the same degree to which they're permitted to contribute to partisan legislative candidates' campaigns—that is, to the tune of one dollar per registered voter per election cycle, according to the PDC website. That means candidates running in smaller municipalities—and, therefore, probably not much on the party committees' radar anyway—aren't eligible to receive particularly large sums of party money. As a result, nonpartisan candidates and officials in Washington's smaller communities very often live up to the "nonpartisan" label as far as their municipal interests or duties are concerned. Such is far less the case, however, with regard to candidates and officials in Washington's larger municipalities.

A case in point is Seattle Mayor Jenny Durkan (2017–2021), who filed her candidacy for the nonpartisan office in May of 2017 following sitting Mayor Ed Murray's announcement, on the heels of sexual abuse allegations, that he wouldn't seek reelection later that year. Durkan, a former U.S. attorney for the Western District of Washington who was appointed to that post by President Obama in 2009, was a newcomer to elective politics, though a May 11, 2017, *Seattle Times* article announcing her candidacy described her as "an insider in Washington state's Democratic Party" (Beekman). According to a C-4 report submitted to the PDC by the Durkan campaign on June 12, 2017, the Washington State Democrats organization provided an in-kind contribution on May 14, 2017, when it shared voter files with the Durkan campaign. While that "sharing" was valued at $500, it may well have been worth a great deal more to Durkan, whose campaign set a record for money raised in a mayoral run in Seattle. In the general election, Durkan defeated fellow Democrat Cary Moon, who, according to the PDC website, received funding from the King County Democrats to help fuel her "nonpartisan" campaign for mayor.

As far as Seattle City Council is concerned, sitting members often have known political affiliations or major party organization endorsements—as is true of councils in larger municipalities across Washington. While municipal candidates on the whole don't receive nearly the

6. Microcosm of the Nation   41

degree of direct financial support from political parties and organizations that legislative candidates do, there are plenty of municipal candidates for mayor or council in medium-sized or larger Washington cities whose fundraising connections and tactics match up well with their openly partisan legislative counterparts.'

The Revised Code of Washington—the state's compilation of current laws—indicates, in RCW 29.A.52.231, that "All city, town, and special purpose district elective offices shall be nonpartisan and the candidates therefor shall be nominated and elected as such." "Special purpose district elective offices" include, among others, public utility commissioner, fire commissioner, port commissioner, park commissioner, and school "director" or board member.

Though a glance at C-1 forms filed in recent years with the PDC reveals that a small number of "special district" candidates apparently forgot they were vying for nonpartisan office and identified political parties on their registration forms, special district offices generally seem to be free of major parties' string-pulling, as those offices are largely charged with providing day-to-day services to district residents and are likely to steer clear of most issues at the top of the big parties' priority lists. While PACs and political party organizations are as free to contribute to special district election candidates as to municipal "nonpartisan" candidates, Washington's special district races, for the most part, aren't funded to ridiculous proportions and, on the surface, show little direct link to any sizable major-party influence—although an October 29, 2017, *Washington Post* article, by Valerie Strauss, on the infiltration of non-transparent "dark money" into school board races identified Washington—along with Colorado, Louisiana, California, Minnesota, and Arkansas—as one state in which school board candidates have been backed by "dark money." As far as Washington State was concerned, Strauss didn't elaborate any further.

The vast majority of school board candidates in Washington tend to be mini-filers who raise and spend little or no money on their campaigns. A relatively small number, however, manage to raise in the tens of thousands of dollars, often with contributions—some of significant size—from mainly Democratic Party institutions or organizations, Democratic Party–aligned labor organizations, or the Democratic-leaning Washington Education Association. While Washington doesn't appear to have had many large out-of-state contributions pouring into recent school board elections, it can be difficult to trace some contributions back to their original sources out of state. It's also difficult to ascertain the nature of every legitimate-looking contribution from an individual or organization *in* Washington—but even so, there's ample evidence that Washington State has had experience with "nonpartisan" school board candidates who weren't nonpartisan at all.

At the county level, meanwhile, while most positions are nonpartisan by law, that doesn't normally prevent candidates for key county offices—or holders of those offices—from letting their major-party colors show. The best example, perhaps, is James Dow Constantine. Constantine, formerly a Democratic state representative and state senator, switched to county politics in 2002, when he parlayed his partisan political connections into a "nonpartisan" seat on the King County Council. In 2009, fueled by well over a million dollars in contributions—a large portion from Democratic Party–aligned organizations and interests—Constantine was elected King County Executive, another "nonpartisan" position. In 2013 Constantine rode nearly a million more dollars to reelection, and in 2017 he rode another million—much of it, again, contributed by Democratic-aligned organizations and interests—to a third "nonpartisan" term as King County Executive in a manner that could be taken as one more slap in the face to citizens who support truth in advertising and integrity in government.

Probably an even harder slap, in some cases, is the "nonpartisan" label worn by judicial candidates and sitting judges in Washington. While voters likely aren't too surprised to find a little partisan leaning from many of their "nonpartisan" elected officials, citizens on the whole seem inclined to expect a higher standard of integrity from people on the bench. Washington's laws regarding the conduct of judicial candidates seem to reflect some of that expectation, as the Washington Courts website reports that "[RCW] Canon 7(B)(2) provides that judges or candidates for judicial office shall not personally solicit or accept campaign funds." But then Canon 7(B)(2) also "provides that judges or candidates for judicial office may establish committees of responsible persons to secure and manage campaign funds." The Washington Courts website continues, "The Code of Judicial Conduct does not place any monetary limitations on the amount an individual may contribute or who may make contributions to a judicial candidate." Aside from that—though there are obvious limits to what they can say regarding legal issues—judicial candidates and sitting judges in Washington, generally speaking, are free to appear at partisan political events to support their own interests or those of other judicial or political candidates. Of course, it goes without saying that some form of financial benefit could result.

While there's a $2,000 limit on judicial campaign contributions per election cycle from party organizations, PACs, corporations, and the like, that limit is double what is generally permitted in legislative, municipal, and county elections. Not surprisingly, then, some judicial candidates—all the way up to the elected State Supreme Court—run well-funded campaigns that may not entirely live up to the spirit of nonpartisanship that some citizens, though probably a dwindling number, might expect of their judicial candidates. The fact is, judicial candidates who choose to keep their distance from major-party organizations and PACs in an effort to display true nonpartisan principles put themselves at a serious disadvantage when it comes to getting elected.

As far as statewide offices in Washington are concerned, the Superintendent of Public Instruction, the overseer of K–12 education across the state, is a nonpartisan office—albeit one that's about as "nonpartisan" as most other nonpartisan posts of any visibility in Washington State. The sitting Washington Superintendent of Public Instruction in 2018, Chris Reykdal, elected to a four-year term in 2016, was a former Democratic state representative who rode some key Democratic Party–aligned endorsements and over $240,000 in contributions—much of it from PACs and labor organizations—to victory in his 2016 race for state superintendent. The previous Superintendent of Public Instruction, Randy Dorn, also a former Democratic state representative, had raised a similar amount—including a $50,000 contribution from the Washington State Democratic Central Committee—en route to getting elected to the nonpartisan Superintendent of Public Instruction post in 2008 before winning reelection in 2012.

Other key statewide executive elective offices in Washington are openly partisan. While smaller-party and legitimately independent or nonpartisan candidates have run for those offices at times since Washington achieved statehood in 1889, on the whole the historical narrative regarding Washington's statewide executive offices very closely mirrors the narrative regarding legislative offices throughout the state's history—i.e., in both cases there's an unmistakable theme of almost utter domination by the Republican and Democratic parties.

Every one of Washington's 21 governors since statehood has been a Democrat or a Republican. One—Washington's third governor, John Rogers—was elected as a Populist in 1896 but joined the Democratic Party after the two parties largely merged during his first term, and Rogers was reelected as a Democrat in 1900. As for the recent era, while gubernatorial races in Washington saw plenty of alternative choices on the ballot from the late 1800s until the early 2000s, no candidate other than a Republican or Democrat has come close to getting on the general election ballot since the top-two primary was instituted in 2008.

The situation is almost identical regarding the state's second-highest executive post, the lieutenant governorship. Washington's only lieutenant governor since statehood who was other than a Republican or Democrat was Thurston Daniels, a Populist elected along with Governor Rogers in 1896. While alternative choices to the big-party candidates for lieutenant governor have appeared on ballots over the years since then, few have caused any concern to the major parties, and not one has made it to the general election since the top-two primary was introduced.

As for the office of Washington Secretary of State, the story is virtually the same. Populist Will Jenkins, elected with Rogers and Daniels in 1896, was a lone chink in an otherwise unbroken chain of Republicans and Democrats to hold the post from 1889 to 2018. As with other partisan statewide elective offices, alternative candidates for Washington Secretary of State have fallen well short in attracting votes and contributions, and since the introduction of the top-two primary no candidate other than a Democrat or Republican has survived to the general election.

Except during that brief period in the late 1800s and early 1900s when the Populist Party swept into Washington, all of Washington's attorneys general since statehood have represented the Democratic and Republican parties. As for fairly recent times, in 2012 Democrat Robert Ferguson narrowly outspent Republican Reagan Dunn $1.683 million to $1.614 million and became attorney general, Washington's top legal official. In 2016, with no Republican opposing Ferguson, Libertarian and lawyer Joshua Trumbull stepped into the vacuum; but unfortunately, Ferguson's $1.4 million to $3,000 "edge" in money spent on the campaign probably made the result a foregone conclusion.

There's nothing positive to report, meanwhile, regarding the

John Rogers, Washington State's third governor (1896–1901), was elected to his first term as a Populist before switching to the Democratic Party a year or two before he died in office in 1901. Rogers' first few years as governor represent the only period of governorship in Washington's history by anyone other than a Republican or Democrat (Governor Rogers, Susan Parish Photograph Collection, 1889–1990, Washington State Archives, Digital Archives, http://www.digitalarchives.wa.gov).

historical success or recent prospects of independent, nonpartisan, or smaller-party candidates for Washington's other statewide elective offices—namely, insurance commissioner, public lands commissioner, state auditor, and state treasurer. Like every other partisan political office in Washington State, those offices have been and remain under almost total control by a gluttonous and well-funded duopoly that seems to be getting hungrier and fatter by the day.

Federal Politics

Since statehood in 1889, Washington has been represented in the U.S. Senate by 11 Democrats and 13 Republicans—*period*. Alternative candidates for the Senate have been on the ballot many times, but not one has seriously challenged the two-party lock on power. Going into the 2018 elections, Washington's U.S. Senate contingent was represented by two Democrats, Maria Cantwell and Patty Murray, with over 40 years of U.S. Senate experience between them and, seemingly, the job security of tenured professors.

Murray, formerly a state legislator, was first elected to the U.S. Senate in 1992. A career politician by any measure, she's served on numerous committees, raised tens of millions of campaign dollars, and generally voted on the Senate floor in a manner that identifies her as a loyal Democrat. Over the course of her five U.S. Senate campaigns, Murray has faced numerous independent, nonpartisan, or smaller-party challengers, and she's also opposed a Republican each time. In the first of her general elections that followed a top-two primary, Murray defeated Republican Dino Rossi in 2010. Six years later she defeated then–Republican Chris Vance, whose Voters' Guide statement voiced frustration with "politicians in both parties who won't tell the American people the truth." Vance's statement continued, "I believe with new leadership we can bring Republicans and Democrats together to solve America's problems." After losing to Murray, 59 percent to 41, Vance would break from the Republican Party and cofound Washington Independents.

That decision was inevitable, he says, when it became clear the Republican Party was following Trump down a path Vance didn't want to travel. "I no longer believed the same things that most Republicans believed," Vance says.

Meanwhile, Cantwell, a U.S. Senator since 2001, was nearing the end of her third term in 2018. She'd been a veteran of state politics before getting elected to the U.S. House of Representatives in 1992, losing a U.S. House reelection bid in 1994, and returning to politics as a Democratic candidate for the U.S. Senate in 2000. In the September 2000 primary Cantwell finished second to veteran Republican Senator Slade Gorton but then, in the general election, narrowly slipped past Gorton following a recount. In the 2006 general election Cantwell had an easier time, handily defeating Republican Michael McGavick along with one Libertarian, one Green, and one independent—each of the latter three taking one percent of the vote. In the 2012 primary Cantwell finished atop a list of eight candidates—seven seeking nomination as Democrats or Republicans and the eighth running as a candidate for the Reform Party and earning one percent of the vote. In the 2012 general election Cantwell defeated Republican Michael Baumgartner 60 to 40 percent.

Rated by ballotpedia.org as "one of the most reliable Democratic votes ... [and] considered a safe vote for the Democratic Party in Congress," Cantwell served on several committees and showed no inclination to hand over the reins as she barreled forward in hopes of winning a fourth term as U.S. Senator in 2018.

Opposing Cantwell in the 2018 primary campaign was a full slate of 28 candidates, including 13 who identified their preferred party as Republican. The majority of those Republicans were newcomers to elective politics, but one notable exception was perennial Washington State political candidate and also-ran Goodspaceguy—born, according to his Wikipedia entry, Michael George Nelson—who, in his Voters' Guide statement, informed the public, "I, freemarket Goodspaceguy, was electorally defeated 18 times." In his most recent previous run for office—for the office of King County Executive in 2017—Goodspaceguy had identified his occupation, in his 2017 primary Voters' Guide statement, as "Part owner: Boeing, Microsoft, PacCar, Disney, Irobot, Orbital, Southwest, etc." In previous years he'd run for a variety of offices, including governor and U.S. Representative, and over the course of his 18 attempts to get elected, Goodspaceguy had sought to align his efforts with a variety of parties, including the Republican, Democratic, and Libertarian parties and the "Employment Party"—the latter difficult to trace to any other organization or entity on earth.

While Goodspaceguy had once previously advanced to a general election—for a position on the Port of Seattle Commission in 2015—such wasn't to be the case in 2018, when his Voters' Guide proposals to begin colonizing space, "[starting] with small habitats, perhaps privately owned by billionaires"; his concerns that "[w]e have unemployed people, criminals, and poverty maintained by welfare"; and his call to "rehabilitate Spaceship Earth [via free market economics] by transforming people into productive people within the labor force" weren't enough to coax voters to push him past the primary, where he took 0.41 percent of the vote.

6. Microcosm of the Nation 47

Of the other 12 Republicans in Washington's 2018 U.S. Senate primary race, 11 finished with results similar to Goodspaceguy's—i.e., they took anywhere from 0.13 percent of the vote to just over two percent. The only Republican to gain traction—and the only Republican Party insider of note, having been Washington State Republican Party Chairman for five years—was well-funded former Seattle TV news journalist Susan Hutchison, who finished far ahead of the dozen other Republican hopefuls combined with 24 percent of the primary vote.

As for candidates identifying themselves as Democrats and challenging Cantwell in Washington's 2018 U.S. Senate primary election, all four such candidates *combined* trailed Cantwell, 55 percent to three. Other parties represented on the primary ballot included the Libertarian Party, the Green Party, the Human Rights Party, the Stand Up America Party, the Freedom Socialist Party, and the FDFR Party—short for "Fuck Democrats Fuck Republicans"—whose senatorial candidate, Brad Chase, in his Voters' Guide entry, directed prospective supporters to his campaign website at www.screwbothparties.com. Senatorial candidates from all those other parties managed to score less than two percent of the primary vote combined.

While voters may have found platforms and views of the smaller-party candidates a little confusing—if they even bothered to look into them—perhaps even more confusing was the issue of affiliation or non-affiliation of the five "independents" listed on the same primary ballot. In their Voters' Guide profiles it was indicated that all five presumably independent candidates had a preference for the "Independent Party," suggesting all five were "Independents" and not "independents." That's a significant distinction because there are political parties in the United States with the word "Independent" prominently in their names. One, the American Independent Party (AIP), had its roots in the 1960s, when it nominated then-segregationist George Wallace for the U.S. presidency. More recently, the AIP, while an invisible presence in most of the country, showed its "independence" by endorsing Donald Trump for president while touting itself, according to the *Los Angeles Times* on April 17, 2016, as "The Fastest Growing Political Party in California."

But after an investigation, the *Times* determined that "a majority of [the AIP's] members have registered with the party in error." The *Times* investigation concluded that many voters in California, intending to register as independent voters, were confused by the use of the word "independent" in the party's name and unintentionally became registered members of a party that endorsed Donald Trump and his border wall.

Two years later the *Times* followed up with an article titled "California voters are joining this party by mistake, but lawmakers aren't doing anything about it." The article, written by John Myers, one of the writers of the April 17, 2016, *Times* report, pointed out that Wyoming, for many years, hadn't permitted new political parties to use the word "independent" in their names. As far as the California/American Independent Party situation was concerned, Myers wrote, "Confusion has been reported by Californians from all walks of life—students, celebrities, even the incoming owner of this newspaper. Dr. Patrick Soon-Shiong, who is buying the *Los Angeles Times* and the *San Diego Union-Tribune*, is registered as a member of the American Independent party. A spokesman says it was a mistake and Soon-Shiong is changing his status to 'no party preference.'"

Stories of that sort may warrant a chuckle—if they weren't so common—but while it may be understandable that individual voters, eager to register their status as "independents" not beholden to either major party, sometimes let their guard down and inadvertently register as members of an "Independent" party, no governmental body should ever mistakenly identify an independent, whether a voter or a candidate, as a member or supporter of an "Independent Party." While it's hard to fathom that any independent (i.e., nonpartisan) candidate for the U.S. Senate in Washington in 2018 would have stood a chance against Cantwell, Hutchison, and their millions regardless of whether such an error had been made, it certainly can be argued that the Washington Secretary of State website—and, ultimately, Democratic Secretary of State Kim Wyman—committed a serious breach by misrepresenting the ideology or alignment of several candidates for the U.S. Senate.

Dave Strider of Tacoma, a Marine veteran and one of the mislabeled "Independent Party" candidates in Washington State's 2018 U.S. Senate race, is unsure when asked whether misrepresentation of his candidacy caused significant voter confusion. Yet he says, "[People] asked me what I was. I said, 'I'm an independent. I don't represent a party whatsoever.'"

In 129 years of statehood leading to the 2018 elections, Washingtonians seeking election to the United States House of Representatives without aligning with the Republican or Democratic party scored exactly the same number of electoral victories as alternative candidates running for the U.S. Senate—none. Going into the 2018 elections, there were six Democratic and four Republican U.S. Representatives serving Washingtonians. While a few chose not to stand for reelection in 2018, and while some congressional districts in Washington had independents and/or smaller-party candidates on the primary ballot, when the dust settled in early August—if not long before—it became evident that Washingtonians wouldn't be sending their first alternative candidate to the U.S. House of Representatives this time either.

In eight of Washington's 10 U.S. House districts, the 2018 general election would be a face-off between a Democrat and a Republican. In one of the other two districts, Congressional District 9, the general election would come down to two Democrats, both named Smith; and in Congressional District 2, a Libertarian whose only "Republican" opposition in the primary was a professional moving man identified in the Voters' Guide and on the ballot as "Moderate GOP" candidate "Uncle Mover," trailed Democratic incumbent Rick Larsen 65 percent to 8 but nonetheless advanced to the general election by outpolling a second Democrat, one Green Party candidate, one independent, and Uncle Mover.

The Washington congressional race getting the most notice was in the 8th Congressional District, where a dozen candidates—none an incumbent—ran for the U.S. House. While five candidates represented smaller parties or declared their nonpartisanship, it was Democrat Dr. Kim Schrier who was most successful in getting across to the electorate her potential as a fresh face in the politics of both Washingtons. In her Voters' Guide statement Schrier, a pediatrician for 16 years, declared, "I am not a career politician and will bring a new voice to Congress." To many Democrats she seemed to represent at least a partial changing of the guard in the Democratic Party to complement or offset the party's "old guard" represented by names like Feinstein, Warren, and Biden. Yet, given Schrier's commitment to the Democratic platform along with her moneyed connections, there probably wasn't much to suggest she was committed to any broader political change than a little reshuffling or re-prioritizing within the Democratic Party agenda.

As it turned out, Schrier—who managed to raise $7 million in her first run for office—edged out fellow Democrat Jason Rittereiser by half a percentage point and advanced to the general election to face Republic Party veteran Dino Rossi, who outpolled Schrier in the primary 43 percent to 19. While there were no guarantees that all of Rittereiser's supporters would get behind Schrier and smooth her path toward winning the general election, it seemed fair to say that, whatever one thought of Schrier's politics or her chances in November, she was one of two medicine-practicing newcomers to Washington State elective politics in 2018 who'd earned some notice and respect from observers of varying political dispositions—the other being State House independent candidate Ann Diamond.

7

A Brief Historical Survey of the U.S. Congress

The Senate

While Washington State hadn't wavered from electing a Republican or a Democrat to the U.S. Senate in all of its 129-year electoral history heading into the 2018 elections, other states, throughout their histories, had seen U.S. Senators with other affiliations or loyalties.

Such was inevitable, of course, in the early decades of the United States before the founding of the Democratic and Republican parties as we know them. In the earliest days of the U.S. Senate—a full century before Washington Territory became a state—party affiliations were often loose or informal, and United States Senators were chosen by state legislatures, as would remain the case until 1914, following ratification of the 17th Amendment to the U.S. Constitution in 1913. As a result, selections to the Senate during decades prior to the 1910s generally reflected power structures and party strengths in the individual states much more than they reflected what was going on nationally with the big political parties.

Parties well represented in the United States Senate between 1789 and 1913 included the Federalists and the Whigs, both of which wielded significant power and influence in their day. Even better represented in the Senate was the Democratic-Republican Party established by James Madison, Thomas Jefferson, and others to counter the Federalists. The Democratic-Republican Party, based on basic principles of republicanism, existed from the early 1790s until the 1820s and was the most dominant and most represented party of its day in the U.S. Senate.

Also represented in the Senate during the century-and-a-quarter era in which U.S. Senators were selected by state legislators were parties that sprang up in response to issues of particular concern in various states or regions—for example, Free Soilers in several northern states and

7. A Brief Historical Survey of the U.S. Congress   51

Nullifiers, Unionists, and Readjusters in the South in the nineteenth century; and, especially toward the end of the nineteenth century, Populists in a large stretch of the country. Various other parties were represented in the Senate as well, but from the introduction of the "modern" Republican Party in 1854, the norm was clearly for state legislatures—nearly always dominated by Democrats and Republicans—to choose U.S. Senators aligned with the major party that had the stronger grip on power in the legislature at the time. That party was usually, and predictably, the Republican Party in much of the North and the Democratic Party in the South.

Only one U.S. Senator from the era preceding ratification of the 17th Amendment in 1913 is widely remembered—or, more accurately, *best* remembered—as an independent. Maryland native and adopted Illinoisan David Davis was a former state legislator, a prominent judge, a Republican, a campaign manager to Abraham Lincoln, and, in 1862, an appointee to the U.S. Supreme Court. While serving on the high court, Davis opposed the Radical Republican agenda and broke from the Republican Party. He left the Supreme Court in 1877 when Illinois legislators appointed him to the U.S. Senate. Well respected and considered impartial, Davis served a single term in the Senate, including two years as president pro tempore, before walking away in 1883.

Former Republican and Lincoln aide David Davis already had a varied and prominent career in government before leaving the Republican Party on principle and serving a term as an independent U.S. Senator from Illinois in the latter days and aftermath of Reconstruction (Brady-Handy photograph collection, Library of Congress, Prints and Photographs Division).

Since U.S. Senators became popularly elected in 1914, many

candidates have run as nominees of parties other than the Democrats and Republicans, but only a handful have been elected. Going into the 2018 elections, the last "third party" U.S. Senator was New York's James Buckley, previously a Republican but elected to the Senate in 1970 as the nominee of the Conservative Party of New York. In 1976 Buckley—brother of author, commentator, and *National Review* founder William F. Buckley, Jr.—failed to get reelected, this time as the Republican Party nominee as well as the Conservative Party of New York nominee.

While a grand total of two recognized "independents" were elected to the U.S. Senate between 1914 and 1999, neither seemed particularly qualified to wear the "independent" label with any conviction. One, Nebraska's George Norris, served in Congress as a Republican for 33 years before getting elected to a final term as an "independent" senator in 1935 and caucusing with the Democrats. The other, Oregon's Wayne Morse, was a Republican senator who left the party in 1952 to become an independent. Three years later Morse joined the Democrats, and he got reelected as a Democrat in 1956.

As for the U.S. Senate's two "independent" members elected since 2000 (and currently serving), one, Vermont's Bernie Sanders—best known at present for attempting to capture the Democratic Party presidential nomination in 2016 and 2020—won the state's Democratic Party nomination for the Senate in 2006, 2012, and 2018, only to decline it each time after the primary, apparently to protect his status as an "independent" going into the general election. The other U.S. "independent" senator elected in the twenty-first century, Maine's Angus King, was aligned with the Democratic Party in the 1970s, serving as a legislative assistant to Maine Democratic Senator William Hathaway. Following a break from politics to practice law and to work in the alternative energy and energy conservation field, King returned to politics in 1993, announcing his intent to run for governor of Maine as an independent in the following year's election. According to the November 18, 1994, *New York Times*—10 days after King's victory over strong Republican and Democratic opponents—part of what may have endeared King to voters in Maine was a pledge "[that] he would never run for any other office." But after serving a second term as governor, from 1998 to 2003, and then sitting out politics for most of a decade to focus on teaching and getting back into the alternative energy industry, King backed away from his pledge and ran for the U.S. Senate after Maine's three-term senator Olympia Snowe, a Republican, decided to call it quits in 2012. King won the election handily and, following a term in which he, like Sanders, caucused and generally voted with the Democrats, King decided to run as an independent for another Senate term in 2018.

The House of Representatives

In the earliest United States Congresses, the seed of two-party domination was definitely planted by designation of candidates as "Pro-Administration"—aligned with the Federalists—and "Anti-Administration," aligned with the Democratic-Republicans. Unlike U.S. Senators, United States Representatives were directly elected starting with the first Congress in 1789, although strict voter "qualifications"—often relating to gender, race, religion, and financial health—usually kept the number of voters low. From the start of the first Congress, when the U.S. House of Representatives comprised only 59 members, until the 17th Congress 34 years later—by which time the House membership had more than tripled—every U.S. Representative, without exception, represented either the Pro-Administration/Federalist camp or the Anti-Administration/Democratic-Republican side.

From the early 1820s until the establishment of the modern Republican Party in the mid–1850s, the two-party system held firm in the House of Representatives, though there was some shifting as to what the two major parties or blocs were at any particular time. Interestingly, things might have taken a different course in the 1820s, as there appeared to be potential for the U.S. House of Representatives to evolve into something more than a two-party chamber. Part of that potential stemmed from the unraveling of the Democratic-Republican Party as a relatively unified entity and the election of large numbers of Democratic-Republicans from three opposing camps in 1822 and 1823. A smaller number of senators were also elected from opposing Federalist factions.

Of numerous smaller-party candidates who ran for the U.S. House of Representatives beginning in the 1820s, a relatively small number got elected to most Congresses through the remainder of the nineteenth century. During that era U.S. Representatives were elected by "qualified voters" in what were often small, peculiarly drawn congressional districts where priorities or concerns resonating with the local populace sometimes worked to the advantage of candidates unaffiliated with the major parties. The first real alternative party established in the United States, the Anti-Masonic Party, opposed the influence and secrecy of the Freemasons, an organization to which many prominent U.S. politicians had close ties. Established in 1828, the Anti-Masonic Party managed to get 40 candidates, most in the Northeast, elected to the U.S. House of Representatives and many more elected to state offices before essentially merging with the Whig Party—by then one of the "big two" parties of its day—in the late 1830s. In the South, meanwhile, the Nullifier Party, whose lifespan roughly mirrored the Anti-Masonic Party's, scored over two dozen victories for 14 of its House candidates—along with a small presence in the U.S. Senate—with its states' rights platform in the 1830s; and in Virginia, two members of an early incarnation of the state's Conservative Party—which would become more of a force during Reconstruction—were elected to the U.S. House of Representatives in 1838 (both having been Democrats in previous years).

The previous Congress, the 25th, had convened in 1837, amid national concerns over economics and slavery, in a Capitol Hill environment dominated by bitter differences between the Democrats and the Whigs. During that same Congress, Kentucky U.S. Representative and Whig William Graves shot and killed Maine U.S. Representative and Democrat Jonathan Cilley in a ridiculous episode having nothing to do with political incompatibility.

Independent candidates of various ideologies began appearing on ballots for the U.S. House of Representatives in the 1840s, though their "independent" status, diluted by past or present connections to the Whig or Democratic parties, was nearly always suspect. Leading up to the debut of the modern Republican Party in the mid-1850s, small parties reflecting particular divisions or concerns in American society of the day—particularly the Free Soilers and Unionist Parties—got some members elected to the House and had a small measure of short-lived influence on political discourse in Washington, D.C.

In 1854, as the modern Republican Party was just coming into being and the Whig Party was nearing the end of its life in America, the Democrats faced off in numerous House races against candidates from the Opposition Party, a Northern party mainly composed of antislavery ex-Democrats and ex-Whigs; and the American "Know Nothing" Party, a force for several years in the North and South with a questionable ideology supporting nativism and a middle ground on slavery. While all those parties showed some strength in the 1854 House elections, starting in 1856—with the new Republican Party fully in the national picture—House elections would snap back to being, essentially, two-horse races.

Yet the Democrats were a divided lot heading into the Civil War, with a full fracture taking place in 1860 when the party split into Northern and Southern branches. Aside from assuring the election of Illinois Republican Abraham Lincoln to the presidency, the Democratic split also resulted in the creation of offshoot political movements and parties that cost the Democrats seats in the House and quickly swung the majority to the Republican Party. Democratic losses in the House increased when House seats of seceding states went vacant. With the brief rise of the Unionist Party in border states during the Civil War and a fairly long and arduous road through Reconstruction in the South, the Democratic Party was

7. A Brief Historical Survey of the U.S. Congress   55

limited as a unified national political force until a decade after the Civil War, when it reclaimed its place as one of only two parties that seemed to matter.

While other parties—in particular, the Greenback Party, the Populist Party, the Progressive Party, the Farmer-Labor Party, and a few others—would have some moderate impact on the electoral history of the U.S. House of Representatives in later years, it was as early as the transition from Reconstruction to the Gilded Age in the 1870s that the Democratic and Republican parties were well on the way to establishing the manner of utter two-party domination in the House that has persisted to the present day. In a century and a half of Democratic-Republican dominance in the U.S. House since the 1870s, those two parties have traded control from time to time but have generally given up few seats to any other parties or to unaffiliated candidates.

That pattern of dominance has been especially pronounced since World War II. In the wake of the war through the 1950s only a few alternative candidates won election to the House of Representatives, and for a 30-year stretch from the 1960s through the 1980s, not a single alternative candidate was elected to the House despite pressing national concerns and bitter debates over Civil Rights, the Cold War, Vietnam, Watergate, Iran-Contra, and more. The drought broke—at least theoretically—in 1990, when Bernie Sanders got elected to the House for the first time as an "independent" who'd go on to caucus with the Democrats in the House of Representatives and, later, the Senate.

Two other "independents" got elected, in 1996 and 2000, during Sanders' eight years in the House, and each, like Sanders, would caucus with a major party while serving as an "independent" in the House. Historically, that was no aberration, as, ever since the earliest "independent" candidates got elected to the U.S. House of Representatives when the Democrats were battling the Whigs, the vast majority of "independent" U.S. Representatives had connections—and often lengthy pasts—with at least one of the two major parties of a particular period. Some were simply labeled "independent" for a time as they made a transition from one major party to another—as illustrated by the case of Virgil Goode, a Democratic state senator from Virginia for over 20 years who, in 1996, was elected as a Democrat to the U.S. House of Representatives. Goode was reelected to the House as a Democrat in 1998 but decided to leave the party prior to running for a third term, successfully, as an independent, in 2000. According to the January 25, 2000, *Washington Post*, Goode indicated "the change allows him to vote his conscience." But then, two years later, before Goode sought and won a fourth term in the House, his conscience led him to join the Republican Party.

An interesting footnote, perhaps, is that, eight years after joining the Republicans, Goode switched to the Constitution Party, and in 2012 he ran as that party's U.S. presidential nominee, barely getting out of the gate with less than 0.1 percent of the votes cast in November.

8

States, Municipalities, and Counties

While party affiliations of elected state officials were often loose or, in many cases, nonexistent in the earliest decades of American independence, over the course of the nineteenth century, party affiliations of legislators in the original and newly established states largely reflected the partisan composition of the United States Congress and Congress' general adherence to the two-party system of the day. But while state legislatures during decades predating the Civil War were most heavily represented by Federalists, Anti-Federalists, Democratic-Republicans, Whigs, and Democrats, smaller parties were widely represented as well, as they were in federal offices. Of course, independents were also part of the picture, though once party affiliations were firmly entrenched in American politics and deemed "respectable" if not a prerequisite for real participation in the democratic process, the majority of "independent" officeholders in state legislatures—as was the case with "independent" federal officeholders—had clear partisan histories or ties that put the lie to their standing as independents.

That wasn't too surprising, since it was the same electorate that chose both state legislators and U.S. Representatives. As far as U.S. Senators were concerned, the fact that they were selected, prior to 1914, by state legislators only reinforced the likelihood that legislatures around the country would reflect the party breakdown—i.e., one characterized by the dominance of two parties—evident in both houses of Congress.

During the early generations of U.S. nationhood, some governors were elected by state legislatures—as in New Jersey, Virginia, and South Carolina—while others were directly elected by a popular vote (albeit a limited popular vote), as in Maine, Illinois, and Delaware. Regardless of how governors came to power, however, their party affiliations closely mirrored the two-party system of their day, as has been the case ever since, particularly since the 1870s.

Of nearly 1,700 state governors to have held office between Reconstruction and 2017, about 40—or, roughly, one in 40—are remembered, if that's the right word, as being other than Republican or Democratic while they were in office. A closer look, however, reveals that the number of governors during that time span who weren't associated with the major parties is actually much smaller. For example, the majority of Populist Party governors elected across several states in the late 1800s would see their allegiances, and their factions' allegiances, slide over, in short order, to the Democratic Party. Some early twentieth-century Progressive governors had close associations with the Republican Party, and some governors associated with North Dakota's Nonpartisan League were, on examination, perhaps more Republican than nonpartisan.

Governors representing other alternative parties—such as the Greenback Party in 1880s Maine, Nevada's Silver Party during the late nineteenth/early twentieth century, and the Prohibition Party during the American "dry" era—also had major-party ties and endorsements and were never considered a serious threat to two-party rule. Since Prohibition, the majority of governors remembered as something other than Democratic or Republican—from Wisconsin Progressive Philip La Follette in the 1930s and Maine's first "independent" governor James Longley in the 1970s to Connecticut's Lowell Weicker, representing the self-established A Connecticut Party in the 1990s, and Rhode Island independent Lincoln Chafee during the first half of the 2010s—had significant major-party ties prior to winning their governorships and, in some cases, afterward. Alaska's Bill Walker, the state's incumbent governor in 2017, was an "independent" who'd twice failed in earlier attempts to win the Republican Party nomination for governor. A previous Alaska governor, Wally Hickel, who served from 1990 to 1994 under the Alaskan Independence Party banner, had previously served as governor, for about two years in the 1960s, as a Republican. Hickel would rejoin the Republican Party during the latter part of his second governorship in 1994.

Florida's Charlie Crist, governor from 2007 to 2011, was another "independent" who put a whole new twist on the word. Two and a half years after getting elected governor as a Republican, Crist became "independent" after leaving Florida's 2010 Republican senatorial primary race when momentum seemed to be favoring candidate Marco Rubio. Unsuccessful in his quest for the Senate—finishing second to Rubio—Crist served out the remainder of his gubernatorial term as an independent. Out of office, he joined the Democratic Party, and in 2014 he ran unsuccessfully, as a Democrat, for governor. In 2016 Crist won election to the U.S. House of Representatives as a Democrat and, apparently comfortable with his latest affiliation, stood for reelection in 2018.

8. States, Municipalities, and Counties

While most "alternative" governors haven't played the field to the extent Crist has, over three-quarters of those approximately 40 "alternative" governors between Reconstruction and 2017 probably wouldn't have scored well in a "truth in advertising" test. The majority had major-party histories, connections, or endorsements; a few jumped from party to party; and others clearly would have worn the cloak of a major party had they been able to. All told, it appears that no more than seven of those nearly 1,700 state governors from Reconstruction to 2017—one in nearly 250, or a mere 0.4 percent—were truly unaffiliated with the major parties or truly independent for reasons that appeared to spring more from principle or ideology than opportunism or gamesmanship.

The Seven

Colorado's eighth governor, **Davis Hanson Waite**, who served from 1893 to 1895, had been associated in earlier years with the Republican Party while serving as a state legislator in Wisconsin and working as a journalist in his native New York State. Waite became a leading member of the Populist Party in Colorado after arriving there from Kansas—another state in which he'd served as a legislator—in the early 1880s. In 1892 he rode the Populist Party nomination to the Colorado governorship; and unlike other Populist governors of the era, Waite kept his distance from the major parties and aimed to maintain the integrity of the Populists' agrarian and working-class platform. Though he lost his bid for a second term and left

Colorado was only into its teens in 1893 and, with a culture and economy largely centered on mining and agriculture, seemed to provide fertile ground for Populism to take root. That year, Populist Davis Hanson Waite (pictured) was elected governor. Nearly 130 years after his failing to get reelected to a second term, Waite, who'd been associated with the Republican Party in earlier years, remains the only governor in the state's history not to have been either a Republican or Democrat while in office (Colorado State Archives).

elective politics at age 69, Waite remained true to the Populist ideology, as a leading Colorado journalist, in his final years.

John Edward Jones was an immigrant from Wales who, a few years after arriving in the Silver State, helped establish the Nevada State Militia in the mid–1870s. After working in the civil service, Jones successfully ran for governor on the Silver Party's largely populist and free-silver (unlimited coinage) platform. As governor, Jones sought to maintain a stand-alone Silver Party, which many other party members aimed to steer into alliance with a major party. Jones died in 1895, after barely a year in office. His successor, **Reinhold Sadler**, an immigrant from Prussia, continued to serve the Silver Party's platform and interests as governor and got reelected in 1898. He served until early 1903—and while Sadler wasn't the last Silver Party nominee to serve as governor of Nevada, he was the last not to have a close association with the Democratic Party.

Julius Meier, a one-term independent governor of Oregon from 1931 to 1935, may well have run for that office as a Republican had the opportunity presented itself. Meier, a civic-minded lawyer, businessman, and public servant with no experience in elective politics, took up the mantle of a friend, George W. Joseph, who died after winning the Republican nomination for governor on a platform supporting public development of hydroelectric power. As the National Governors Association website reports, after the Republicans' replacement nominee favored private and not public development of hydro, Meier decided to run for governor as an independent to uphold his friend's position. Meier won the governorship and, though not entirely successful in implementing Joseph's vision for hydro, went on to earn generally high marks while in office and conducted himself in a manner that seemed consistent with the spirit of his self-designation as an independent. Following his single term as governor, both major parties showed interest in backing a Meier bid for the U.S. Senate, but, whether because of Meier's commitment to independence, his failing health, or his desire to get out of politics, nothing came of the offers, and Meier passed away two years later.

Meanwhile, Minnesota's Farmer-Labor Party, founded in 1918, reached its height during the Depression and was allied with a national Farmer-Labor Party that exerted some influence in other states. While the Minnesota Farmer-Labor Party would merge with the Democratic Party during World War II, two Depression-era Farmer-Labor governors of Minnesota seemed set on steering clear of major-party connections and influences as they tackled hard problems of the day. One, **Floyd B. Olson**, had failed in earlier attempts to get elected, as a Democrat, to the U.S. House and, as the Farmer-Labor nominee, to the governorship. Known as a tough but fair and independent-minded prosecuting attorney

8. States, Municipalities, and Counties

before winning the governorship in 1930, Olson had detractors but, in the view of many, seemed to maintain his reputation for fairness and principle until passing away in 1936, during his third two-year term as governor. **Elmer Benson**, was a close friend of Olson's with a similar commitment to public service and the social democratic principles of an independent Farmer-Labor Party. After serving for about a year in Washington, D.C., as a Farmer-Labor U.S. Senator, Benson was Governor of Minnesota from 1937 to 1939 before losing his bid for a second term. Afterward, he remained active in Farmer-Labor affairs until his party was absorbed by the Democrats.

After the Olson and Benson governorships in the 1930s all the way to the present day, probably the only other U.S. governor demonstrably faithful to third-party interests or real independence while keeping a convincing distance from major-party entanglements, influences, dollars, endorsements, and caucuses was another Minnesotan, **Jesse Ventura**, governor from 1999 to 2003. Ventura, born James Janos, was a Navy SEAL in Vietnam, a high-profile professional wrestler for a decade, and a Hollywood actor before kicking off his political life with a successful run for mayor of Minneapolis suburb Brooklyn Park in 1991. Seven years later, running as the nominee of the Ross Perot–founded Reform Party—though without explicit support from the party's national leadership—Ventura squeezed past Republican and Democratic candidates to earn the governorship with 37 percent of the vote. Focusing largely on lowering taxes, improving mass transit, and expanding trade opportunities for Minnesotans, Ventura had some successes despite seeing his efforts stifled at times by major-party state legislators who appeared to regard him as either a threat or an intruder. Citing media attacks on his family, Ventura declined to pursue a second term in 2003. Had he run for reelection, it wouldn't have been under the banner of the Reform Party, which Ventura left in 2000 when the party put its weight behind Pat Buchanan's effort to get elected president. Instead, Ventura would almost certainly have run as the nominee of the Independence Party of Minnesota, which, like Ventura, had broken off from the Reform Party during his term as governor. There appears to be no chance that Ventura would have considered aligning with one of the major parties to seek a second term.

The very fact that Ventura won a *first* term has to be seen as a major coup—if not a blueprint for any candidate or movement aiming for meaningful change in one of the upper levels of government. While Ventura was known to speak his mind in an often-unpredictable manner, it wasn't simply his standing as an anti-politician or a strapping everyman that had won him an unlikely governorship. As the *Washington Post*'s Jon Jeter reported on November 5, 1998—two days after Ventura became governor-elect—while "Ventura's celebrity, tough-guy image and shoot-from-the-hip theatrics played a big role in his success," his "surprising win" also "demonstrated the possibilities that come with decoupling money from politics." Specifically, as Jeter reported, a decade before Ventura's run for governor, Minnesota had enacted reforms to provide subsidies to candidates from outside the major parties who received five percent or more of the vote in a primary election. Ventura took 10 percent of the primary vote; and, as Jeter reported, pollsters, political scientists, and party officials concluded, "That, as much as anything, got Ventura's cash-poor campaign into the game." Without campaign finance reform, Ventura's showing of 10 percent in the primary, coupled with a general lack of funds, would have kept him at a serious disadvantage in the general election. But rules limiting campaign expenditures by the major-party candidates, Republican Norm Coleman and Democrat Hubert Humphrey III, kept the playing field relatively flat and prevented Coleman, Humphrey, and their parties "from running away with the campaign with a blitzkrieg of television ads." Jeter continued, "Unable to saturate the airwaves with political ads, the three candidates were forced to rely more on television debates to define themselves and their opponents to the voters. In that forum, Ventura clearly shined, appealing to blue-collar workers and young people with his candor, compassion and anti-establishment pronouncements."

Municipalities and Counties

It's difficult to measure or even estimate the degree of major-party influence and party affiliations across the board when it comes to municipal and county politics in the United States over the years. One difficulty is in determining to what degree "nonpartisan" candidates or officeholders at those levels have truthfully been nonpartisan, as many were simply required to wear the label regardless of how deeply mired they may have been in partisan politics. To the current day, municipal and county governments are as mixed a bag as there is in U.S. government, with many states requiring offices at those levels to be "nonpartisan" and other states sanctioning partisanship in municipal or county elections and offices. In some cases, states allow the municipalities and counties to make the call themselves, which, of course, mixes the bag even more. Judicial offices across the country are likewise mixed, with many adhering to "nonpartisan" requirements—often little more than a veneer—and many others openly partisan and frequently won as a result of advantages gained through victory in party primaries. Such is the case all the way up to several states' supreme courts.

8. States, Municipalities, and Counties 63

As far as municipalities are concerned, the major parties, obviously, are hungrier to exert their influence in larger cities than in smaller ones—and, in fact, a key reason nonpartisan municipal elections became common during the Progressive era of the late nineteenth/early twentieth century was to limit party influence in big-city governments. In the current era, according to ballotpedia.org, most of the hundred largest cities in the United States continue to have "nonpartisan" elections for mayor and city council. But while "[c]andidates in these cities do not officially run under party labels or compete in partisan primaries ... [t]here are local partisan stories to tell." That's a major understatement.

Ballotpedia.org reports that, while 84 of the hundred largest U.S. cities officially held "nonpartisan" elections as of the end of 2016, there were 63 of the top hundred cities' mayors at the end of 2017 "affiliated with the Democratic Party," and another 29 were Republicans. That's a total of 92 of the nation's hundred largest cities that had mayors with ties to the Democratic and Republican parties.

The remaining mayors, all eight non–Democrats/non–Republicans who served as mayors of the top hundred cities at the end of 2017, are identified by ballotpedia.org as "independent" or "nonpartisan." Any halfway serious investigation, however, suggests that, of the eight, only four had bothered to look up the definitions of "independent" and "nonpartisan." Two of the four were in California: Fremont's Lily Mei and Riverside's William "Rusty" Bailey III. While Mei had a few endorsements leading to the 2016 Fremont mayoral election that might have caused one to question her nonpartisanship, there's no obvious indication she did anything to compromise her integrity as a nonpartisan during the campaign or afterward. Meanwhile, though Bailey had an internship with 1988 Democratic presidential candidate Michael Dukakis years after Dukakis' departure from elective politics, nothing about Bailey's record in city government seemed to suggest he was anything but a citizen-politician—a high school teacher, doubling as a mayor, who steered clear of dirty partisanship.

As far as the other two possible "truly nonpartisan" mayors of top-hundred cities—San Antonio's Ron Nirenberg and Las Vegas' Carolyn Goodman—were concerned, unlike Mei and Bailey, both had a history of accepting $1,000-plus donations from individuals, corporations, and PACs that made it difficult to confirm with confidence that one or both didn't have hidden or indirect partisan connections. Even if Goodman and Nirenberg could rightly be considered true nonpartisans—and the debate there seems unsettled—that would still mean only four of the hundred biggest-city mayors in the United States heading into 2018 (Mei, Bailey, Goodman, and Nirenberg; none facing reelection in 2018) were genuinely independent or nonpartisan. That's a mere 4 percent—or 21 times less than the 84 percent ballotpedia.org says represents the proportion of the nation's largest hundred cities that held officially "nonpartisan" elections. Even more alarmingly, that small number—4 percent—far exceeds the percentage of truly independent or nonpartisan representation at any other level of elective government outside the smallest jurisdictions in the United States.

9

Lay of the Land, 2018 (Alabama–Montana)

Following is a summary of where each state and the District of Columbia stood, going into the 2018 general election, with regard to participation in the democratic process by independents/nonpartisans and parties other than the Republicans and Democrats. Included are statements addressing past successes of alternative candidates, officeholders, and parties, along with comments on their prospects in the 2018 general election and beyond.

Alabama—Duopolistic stronghold. No independent or smaller-party elected officials at the federal level. At the state level, the only "alternative" officeholder going into the 2018 general election appeared to be "independent" State Senator Harri Anne Smith, a 20-year veteran of the State Senate who'd been a Republican until falling out with the GOP in 2010 when she endorsed a Democratic Party nominee for the U.S. Congress. Smith went on to demonstrate her "independent" standing by caucusing with the Republicans. She didn't file for reelection in 2018. ... Several independents and two Libertarians filed to run for the state legislature in 2018, and three candidates for partisan judicial offices across the state filed as independents. "Nonpartisan" mayors of the key Alabama cities, meanwhile, were openly affiliated with the major parties.

Alaska—Duopolistic stronghold. No independent or smaller-party elected officials at the federal level. "Independent" governor Bill Walker, formerly a Republican, suspended his campaign three weeks before the November 6, 2018, general election when reelection prospects looked poor. ... A Libertarian candidate was on the general election ballot to succeed Walker as governor. Also at the state level, two Libertarians filed to run for the legislature. ... Independent Attorney General Jahna Lindemuth and Lieutenant Governor Valerie Nurr'araaluk Davidson, the latter a nonpartisan devoted to Native health issues, were appointed to their posts by Walker in 2016 and 2018, respectively. Walker's departure from the 2018 gubernatorial race appeared to signal the end of the road for both as far as service in those posts was concerned. ... A small number of candidates other than Republicans, Democrats, or Libertarians filed to run for the state legislature in 2018, including independent incumbent State Representatives Jason Grenn and Daniel Ortiz, both Unite America endorsees in 2018 despite the latter's history of participating in the Democratic Party caucus. ... There are no partisan judicial elections per se in Alaska, as judges statewide—as in many other states—instead face "retention" elections in which incumbency nearly always assures continuation.

Arizona—Duopolistic stronghold. No independent or smaller-party elected officials at the federal or state level. ... Arizona's Libertarian and Green parties were recognized as official parties in 2018, and a small number of independents, Libertarians, and Greens filed as candidates at the federal and state levels. The Green Party's Angel Torres was set to be on the 2018 general election ballot in her bid for governor, along with two fellow Greens in their bids for the U.S. Senate and the U.S. House. ... Independent Kathy Knecht, a Unite America endorsee with over a decade of experience as an elected member of the Peoria (Arizona) School District, appeared to be running strongly in her District 21 race for state senator. She faced only a single opponent but one who was favored to win: former Republican state representative Rick Gray, who'd been appointed in early 2018 to fill District 21's State Senate seat. ... In Phoenix, "nonpartisan" mayor Greg Stanton, a Democrat, stepped down in May 2018 to devote his time to a congressional run. His interim replacement as Phoenix's officially "nonpartisan" mayor was Republican vice mayor Thelda Williams, who declared, "I want us to be as nonpartisan as possible" (Flaherty). Williams, who'd been Phoenix's replacement mayor before, chose not to file as a mayoral candidate in the November 2018 special election.

Arkansas—Duopolistic stronghold. No independent or smaller-party elected officials at the federal level. ... In State House District 11, Mark McElroy, elected to a third term as a Democrat in November of 2016, left the party in 2018 and told independentarkansas.com, as reported on September 2018, that he was "too conservative to really be a Democrat [but] too poor to be a Republican." The report continued, "Earlier this year, he decided he didn't want either label, and now he's campaigning to see if his district's voters will send him back to the Capitol as an independent." ... A small number of independents and Libertarians filed for candidacy in state races in 2018—the Libertarian candidates representing Arkansas' only officially recognized third party in 2018. ... "Nonpartisan" races in Arkansas' state executive and judicial branches and in some municipal and county jurisdictions seemed to warrant the same sort of questions, concerns, or suspicions as similar races in other states.

California—Duopolistic stronghold. No independent or smaller-party elected officials at the federal or state level. ... In 2018 California's top-two primary system yielded very similar results to Washington State's, with general election races overwhelmingly coming down to a Democrat vs. a Republican or, in some cases, two candidates from the same major party opposing each other. ... One race of particular interest was independent Steve Poizner's bid to get elected State Insurance Commissioner. Poizner had been a Republican when he made a bid for governor in 2010 while serving his first term as Insurance Commissioner from 2007 to 2011. A long-time Silicon Valley entrepreneur noted for strong concerns about undocumented immigration, Poizner sat out politics for seven years before announcing his candidacy in February of 2018—this time as an independent—for another term as Insurance Commissioner of California. If successful, he'd become the first independent ever to hold statewide office in California. On June 5, 2018, Poizner finished first in the four-way primary, ahead of two Democrats and a candidate representing the Peace and Freedom Party, ensuring his place on November's general election ballot.

Colorado—Duopolistic stronghold. No independent or smaller-party elected officials at the federal level. ... Cheri Jahn, a Democratic state senator since 2011, declared herself independent in late 2017 but couldn't run for reelection in 2018 due to term restrictions. ... A fairly small number of alternative candidates—mainly Libertarians and, to a lesser degree, Unity Party of America nominees and independents—stood for election in 2018 at the federal and state levels. Among them were Scott Helker (Libertarian) and Bill Hammons (Unity Party), both running for governor; William Robinson, Libertarian candidate for attorney general; and U.S. House candidates Mary Malarsie and Nick Thomas, both independents.

Connecticut—Duopolistic stronghold. No independent or smaller-party elected officials at the federal or state level. State Senator Ed Gomes, an ex–Democrat, won election as the Working Families Parties candidate in 2015 but returned to the Democratic Party before getting reelected in 2016. Gomes didn't seek reelection in 2018. ... As in many states, candidates in Connecticut running as independents or nominees of other than "established political parties" had to petition to get on ballots. A small number of mainly Green Party, Independent Party of Connecticut, Libertarian, and nonpartisan candidates petitioned successfully in 2018, but major-party domination was evident at all levels of government. ... The disqualification of Socialist Action U.S. Senate candidate and Iraq War veteran Fred Linck from appearing on the general election ballot, despite claims of having turned over far more than the 7,500 signatures required to be on the ballot, raised suspicions and drew strong criticism in some quarters.

Delaware—Duopolistic stronghold. No independent or smaller-party elected officials at the federal or state level. Delaware's closed primary system limits participation to registered members of "established" parties, thus ensuring a Democratic–Republican showdown—or an unopposed major-party candidate—in almost every general election contest. While Libertarians and Greens were eligible to place a candidate in any partisan race on the general election ballot, both parties had limited resources and ran only a small number of candidates for federal and state offices in 2018. No other alternative parties had any activity of note in Delaware's 2018 electoral process. ... Nonpartisan candidates had two paths to getting on the general election ballot: petitioning and collecting signatures equal to one percent of eligible voters by the end of the year before the election; or filing as write-in candidates. Neither path had a history of success in Delaware.

Florida—Duopolistic stronghold. No independent or smaller-party elected officials at the federal or state level. After gaining notice in the recent era for allegations of Russian hacking and an apparent difficulty when it comes to counting ballots, the Sunshine State held steady as a bastion of "duopolism" heading into the 2018 elections. ... Florida is a closed-primary state, which ensures both major parties are represented in every partisan federal- or state-level race in which they want to participate. While Florida has had a small share of alternative candidates in partisan state and federal races over the years—including qualifying nonpartisan candidates and write-in filers in 2018—the past century, at the state and federal levels, has been characterized by duopolistic domination across the board.

Georgia—Duopolistic stronghold. No independent or smaller-party elected officials at the federal or state level. Georgia allows eligible voters to participate in either major party's May primary without registering as a members of the party. Voters also have the option of participating in nonpartisan primaries—an option that denies any say in choosing the major-party nominees. ... Georgia's system may be a little different from Florida's, but the result is similar: While Georgia has had some alternative candidates over the years—including a small number of Libertarians and write-in filers in 2018—the last century has been a story of utter domination by the two major parties characterized, in recent decades, by a power shift from the Democrats to the Republicans. ... As far as 2018 was concerned, much of the statewide call for political change focused on calls to swing the governorship from a Republican who used to be a Democrat to a Democrat who seemed to stand against everything President Trump and his backers stood for—except the two-party system. That contest, pitting African American State Representative Stacey Abrams against Republican opponent Brian Kemp in a race to succeed retiring

Democrat-turned-Republican and sitting governor Nathan Deal, had blatant racial overtones, figured to be one of the most divisive races in the country, and appeared likely to go right down to the wire. Even more, it seemed certain to overshadow, if not stifle, any talk of Georgia's politics evolving into something more than a two-party power grab.

Hawaii—Duopolistic stronghold. No independent or smaller-party elected officials at the federal or state level. The Libertarian, Green, and Constitution parties, along with nonpartisans, had limited participation in the 2018 primaries, with a small number of Libertarians and nonpartisans qualifying for the November general election. At the state level, in several districts—State Senate Districts 3 and 6 and State House Districts 3, 13, and 17—one of the major parties (in most cases, the Republican Party) essentially sat out the election, as the opposing major party appeared to have victory in hand. The stepping-aside of one major party in those races paved the way for smaller-party candidates—three Libertarians and two Greens—to go one-on-one with lone major-party candidates in the general election, which, in a perfect world, might have been a blessing.

Idaho—Duopolistic stronghold. No independent or smaller-party elected officials at the federal or state level. … The May 2018 primaries focused mainly on giving the major parties—the only parties participating—an opportunity to sort out preferences and settle on candidates going into the general election. The general election campaign would see the addition of a small number of nonpartisan candidates, along with several others from the Libertarian and Constitution parties—none expected to make much of a showing in November's election. While Idaho's judicial and municipal races, along with school board elections, are officially nonpartisan, the "nonpartisan" requirement—especially as far as municipal elections are concerned—has been under some fire from two opposing groups: those favoring honest nonpartisanship, as opposed to the nominal variety; and those favoring open partisanship in Idaho's municipal politics.

Illinois—Duopolistic stronghold. No independent or smaller-party elected officials at the federal or state level. Heading into 2018, there were few expectations that smaller-party or independent candidates in partisan elections across Illinois would take significant steps toward getting elected. … Illinois' closed primary elections have a notable peculiarity. Journalist Greg Bishop quotes Drew Penrose, law and policy director of the nonpartisan organization Fair Vote: "[In Illinois] you declare a [major] political party affiliation and then the person who is handing you a primary ballot has to announce in a voice loud enough for people to hear in the polling place which party … you are affiliating yourself with." As

Bishop reports, Illinois counties' custom of compiling voter lists complete with declared party affiliations can "disenfranchise voters who don't want to be singled out for publicly affiliating with one party over another." But more important, as far as stifling opposition to political "duopolism" in Illinois is concerned, is that "Illinois' primary system ... freezes out independent voices that may have important policy issues to add to the conversation that aren't being addressed by the major party candidates" (Bishop, quoting Penrose).

Indiana—Duopolistic stronghold. No independent or smaller-party elected officials at the federal or state level. ... Participation in Indiana primaries is limited to voters selecting a Republican or Democratic Party ballot, except in cases where voters choose to weigh in only on referendum issues. ... Although success has been elusive for alternative candidates vying for federal or state office, a small number of independents and Libertarians—the latter representing the only party in Indiana other than the Republicans and Democrats to have ballot access—were serving in partisan elective municipal and township positions across the state heading into the 2018 elections. Several more seemed to have a realistic chance of getting elected in 2018.

Iowa—Duopolistic stronghold. No independent or smaller-party elected officials at the federal level. The only alternative elected officeholder at the state level going into the 2018 elections was State Senator David Johnson, a 21-year state legislator and a Republican for about 19 of those years until declaring himself independent in 2016 in opposition to the Republican Party's embrace of Donald Trump. In May of 2018 Johnson announced he wouldn't stand for reelection. ... While a relatively small number of Libertarians, Greens, and independents had run unsuccessfully in a variety of partisan races in recent years, the Hawkeye State, going into the 2018 elections—and for nearly half a century prior to that—was best known to most people, politically speaking, as the setting of statewide caucuses held every presidential election year and designed, as it appears, to perpetuate the two-party system for eternity.

Kansas—Duopolistic stronghold. No independent or smaller-party elected officials at the federal level. ... John Doll, who was elected, for the third time, to the State Senate as a Republican in 2016, announced in March 2018 that he was ending his affiliation with the Republican Party and planning to run as an independent for Lieutenant Governor that year. His running mate, independent gubernatorial candidate Greg Orman, was another ex–Republican but, unlike Doll, one who'd been a registered Democrat as well. ... While Kansas' 2018 primaries were closed, with participation limited to the Democratic and Republican parties and voters who belonged to those parties or declared a preference for one or the other, it was widely believed that many normally unaffiliated voters, along with many others who normally supported smaller parties, participated in the primaries for strategic reasons designed to boost the chances of non–Democratic/non–Republican candidates they actually preferred. … Candidates representing the Libertarian Party—Kansas' third officially recognized political party—were slated to participate in a variety of partisan races in Kansas' general election, and a fairly small number of independents successfully petitioned to appear on the general election ballot.

Kentucky—Duopolistic stronghold. No independent or smaller-party elected officials at the federal or state level. As in Kansas and other states, participation in Kentucky's 2018 primaries was limited to the Republican and Democratic parties. … In 2016 the Libertarian Party of Kentucky gained official recognition as a political party in the state, which allowed Libertarians in partisan races to have the party designation on ballots along with their names. One Libertarian was elected to partisan county-level office that year, and heading into the 2018 elections, three other Libertarians appeared to hold municipal or county elective offices in Kentucky. … While Libertarians and independents—some representing unofficial parties or "political organizations"—were slated to be on the ballot in many partisan races in the November 2018 general election, prospects didn't look good for any at the federal or state level.

Louisiana—Duopolistic stronghold. No independent or smaller-party elected officials at the federal level. Louisiana's primary election system delays primaries in many races until early fall. Those primaries, essentially, are of the top-two variety, though winners are automatically elected if they earn a majority of the primary vote. If no candidate wins a majority in the primary, the top two finishers face off in the general election, regardless of party affiliations, as in Washington State and California. … In years leading to the 2018 elections, Louisiana had seen plenty of activity but limited success by the Libertarian and Green parties. Nonetheless, both were officially recognized in the state in 2018. … With Louisiana also recognizing the Independent Party of Louisiana, the Louisiana Secretary of State website sang a familiar refrain: "There has been confusion over 'Independent.' Some voters register as a member of the Independent Party. Some voters do not wish to be affiliated with a political party and refer to themselves as independent. If a candidate indicates 'Independent' on qualifying papers, please confirm whether this is a party designation, because it determines whether the candidate is identified as 'Independent' or 'No Party' on the ballot." It doesn't appear that Louisiana's three independent state representatives serving in 2018—Terry Brown, Joseph Marino, and Jerome Richard, all legitimately independent and none facing the end of their four-year terms in 2018—were elected due to any voter confusion.

Maine—Duopolistic stronghold. No independent or smaller-party elected officials at the federal level except U.S. Senator Angus King. King, a former Democrat with an "independent" pedigree spanning a quarter-century, had been caucusing with the Democrats since joining the Senate in 2013. ... At the state level, eight officeholders in Maine were independent or aligned with smaller parties heading into the 2018 elections. Of the eight, several were ex-members of a major party, two would reach the end of their consecutive term limits in 2018 and be ineligible to seek reelection until 2020, one chose not to run in 2018 despite being eligible, and one decided to run for Congress in 2018. ... Appointed State Treasurer Teresea "Terry" Hayes, an independent since leaving the Democratic Party in 2014, filed in 2017 to run for governor as an independent in 2018. Hayes, a former Democratic state representative, received the endorsement of Unite America for her gubernatorial run. ... In 2018 Maine employed a ranked-choice voting system in state and congressional primary races (which would continue into the congressional general election). While the new system, approved by voters in 2016, came under some fire, there was hope that allowing voters' backup choices to factor into some election results could mean the partisan (and nonpartisan) balance of elected officials and elective bodies would more accurately reflect the will of voters than the vote-for-one, winner-take-all system traditionally had done.

Maryland—Duopolistic stronghold. No independent or smaller-party elected officials at the federal or state level. Heading into the 2018 elections, every level of partisan elective politics in the state was dominated, if not controlled, by the major parties, and appointees to various nonpartisan state executive offices typically had clear and often lengthy partisan histories. ... Maryland has one of the most closed primary election systems in the country, with minimal activity or participation by any entity unaffiliated with the Republican Party or the Democratic Party. Despite being banished from the primaries, a fairly small number of mainly Libertarian, Green, unaffiliated, and write-in candidates were set to appear on the 2018 general election ballot.

Massachusetts—Duopolistic stronghold. No independent or smaller-party elected officials at the federal level. Two independent state representatives—recent converts from opposing major parties—held office going into the 2018 elections. ... Massachusetts' hybrid primary system allows independent voters to participate in primaries while retaining their standing as independents. In 2018 such voters could select the party ballot of their choice—Democratic, Republican, or Libertarian—without being required to register with the party. ... In recent times Massachusetts has had a fairly long list of "legal political designations" from which voters can choose candidates to support—though not in a primary. Those designations, which don't equate to official party status in the Bay State, include known entities such as the Green Party, the Reform Party, the American Independent Party, and the Socialist Party, along with others flying more under the radar—for example, the Prohibition Party, the Pirate Party, and the Pizza Party (all listed, along with about 20 other "legal political designations," on the Massachusetts Secretary of State website).

Michigan—Duopolistic stronghold. No independent or smaller-party elected officials at the federal or state level. The major parties have maintained a lock on power at nearly every level of elective government in Michigan, and their influence is often evident in nonpartisan races and offices. ... The Libertarian Party became primary-eligible in 2018—Michigan's only "third party" to do so in the previous 20 years—on the basis of the party's modest showing in 2016, and Libertarians were slated to be on the general election ballot in many races across the state in 2018. The Green Party, the Natural Law Party, the U.S. Taxpayers Party, and the Working Class Party, all excluded from primaries, were eligible to be on the state ballot and would run candidates for various federal and/or state-level offices in 2018. As for independents, Michigan's onerous petition-signature requirements were challenged in court by former federal prosecutor Chris Graveline, who filed to run as an independent for attorney general in 2018. Despite falling far short of the required 30,000 signatures to get on the ballot, Graveline received a court injunction allowing him to run. According to Paul Egan of the *Detroit Free Press*, U.S. District Judge Victoria Roberts, who issued the preliminary injunction, "noted that no independent candidate had qualified for the statewide ballot since the current rules were adopted in 1988."

Minnesota—Duopolistic stronghold. No independent or smaller-party elected officials at the federal or state level. Minnesota's Democratic Party is formally known as the Democratic Farmer-Labor Party, reflecting the history of the state's Farmer-Labor Party, which had numerous candidates elected to federal and state office from the 1920s to the 1940s before the party was swallowed by the Democrats. In 2018 any illusions of an alternative nature to the Democratic Farmer-Labor Party were long gone, as the party was at best a thinly disguised version of the Democratic Party. ... Minnesota is an open primary state, and in 2018 there were seven officially recognized parties—two centered largely on marijuana legalization. Others included the Independence Party of Minnesota—the outgrowth of Ross Perot's Reform Party, which Ventura represented in his successful 1998 run for governor—and the Libertarian Party of Minnesota, which, heading into the 2018 elections, had several members holding nonpartisan municipal offices, particularly in the Minneapolis suburb of Crystal. ... In the wake of the 2018 primaries, while many races were set as one-on-one contests between major-party candidates, other races featured at least a short list of smaller-party, unaffiliated, or write-in candidates, nearly all of whose chances looked slim.

Mississippi—Duopolistic stronghold. No independent or smaller-party elected officials at the federal or state level. Alternative-party activity or ballot presence of any note—none in the primaries—was predominantly represented by the Independence (formerly Reform) Party and the Green Party, neither of which, heading into the 2018 elections, had a member serving in any partisan elective office in Mississippi. ... Libertarian Steve McCluskey was elected mayor of McClain, Mississippi (population 440), in a 2017 nonpartisan election. While McCluskey didn't face reelection in 2018, his story was one of the few bright spots concerning prospects of alternative candidates going into Mississippi's 2018 general election.

Missouri—Duopolistic stronghold. No independent or smaller-party elected officials at the federal or state level. ... While three alternative "established parties" participated in the 2018 primaries—the Libertarians, Greens, and the Constitution Party—candidates from those parties who made it to the general election weren't expected to fare much better than independents who managed to get on the ballot. Write-in prospects, meanwhile, looked dismal as usual. ... A small number of legitimate independents and people connected to alternative parties were serving in local nonpartisan offices in 2018. One, Ismaine Ayouaz, declared himself a "Blue Republican" in 2014 before aligning with the Libertarians and getting elected to council in Crestwood, Missouri's April 2018 municipal election. A second, Russ Monchil, had run unsuccessfully three times for the U.S. House of Representatives as a Libertarian before getting elected to northwestern Missouri's tiny Mirabile School District in 2017, apparently not for the first time.

Montana—Duopolistic stronghold. No independent or smaller-party elected officials at the federal or state level. Montana's open primary system allows voters to select the "qualified" party ballot of their choice. In 2018 the Green Party qualified and participated, alongside the Republicans and Democrats, in the state's June 2018 primary—only to have a judge, one month later, side with a Democratic Party complaint and rule the Green Party ineligible for the general election ballot as a result of having too few valid signatures, and too many suspicious ones, on the petition it had submitted to the state to become a "qualified" party. ... Libertarians were on the 2018 general election ballot in a few statewide races and in 17 races for the state legislature. Only two independents, however, both running for the legislature, made the November ballot. One, 80-year-old Bob

Sivertsen, a state legislator when he was in his forties, was set to oppose a Libertarian and a 20-year-old Democrat. In a July 17, 2018, article in his hometown newspaper, *The Havre Herald*, Sivertsen, a 2013 inductee to the Montana Cowboy Hall of Fame, said he decided to make his political comeback after a 37-year layoff "[b]ecause the people have been asking me." Writer Paul Dragu added, "All he cares about are the issues, and that's what he views as the factor separating him from the politicians. He proudly wears his independent badge." While that may have made good copy, the reality was clear: Montana's 2018 general election looked to be a clean two-party sweep, as was customary, in every partisan race of any significance across the state.

10

Lay of the Land, 2018 (Nebraska–Wyoming and DC)

This chapter continues a summary of where each state and the District of Columbia stood, going into the 2018 general election, with regard to participation in the democratic process by independents/nonpartisans and parties other than the Republicans and Democrats.

Nebraska—Duopolistic stronghold. No independent or smaller-party elected officials at the federal level. ... At the state level, Nebraska has had a unicameral legislature since the Depression. Every legislator is a senator, elected for four years at a time, with a limit of two consecutive terms. Notably, legislative primaries, general elections, and elective offices in Nebraska are officially nonpartisan (unlike various state executive offices up to governor). The reality, however, is that Nebraska's unicameral legislature, for all practical purposes, is highly partisan, with parties endorsing candidates and senators generally not doing much to hide their partisan leanings or connections. Heading into the 2018 general election following the state's top-two "independent primary," Nebraska's 49 senators—24 facing reelection or preparing to step down in 2018—included two known Republicans who switched parties in 2016 or 2017, one to the Libertarian Party and the other to the Democratic Party, all the while officially maintaining "nonpartisan" status. Another sitting senator, 81-year-old Ernie Chambers, was a long-time and legitimate independent and the longest-serving legislator in Nebraska's history. Chambers, who didn't face reelection in 2018, is probably best known outside Nebraska for his 2007 lawsuit against God—intended mainly as a tongue-in-cheek statement against the ease of bringing frivolous lawsuits to court. ... Like state legislative elections and offices, various lower-level elections and offices in Nebraska are officially nonpartisan. Fortunately, the major parties aren't as invested in races such as those for municipal or county boards or districts, so those races and elective offices don't make such a mockery of the term "nonpartisan."

Nevada—Duopolistic stronghold. No independent or smaller-party elected officials at the federal or state level except one: State Senator Patricia Farley, elected in 2014 to a four-year term as a Republican before announcing in 2016 that she was becoming nonpartisan—despite her intention to caucus with the Democrats. In 2017 Farley survived a recall attempt unrelated to her switch, and that same year she announced her intention not to seek reelection in 2018. ... Nevada's primaries are closed, with voters who aren't registered Republicans or Democrats allowed to participate only in nonpartisan contests. ... Along with the major parties, the Libertarian and Independent American parties had general election ballot access in 2018. Candidates associated with parties not officially recognized—i.e., all others—could petition to get on the ballot but without party designations. Though petition signature requirements in Nevada weren't too onerous for such candidates, prospects didn't look good for alternative candidates lined up for races of any significance in the Silver State's 2018 general election.

New Hampshire—Duopolistic stronghold. No independent or smaller-party elected officials at the federal level. Heading into the 2018 elections, three young sitting state legislators were neither Republican nor Democratic: Brandon Phinney and Caleb Q. Dyer, both elected in 2016 as Republicans before switching to the Libertarian Party in 2017; and Joseph P. Stallcop, elected in 2016 as a Democrat before switching to the Libertarian Party in 2017. ... Libertarians also had some minor penetration at the local level of government in New Hampshire. ... The Libertarian Party, the only party other than the Democrats and Republicans with official status in New Hampshire in 2018, participated in the New Hampshire primary—which, of course, is far better known during presidential election years for its part in helping kick off the Democratic and Republican presidential nomination process. ... Despite minor successes by New Hampshire Libertarians in recent years, 2018 general election prospects looked dim for candidates in the Granite State who were running in partisan races without a major-party nomination.

New Jersey—Duopolistic stronghold. No independent or smaller-party elected officials at the federal or state level. The Garden State, even in fairly recent times, has made it difficult for alternative parties to gain a foothold. As Eric Kiefer reports at patch.com, "[U]ntil as recently as 2001, New Jersey voters weren't allowed to register with third-parties. To this day [22 August 2018], third-parties are still prohibited from holding primaries or occupying the first two columns on the general election ballot." It's no surprise, then, that, going into the 2018 elections, only the Republicans and Democrats had official party status in the state. ... While much was made in some circles of the state Libertarian Party reaching 10,000 registered members in 2018, that total was far less than one percent of registered Democrats *or* registered Republicans in New Jersey. ... Given difficult "official party" qualification standards, it seemed farfetched that the Libertarians or, especially, smaller parties ranging from the Constitution Party and the Greens on down to the Make It Simple; New Day NJ; and Stop the Insanity "parties"—the latter three essentially slogans apparently aimed at bolstering the prospects of independent candidates who seemed to be in over their heads—would make even a scratch in the state's long-established tradition of two-party dominance anytime soon.

New Mexico—Duopolistic stronghold. No independent or smaller-party elected officials at the federal or state level. In 2018 the Libertarian Party had official status in New Mexico—the only official party in the state other than the Republicans and Democrats—and 1995–2003 Republican governor Gary Johnson, better known nationally in 2018 as the 2012 and 2016 Libertarian nominee for president, headed into New Mexico's 2018 general election as the Libertarian Party of New Mexico's nominee for the U.S. Senate. His chance of winning looked slim but seemed to far surpass the chance of nearly any other New Mexican non–Republican or non–Democrat getting elected to a partisan executive, legislative, or judicial office in any race above the county level. One possible exception, though still a decided long shot, was in Legislative District 50, where independent Jarratt Applewhite, according to his campaign website, aimed to "give voters an alternative to the dysfunctional two-party system that is degrading our democracy." Applewhite had the luxury of facing a single general-election opponent—a Democratic incumbent the Republicans didn't bother opposing—and had the endorsement of Unite America in his independent run for the legislature.

New York—Duopolistic stronghold. No independent or smaller-party elected officials at the federal level. ... Fred Thiele, a New York State Assemblyman since 1995, switched from the Republican Party to the Independence Party in 2009 and, prior to 2018, got reelected four times as an Independence Party candidate. However, he caucused with the Democratic Party and didn't face any Democratic opposition in his reelection bids after leaving the Republican Party. That was no surprise, since Thiele also got the Democratic nomination in 2010, 2012, 2014, and 2016. Heading into the 2018 general election, Thiele, who had the backing of the Independence Party and several other small parties, was recognized again as the Democratic candidate in Legislative District 1 and appeared likely to win another term. ... As far as the New York Democratic Party was concerned, 2016's "Independent Democratic Conference" highlighted some recent rupturing among state Democrats, but the result, for disgruntled Democrats, leaned more toward collaboration with Republicans than formation of a new or independent body. ... Perhaps more interesting, heading into 2018, were the sometimes determined, though generally unsuccessful, efforts of some members of New York's fairly long list of third parties to make a little headway in the democratic process. While Libertarian- or Green-affiliated officials held a few local nonpartisan posts, the most compelling of New York's smaller parties, at least to entertainment lovers, was probably the Rent Is Too Damn High Party, whose founder, Jimmy McMillan, attracted plenty of attention in a series of unsuccessful runs, sometimes as a Republican as well as his own party's "nominee," for New York governor, New York City mayor, and New York City councilor, between 2005 and 2017—but especially for a *Saturday Night Live* spoof in 2010 and a McMillan appearance on that same show in 2013. In 2018 McMillan failed in an attempt to get on the ballot for governor.

North Carolina—Duopolistic stronghold. No independent or smaller-party elected officials at the federal or state level. ... The passage of NC Senate Bill 656 in 2017 lifted some of the burden of what one North Carolina Green Party official, quoted at the Blue Ridge Public Radio website, called "the most restrictive ballot access law in the country" (Vaillancourt). The bill's reduced signature requirements in 2018, from two percent of registered voters in the last election (98,000 signatures as reported) to a quarter of one percent (about 11,000 signatures as reported), brought about an increase in the number of officially recognized political parties in North Carolina from three (the Republican, Democratic, and Libertarian parties) to five (with the addition of the Green Party and the North Carolina Constitution Party—the latter having to overcome multiple legal obstacles en route to gaining ballot access). All five recognized parties were slated to run candidates in partisan races in the 2018 general election, joining a small number of unaffiliated candidates on the ballot. Unfortunately, victory for big-party nominees seemed a foregone conclusion almost across the board.

North Dakota—Duopolistic stronghold. No independent or smaller-party elected officials at the federal or state level. In North Dakota, the Democratic Party is represented by the Democratic-Nonpartisan League Party. Like Minnesota's Democratic Farmer-Labor Party, the Democratic-Nonpartisan League Party hearkens back to an alternative party that flourished for a time in the first half of the twentieth century before merging with the Democratic Party in the 1940s or 1950s. Since its founding as such in 1956, the North Dakota Democratic-Nonpartisan League Party has functioned as the de facto state Democratic Party and a duopolistic partner in every way. ... Besides the "big two," North Dakota recognized only the Libertarians as an official party in 2018. Qualifying nominees or representatives of other parties were set to appear on the general election ballot as independents, but no independent of any persuasion appeared likely to earn victory in any of North Dakota's partisan races. As for nonpartisan races, particularly at the county and municipal levels, while many "nonpartisan" candidates were affiliated or connected with the major parties, low-profile nonpartisan races across sparsely populated, largely rural North Dakota seemed relatively free of major-party meddling.

Ohio—Duopolistic stronghold. No independent or smaller-party elected officials at the federal or state level. Heading into 2018, one statewide official, Ohio Public Utilities Commission chair Asim Haque, was an independent. Haque was appointed to the commission by Republican Governor John Kasich in 2013 and reappointed for a second term by Kasich in 2016. Other members of the same commission in 2018, all appointees, had major-party affiliations. ... Ohio recognized the Republicans, Democrats, and Greens as official parties heading into the 2018 elections, and all three participated in the May 8 state primary. ... Libertarians, meanwhile, had to scramble to regain ballot access, which the party lost in 2014 when rules were tightened. As it turned out, the Libertarian Party mounted a successful effort, gathering over 60,000 signatures, to get back on the general election ballot in 2018. As State Libertarian Party Executive Committee Vice-Chair Scott Pettigrew put it in a post by Dustin Nanna at the state party website, "This isn't just about [Libertarians].... Sure, we want the chance to make our voices heard, but we also believe that it's unfair for the two legacy parties to dictate voters' choices." A three-percent general-election showing by the Libertarian Party's 2018 gubernatorial candidate, activist Travis Irvine, would be required for the party to qualify automatically for state ballot access in 2020. The Green Party needed a similar three-percent showing by its gubernatorial candidate, Constance Gadell-Newton, to remain on the ballot in 2020. Such a showing was by no means guaranteed for either candidate or party.

Oklahoma—Duopolistic stronghold. No independent or smaller-party elected officials at the federal or state level. ... Oklahoma had three officially recognized parties—the Republicans, Democrats, and Libertarians—going into the 2018 elections. Heading into the primaries, the Democratic Party was set to allow "no party" or independent registrants to participate in Oklahoma's Democratic primary, but the Republicans, running well ahead of the Democrats in the Sooner State, were making no such concessions. Libertarians, meanwhile, had limited activity or presence in Oklahoma's June 2018 primary. ... As for the 2018 general election, no Libertarian, nonpartisan, or small-party "independent" appeared to have a reasonable chance of winning a partisan election, though several—including alternative candidates for State Treasurer and State Auditor and

Inspector—were slated to face only a single opponent, as the Democrats strategically sat out many races.

Oregon—Duopolistic stronghold. No independent or smaller-party elected officials at the federal or state level. Heading into the 2018 primaries, Oregon officially recognized eight political parties, three as "major parties"—the obvious two and, surprisingly, the Independent Party of Oregon (IPO), which in 2015 reached the membership threshold of over five percent of registered voters (or over 109,000 registered members) statewide to qualify for major-party recognition. As numerous observers have pointed out, the fairly rapid rise of the Independent Party of Oregon since its inception in 2007 seems to have been connected to its name, as has been the case with "independent parties" elsewhere. As the *Portland Tribune* reported on July 24, 2018, leaders of the IPO "chose a name destined to swell their organization's ranks. People wanting to declare their independence from political parties, but unaware that the way to do that in Oregon is by signing up as a 'non-affiliated voter,' have registered instead for the Independent Party." It also appears the Independent Party of Oregon settled on another political shortcut in trying to smooth its path to power. In 2018, as in previous years, the vast majority of IPO nominees were "cross-nominees"—i.e., Democratic or Republican nominees who, according to the IPO website, "responded to our survey and agreed to support parts of our legislative agenda and platform or [have] supported past priorities of the party." … Compared to most other states, Oregon sets the bar relatively low when it comes to party qualification for "official" status, as a one-percent showing by a single candidate representing a political organization in the race for president or in any other partisan statewide race in Oregon's last general election qualifies that organization for official recognition as a "minor" party. Minor parties going into the 2018 elections were the Libertarian Party, the Green Party, the Working Families Party, the Constitution Party, and the Progressive Party—the majority running few candidates, all decided underdogs.

Pennsylvania—Duopolistic stronghold. No independent or smaller-party elected officials at the federal or state level. Going into the 2018 election season, Pennsylvania officially recognized four parties—the Republicans, Democrats, Libertarians, and Greens. … Pennsylvania has seen a grassroots acceptance of the Libertarians and Greens in a manner beyond what is evident in most of the country. Heading into the 2018 elections, about 40 Libertarians were serving in elective office in Pennsylvania, along with roughly half as many Greens. All held municipal or county offices, many officially partisan; but it remained to be seen—though it looked highly unlikely—whether a Libertarian or Green candidate could defy the odds and get elected to a state office in 2018. … While reduced petition signature requirements in 2018 theoretically opened the way for an increased number of alternative candidates in Pennsylvania to stand for election in state and federal races, no such candidate appeared to have traction heading into the general election.

Rhode Island—Duopolistic stronghold. No independent or smaller-party elected officials at the federal or state level. Other than the Democrats and Republicans, Rhode Island's only official party heading into the 2018 elections was the Moderate Party, founded in 2007 by Ken Block. Block ran in 2010 as the Moderate Party candidate for governor, finishing fourth in the general election. He made another run for governor in 2014, theoretically upping his odds by running as a Republican, but got knocked out in the primary. ... In 2018 the Moderate Party was a quiet presence—making barely a whisper—in the lead-up to the November general election. Getting more attention was the Compassion Party of Rhode Island—"compassion" in this instance largely synonymous with a sympathetic attitude toward cannabis use. Attention spiked in early October of 2018, one month before the general election, when the Compassion Party's candidates for governor and attorney general were arrested for allegedly having 48 pounds of marijuana in their possession in the presence of a minor. ... Also drawing some attention was a father-son race between David A. Quiroa, Sr., a Trump Republican, and independent David A. Quiroa, Jr., in the District 73 contest for representative in the state's General Assembly. According to Michelle R. Smith in the June 29, 2018, *Chicago Tribune*, father and son, aged 47 and 22, were living at the same address when they filed for candidacy.

South Carolina—Duopolistic stronghold. No independent or smaller-party elected officials at the federal level. At the state level, members of the officially nonpartisan South Carolina Public Service Commission, whose members are elected by the General Assembly, appeared to maintain nonpartisan neutrality. ... While South Carolina officially recognized 10 political parties in 2018, only the Republican and Democratic parties were represented in the state primaries. Registered voters, however, could participate in either primary, regardless of party affiliation or non-affiliation. ... One major party or the other sat out the 2018 primaries in the majority of state races—including nearly two-thirds of "contests" for the State House of Representatives. Alternative candidates weren't expected to capitalize on the major parties' strategic absences from races. Instead, the majority of State House contests in the general election weren't stacking up as contests at all, with a single major party candidate standing unopposed or facing only the prospect of write-in opposition.

South Dakota—Duopolistic stronghold. No independent or smaller-party elected officials at the federal or state level. ... In 2016 the South

Dakota Libertarian Party joined the Republicans and Democrats in the exclusive club of official parties in the Mount Rushmore State. That same year, a known Libertarian was elected to public office in South Dakota, apparently for the first time. The electee was Tricia Weathers, to a three-year nonpartisan post on the Box Elder, South Dakota, city council. While Libertarians were aiming for further success in South Dakota's nonpartisan municipal elections in 2018, that wouldn't be an easy task, as, "more often than not, city councilors and mayors are affiliated with one of the two major political parties"—putting the lie to any notion that "[m]unicipal offices across South Dakota are supposed to be devoid of partisan politics," according to Joe Sneve in the March 9, 2018, Sioux Falls *Argus Leader.* ... At the federal and state levels, meanwhile, prospects generally looked bleak for the small number of alternative candidates slated to be on the 2018 general election ballot.

Tennessee—Duopolistic stronghold. No independent or smaller-party elected officials at the federal or state level. ... According to an August 2016 report at Nashville's fox17.com, the Green and Constitution parties successfully sued to get on the state ballot in 2012 and 2014—though neither party had similar success in 2016. The same report, addressing the frustration alternative "organizations" and voters sometimes faced when a smaller-party designation wasn't allowed on the ballot next to a candidate's name, quoted a Green Party member: "I've had a lot of people tell me I want to vote for the Green [P]arty candidate but I couldn't remember which one was running for the office so since they were all independents they weren't able to do that." ... Heading into the 2018 elections, the Green and Constitution parties were still off the ballot and the Volunteer State recognized only the Republican and Democratic parties as official. ... At least three Libertarians—all officially independent—were elected to partisan county or municipal offices in August 2018; but as far as the November general election seemed to be shaping up, despite the presence on the ballot of a fairly significant number of "independent" candidates—along with others who were independent by design—the most likely result by far seemed to be a clean sweep in all but the smallest races by Tennessee's only two official parties.

Texas—Duopolistic stronghold. No independent or smaller-party elected officials at the federal or state level. In early 2018 only three parties—the Democrats, Republicans, and Libertarians—qualified for the general election ballot. The Green Party, which had been on the state ballot in 2016, didn't do well that year and had to petition to stay on the ballot in 2018. A May 30, 2018, *Texas Tribune* headline tells how that went: "The Green Party needed nearly 50,000 signatures to make it onto the November ballot in Texas. It got about 500" (Samuels, Alex). To its credit, the

Texas Green Party didn't resort to the seemingly shady and undemocratic practice some parties across the nation do when trying to gather enough signatures to get on a ballot—i.e., hire companies to gather the signatures they need. ... *The Texas Tribune* quoted Green Party gubernatorial candidate Janis Richards: "It's really important to me that we offer an alternative solution to what's already on the ballot. ... I want to try to speak for people who might not already have a voice on the ballot" (Samuels, Alex). Unfortunately, Richards, who appeared to have an impossible hill to climb—especially without Green Party ballot access—bowed out before the general election. ... The Libertarians and Greens each appeared to have one elected official serving in a nonpartisan municipal office heading into the 2018 general election. No further alternative-candidate gains beyond the municipal level looked likely as the general election neared, and much of Texans' talk of political change in 2018 seemed to focus more on Democratic U.S. Representative Beto O'Rourke's effort to unseat Republican Senator Ted Cruz in what figured to be a tight race.

Utah—Duopolistic stronghold. No independent or smaller-party elected officials at the federal or state level. Utah entered the 2018 election season with seven officially recognized parties, including the two major parties, the Libertarians, the Greens, and the Constitution Party. The remaining two official parties were the Independent American Party and the United Utah Party, the latter founded in 2017 and aiming, according to the party's website, to "[unite] all who want to end the extreme partisanship that has corrupted our political conversation [and to focus] on common sense and common ground." ... The 2018 general election seemed to be shaping up as a major-party sweep and, particularly, a Republican landslide. No independent or smaller-party candidate appeared to hold a partisan elective office in Utah heading into the general election, and it seemed safe to predict that wouldn't change coming out of the election.

Vermont—If any state could have been considered other than a "duopolistic stronghold" heading into the 2018 elections, it was tiny Vermont—and not because of Bernie Sanders' long and dubious history as an "independent." What set Vermont apart wasn't the fact that the Green Mountain State had six official political parties—some states had more—but the fact that multiple smaller parties had been successful in getting candidates elected to both local/municipal and state legislative offices. ... Leading the way in recent times among Vermont's smaller official parties was the Vermont Progressive Party, established in 2000 but traceable, according to the party's website, to "the coalition that worked to elect Bernie Sanders" mayor of Burlington in 1981. Since 2000 Sanders has continued his affiliation with the Vermont Progressive Party and received endorsements from the party, whose clear social-democratic and social-justice bent has resonated with a significant body of voters in Vermont. Heading into the 2018 general election, the Vermont Progressives had elected officials serving in several municipalities and in both houses of the state legislature—though some were also endorsed by the Democrats. Two statewide elected officials, Lieutenant Governor David Zuckerman and Auditor of Accounts Doug Hoffer, were affiliated with and backed by both the Progressives and the Democrats. Such dual affiliations would be fairly common on Vermont's 2018 general election ballot, and there were even some self-identified Democratic/Republicans lining up hoping to get elected. In short, Vermont's 2018 general election ballot seemed to be shaping up as a political smorgasbord. ... While Vermont voters have shown a willingness to consider and even back alternative candidates to a degree not generally seen in other states, the Libertarian and Green parties—considered leaders among alternative movements nationwide—haven't been at their strongest in Vermont. While the Libertarians had minor success at the local level of government in years leading to 2018, the Vermont Green Party had a short but turbulent existence before, essentially, getting absorbed by the Vermont Progressive Party in the early 2010s.

Virginia—Duopolistic stronghold. No independent or smaller-party elected officials at the federal or state level. In 2018 Virginia recognized only the Republicans and Democrats as official parties. According to the Virginia Department

The United States' most prominent independent politician in recent years has made it clear that he's not as independent as billed. Vermont's Bernie Sanders has maintained a close association with the Democratic Party, whose presidential nomination he has unsuccessfully tried to win twice, all the while abstaining from actually joining the party in order to maintain his claim to independent status (Gage Skidmore).

of Elections website, "All other party organizations are required to register as Political Action Committees"—though there are some exceptions to that general rule for county, city, or local party committees intending to raise or spend relatively small amounts of money. While Virginia's petition-signature requirements for independents to get on the ballot weren't particularly onerous, there seemed to be no chance, going into the 2018 general election, that any nonpartisan candidate would win election to a partisan state or federal office. The same was true of "independents" qualifying for the ballot who chose to have their official Political Action Committee preferences listed by their names, as allowed in Virginia. ... One independent candidate for the U.S. House of Representatives, Shaun Brown, was disqualified from the ballot, according to a September 5, 2018, *Washington Post* report by Gregory S. Schneider, for presenting forged signatures gathered "by staffers working for the incumbent Republican, Scott Taylor." According to Schneider, it was the Democratic Party of Virginia that brought forward the suit to keep Brown off the ballot. Brown had run as a Democrat for the U.S. House in 2016, losing to Taylor. On October 30, 2018, the *Post* would follow up with a report on Brown's conviction for defrauding a federal government program that helped feed low-income children. ... While there's been no history of success in recent decades for true independents or smaller-party candidates in state or federal election races in Virginia, candidates without Democratic or Republican party affiliations or leanings have tasted victory in local contests. The Libertarians and Greens had a few registered members holding local elective offices going into the 2018 general election, and it appeared the best any smaller party/PAC or unaffiliated candidates could do, at least in the near future, was aim for victory in municipal or county races.

West Virginia—Duopolistic stronghold. No independent or smaller-party elected officials at the federal or state level. ... Rupert "Rupie" Phillips, a Democratic state delegate (representative) since 2010, announced in January 2017 that he was declaring himself an independent. "It is clear to me that the citizens of [District 24] want a true Independent voice in Charleston," he said, as reported at wdtv.com. But in May of 2017 Phillips announced his plan to join the Republicans in a bid for Congress, and a year later, in May of 2018, he failed to win the Republican nomination in West Virginia's 3rd Congressional District. Phillips didn't run for reelection to the House of Delegates in 2018 (though, two years later, he'd return to elective office in West Virginia as a Republican state senator). ... In 2018 West Virginia recognized four official parties: the Republicans, Democrats, Libertarians, and the Mountain Party (the Mountain State's Green Party affiliate). Only the Democrats and Republicans, however, had any history of success in partisan elections. ... Long a Democratic stronghold, West Virginia in recent times has turned against Democratic policies and regulations blamed for choking the state's struggling coal industry. Third parties and independents haven't benefited significantly from the Democratic Party's overall decline in West Virginia, as the Republicans have picked up the slack, and Mountain State politics has remained essentially a two-horse race. ... As far as 2018 was concerned, not a single non–Republican or non–Democrat appeared to be holding a partisan office heading into West Virginia's primary and general elections, and there were few illusions that that would change coming out of the elections.

Wisconsin—Duopolistic stronghold. No independent or smaller-party elected officials at the federal level. ... Wisconsin recognized five official parties in 2018: the Republicans and Democrats, the Constitution Party, and the Libertarians and Greens. ... Heading into the 2018 elections, the Libertarian and Green parties had a few members holding local nonpartisan elective offices, and a couple of Greens held elective positions in the Wisconsin Conservation Congress. Even so, alternative candidates—except possibly in a few cases where a single opponent would be on the ballot—appeared unlikely to attract much support at the polls in 2018, and the usual sweep in partisan elections by the Republican and Democratic parties seemed inevitable.

Wyoming—Duopolistic stronghold. No independent or smaller-party elected officials at the federal or state level. While Wyoming had four official parties in 2018, the state was in every way a duopolistic stronghold and, increasingly in recent years, one overwhelmingly dominated by the Republicans. ... Candidates representing Wyoming's official "minor parties"—the Libertarian and Constitution parties—were set to participate in 2018's general election. Both parties had a candidate running for governor, and the Libertarians ran a few other candidates for federal and statewide offices, along with a single candidate for the state legislature. Five independents, meanwhile, were on the general election ballot, all running for the state legislature. ... A surprisingly high number of Republicans were slated to run unopposed in races for the state legislature, where Republicans already had a firm grip on power. Prospects generally looked poor for Democrats running for the legislature and downright bleak for minor-party and independent candidates hoping to get elected to a seat in Cheyenne—with two notable exceptions. In State House District 55, the only Libertarian candidate for the legislature, Bethany Baldes, appeared to be running a strong grassroots race against 10-term Republican incumbent David Miller. In 2012 Baldes had run unsuccessfully in a three-way race against Miller, who was reelected, unopposed, in 2014 and 2016. In

2018 Baldes, armed with strategy assistance from the national Libertarian Party and some key local endorsements, would get to oppose Miller one-on-one. Meanwhile, in State House District 22, Jim Roscoe, who'd served the district for two terms as a Democratic state representative from 2009–2013, got back into state politics in 2018 after declaring his intent to run for his former legislative seat as an independent. On his campaign website, Roscoe revealed that, apart from having served in the legislature as a Democrat, "I was a registered Republican for 30+ years." He went on to set a conciliatory tone: "I know [firsthand] that there's wisdom in both parties. ... As an Independent, I can lift the best ideas from both parties without being beholden to either." Going into the 2018 general election, Roscoe seemed to be running an active grassroots campaign. Facing only a lone candidate—though an incumbent in Republican State Representative Marti Halverson—Roscoe looked to be competitive in his bid to be Wyoming's first non–Republican or non–Democrat to get elected to the state legislature in 36 years.

District of Columbia—The nation's capital, municipally speaking, has been a Democratic Party bastion, especially in recent decades, with every mayor since partisan elections for that office were established in the 1970s having been a Democrat. The District of Columbia doesn't have a legislature per se but a 13-member council to which independents in recent years have been more likely to get elected than Republicans. Heading into the 2018 elections, two DC Council seats were held by independents, with one sitting independent, Elissa Silverman, up for reelection in November. In many of DC's races in 2018, independents, Libertarians, and DC Statehood Green Party candidates figured to be the stiffest, or only, competition Democratic candidates would face. ... The DC Statehood Green Party, affiliated with the national Green Party, explained, on its website, why it was a good option for voters: "The Republicrats (that is, the 'Democrats') are not the answer—unless you want more of the same: poorly performing schools, poor public safety, corrupt government, high unemployment, inadequate city services, and politicians for sale." Yet, going into the 2018 DC general election, it appeared all but certain the "Republicrats" once again would dominate partisan races in the District.

* * *

And, to recap the scenario in the other Washington—Washington State (Chapters 5 and 6)—the best bellwether of prospects for alternative candidates in the current era clearly lay in the fortunes of Dr. Ann Diamond—a personable independent, long known in her community, who seemingly had done everything right in pursuit of a legislative seat that had been in Republican hands since the 1960s. While Washington State had a few Libertarians quietly holding municipal or county nonpartisan offices going into the 2018 general election, clearly it was the fortunes of Diamond and her active grassroots campaign that would tell the story.

11

Coming Out of the 2018 Midterms (Pacific Coast, Western Interior, Midwest, and Southwest)

It didn't take long after the closing of the polls in Washington State on November 6, 2018, to determine what everyone already knew: that regardless of how Ann Diamond and the relatively few other alternative candidates who'd made it through their top-two primaries fared in the general election, it would once again be the Democrats and the Republicans feasting at the banquet table. The only question that remained was whether any independents or smaller-party candidates would be making off with any scraps.

In recent years, smaller-party candidates in Washington—unlike their peers in many other states—had been able to get on the primary election ballot and state their party preferences there without having to jump through hoops. But the reality, proven time and time again, was that smaller-party candidates normally got shut out in Washington's primaries when facing candidates aligned with both major parties. Another reality was that each major party, especially in districts where the opposing major party's candidate was regarded as unbeatable, tended to sit out certain races, sometimes opening a path for smaller-party or nonpartisan candidates to get on the general election ballot.

With the stakes so high in federal races, there were no such races—where one major party sat on the sidelines—in Washington State's 2018 elections for the U.S. Senate or U.S. House. In Washington's 2018 U.S. Senate election, Democratic incumbent Maria Cantwell—whose Senate career had gotten off to a rocky start in the early 2000s when she was admonished by the Federal Election Commission for campaign finance issues—defeated Republican Susan Hutchison to win a fourth term.

In Washington State's 2018 U.S. House elections, Democrats won seven of the 10 races, picking up one seat to reflect a general Democratic upswing in U.S. House races across the country. In Washington's Congressional District 2, Libertarian Brian Luke, who'd beaten out "Moderate GOP" candidate Uncle Mover to advance from the top-two primary to the general election, lost to Democratic incumbent Rick Larsen. While Luke had trailed Larsen 65 percent to eight in the primary, he narrowed the gap in the general election, trailing the incumbent 71 percent to 29.

As it turned out, the nature of Washington voters' call for "change" was perhaps evident in the results from Congressional Districts 7 and 8. In District 7 India-born Pramila Jayapal, the Democratic incumbent, formerly a civil rights activist supporting immigrants' rights, soundly defeated a Republican challenger who, in his Voters' Guide statement, took aim at "politicians who exploit immigration fraud" and "SSN theft committed by illegal aliens." The Republican challenger, Craig Keller, added, "The incumbent [Jayapal] would vote illegal aliens an amnesty 'pathway' to your Social Security and thereby blow up an already insolvent *Old-Age and Survivors Disability Insurance* program [italics in original]. That's insurance fraud!" Meanwhile, in District 8, Democrat Dr. Kim Schrier edged out Republican Dino Rossi to win outgoing U.S. Representative David Reichert's seat in the House of Representatives. The victories of Jayapal and Schrier reflected what could be viewed as an incongruity that seemed to run throughout the U.S. state and federal elections in 2018—that is, the tendency of voters, concerned about where Trump and his allies were taking the country, to look for change in seemingly appealing "alternative" candidates, often female and/or "minority," aligning themselves with the Democratic Party, which, despite numerous reports suggesting voters were getting tired of the two-party system and a fairly large percentage now considered themselves "independent," clearly remained the only viable alternative recognized by most voters opposed to the Republicans.

At the state level in Washington, the moment of truth came on November 6, 2018, for seven independents or nonpartisans and four Libertarians who'd survived the primary and made it to the general election. All but one—Okanagan County's Dr. Ann Diamond—had survived the primary mainly as a result of having had the good fortune of facing only one major-party candidate, and nine of the 10 not counting Diamond had faced only a single opponent of any sort in the primary. One "independent" appeared to wear the label dubiously, as a Republican Party organization had contributed to the State Senate campaign of Legislative District 29 "independent" candidate Pierre Malebranche.

All four Libertarians lost to Democrats by wide margins, three in northwest Seattle's Legislative District 36. District 22 Libertarian Allen

Acosta, meanwhile, finished at 30 percent in the general election, up from a 77–23 deficit in the primary.

Acosta, who says he could have received some quiet Republican funding had he agreed to oppose his Democratic opponent as an "independent" rather than sticking to his principles and running as a Libertarian, reports that the key challenge of his campaign lay less in explaining to voters what Libertarianism was about than in making them aware that there was *any* opposition to the Democratic Party nominee in his race in what was considered a hands-off Democratic district. "I just got sick and tired of seeing … no choices on the ballot," he says, and his hope was to connect with voters who shared that frustration. A community activist, Acosta says he "continued to engage the community" while going door-to-door, sign-waving, and doing what he could to "make people aware that they had another choice on the ballot." His efforts resulted in increasing his vote total from just over 8,000 in the primary to just over 20,000 in November. As far as independents/nonpartisans were concerned, five of the seven contending for state legislative seats in Washington's 2018 general election improved on their primary showings to close out the general election at 30 percent or better. One, former Poulsbo mayor Betsy Erickson, improved on her 36 percent primary showing to break the 40 percent barrier in the general election.

As for Dr. Ann Diamond, the independent candidate facing Republican Keith Goehner in rural State Legislative District 12, hopes were high for an unaffiliated newcomer who'd filed early as a candidate, raised small contributions from many voters in her district, and run what seemed to be an effective grassroots campaign in her Republican-heavy district. Chris Vance, whose Washington Independents organization provided major support to the Diamond campaign, says that, right to the end, "We were hoping she'd win." But in the end, that wouldn't happen, as Diamond fell, 56 percent to 44, to Goehner.

* * *

Following is a general, region-by-region accounting of political affairs in the wake of the 2018 U.S. midterm elections. Given particular focus are developments that seemed to speak, one way or another, about changes concerning the American major-party duopoly or the prospects of individuals or entities committed to the development of a more democratic form of election and government.

Pacific Coast

Down the coast from **Washington**, dozens of Libertarians and, especially, Greens were serving at the local/municipal level in **California** before the November 2018 general election, and election results ensured that would remain the case in 2019 and beyond. But, to probably no one's surprise, at the state and federal levels, California's 2018 general election resulted in a clean sweep for the two major parties. ... Some attention was given to the efforts of three Green Party candidates for the state legislature in 2018—Kenneth Mejia, Laura Wells, and Rodolfo Cortes Barragan—all of whom, without Republican opponents in California's top-two primary, had advanced to the general election. All three lost to Democrats in November, though Wells managed to reduce her margin of loss from 99.5 to 0.5 percent in the primary to 88.4 to 11.6. Eight years earlier, Wells had run for governor, representing the Green Party and finishing third with two percent of the vote. ... Steve Poizner, who'd served as California Commissioner of Insurance as a Republican from 2007 to 2011, fell short in his effort to return to the post as an independent in 2018 despite having finished first in the primary. When the general election ballots were counted, Poizner trailed Democrat Richard Lara 52 percent to 48 in his attempt to become the first independent ever to hold statewide elective office in California.

In **Oregon**, a small number of Green- or Libertarian-affiliated officials were serving in elective local nonpartisan offices heading into the 2018 general election, and a similar small number were set to serve in such offices coming out of the election. ... The Independent Party of Oregon, while seeing some of its "cross-nominees"—Republicans or Democrats with IPO endorsement—win federal or state races in 2018, didn't have a candidate of its own (i.e., one who wasn't a Democrat or Republican) come close to winning such a race.

Up north in **Alaska**, the departure of "independent" Bill Walker from the governorship in late 2018 led to the departure of his nonpartisan appointees, Lieutenant Governor Valerie Nurr'araaluk Davidson and Attorney General Jahna Lindemuth, who would both be replaced under the incoming administration of Republican Mike Dunleavy. ... The 2018 general election, as expected, was a Republican/Democratic shutout. One federal race, in U.S. House District 1, resulted in a dead tie between big-party candidates following the initial vote count, with 17 votes in the district going to other than the Republican or Democratic candidate. Given how close the vote was, it's safe to say those few "other" votes influenced the outcome of the election. ... Some observers saw a bright spot in the 2018 reelection, in State House District 36, of "nonpartisan"

Daniel Ortiz, whose nonpartisan credentials had to be considered suspect since he caucused with the Democrats. Two other nonpartisans, without any obvious party alignment, fell slightly short in their runs for the State House: Chris Dimond in District 33, trailing Democrat Sara Hannon 57 percent to 43; and incumbent State Representative Jason Grenn, who finished well ahead of Democrat Dustin Darden but trailed Republican winner Sara Rasmussen 47 percent to 41.

In **Hawaii**—historically reluctant to make any movement away from the two-party system that began to take hold during the territorial era predating statehood—partisan elections over the years have been anything but friendly to alternative candidates, and such was certainly the case in November of 2018. While a few Green and Libertarian candidates ran fairly strong races for the state legislature—taking over a quarter of the vote in a couple of instances—the statewide result was exactly what history had conditioned Hawaiians to accept: yet another clean sweep by the duopoly (led by the Democratic Party).

Western Interior

While a couple of key races in **Idaho**'s 2018 general election had fairly large and mixed fields of candidates, the Gem State clearly dug in its heels once again as a bastion of duopolistic power-sharing. Legislative races went in a similar manner as in most of the country (i.e., resulting in a major-party shutout), and the vast majority—95 of 105 races (two for state representative and one for state senator in each of Idaho's 35 legislative districts)—didn't have an alternative candidate on the ballot. Even at the local level, there didn't appear to be any new ground broken as far as independent candidates were concerned. ... In neighboring **Montana**, Libertarians, on the general election ballot but facing dismal prospects, finished a distant third in statewide races in which the party fielded candidates. The same was true in legislative races where Libertarian candidates faced opponents from both major parties. The all-too-predictable result was that no Libertarian candidate—or alternative candidate of *any* persuasion—came close to winning a partisan election at any level in Montana's 2018 general election.

In **Wyoming**, where prospects generally looked poor for alternative candidates in the 2018 general election, two candidates for state representative had some success swimming against the tide. In District 22, independent Jim Roscoe—who'd served as a Democratic state representative from 2009 to 2013—defeated Republican opponent Marti Halverson by a 56–44 margin to ensure his return to the State House as the first independent representative to get elected since the 1980s. In District 25, meanwhile, Libertarian Bethany Baldes ran a strong campaign—despite injuring her leg and needing help getting around—and, taking 49 percent of the vote, fell just short of upending Republican incumbent David Miller.

Colorado appeared to have one person other than a Republican or Democrat holding a partisan office heading into the 2018 general election: "independent" State Senator Cheri Jahn, who'd been elected as a Democrat in 2010 and 2014 before leaving the party in late 2017. Jahn was unable to run for reelection in 2018 due to term limit restrictions and, following the general election, was set to be replaced as District 20 state senator by a Democrat. With Jahn out of the picture, there didn't appear to be a single alternative partisan officeholder on deck coming out the election. ... While alternative candidates weren't competitive in any federal or state race that included candidates representing both major parties, Libertarians or independent/unaffiliated candidates managed to take a quarter or more of the vote in a few state legislative races when facing only single opponents. Independent candidate for state senator in District 59, Paul Jones, endorsed by Unite America, led the way among alternative candidates facing single opponents in the general election, earning 44 percent of the vote.

The picture in **Utah**, leading to November 2018, seemed clear: There didn't appear to be a smaller-party or nonpartisan candidate serving in any partisan elective office in the state. The prognosis—more of the same—seemed equally clear and was borne out in the 2018 general election. ... To some observers, the freshest "new blood" pumped into the 2018 Utah general election seemed to be in the form of 2003–2007 Massachusetts governor and 2012 Republican Party presidential nominee Mitt Romney, who made his successful return to elective politics by getting elected, as a Republican, to serve as Utah's junior U.S. Senator.

Nevada, like Colorado, had an independent state senator in 2018 who hadn't won election as an independent. Nevada State Senator Patricia Farley, elected as a Republican in 2014, announced her intention to caucus with the Democrats after becoming "nonpartisan" in 2016. Likely with a good view into the future, Farley didn't seek reelection in 2018. ... While a few alternative candidates managed to earn a quarter or more of votes in two-person state legislative races, Nevada's 2018 general election seemed to bear out what had hardly been a secret going into the election: that, while many Nevadans supported or worked in the gambling industry in places like Las Vegas, Henderson, and Reno, the majority of voters in the Silver State didn't seem at all prepared to take a gamble on a political candidate who wasn't either a Democrat or a Republican.

Midwest

While progress toward a more inclusive brand of democracy in the Midwest was slight at best coming out of the 2018 general election, there at least appeared to be grounds for faint optimism in some quarters. ... Legislative candidates in 2018 spent heavily on campaigns in **Nebraska**, though not necessarily at levels exceeding spending in most other states—but then none of those other states, unlike Nebraska, made a claim that its legislative elections and legislative body were nonpartisan. In 2018 and prior, political affiliations of Nebraska's sitting legislators and candidates were generally no secret, and the big political parties donated generously to "nonpartisan" candidates who supported party positions. During the primary phase of the 2018 election, the biggest spender among legislative candidates in Nebraska, according to the *Omaha World-Herald*, was incumbent senator (legislator) Laura Ebke, who, while officially holding a "nonpartisan" office, had left the Republican Party to join the Libertarians in 2016. According to the *World-Herald*, Ebke ramped up her spending in 2018 to defend her campaign against attack ads by those opposing her departure from the Republican Party. Indeed, attack ads—often highly partisan in nature—were as much a part of the political landscape in Nebraska in 2018 as in most other parts of the country. As it turned out, "nonpartisan" Libertarian Ebke lost her seat to "nonpartisan" Republican Tom Brandt.

In **Iowa**, four-term state senator David Johnson, a long-time Republican who left the party in 2016 in opposition to its embracing Donald Trump as the party's presidential candidate, served out the remaining two years of his term as Iowa's first independent legislator in over four decades but, in 2018, decided not to run for reelection in his predominantly Republican district.

As for appointees to state-level offices, two independents/nonpartisans—**Illinois** Commerce Commission member Anastasia Palivos and **Ohio** Public Utilities Commission chair Asim Haque—held key positions in 2018, which they would retain until early the following year. ... The inclusion of two Greens, at least through April 2019, on the popularly elected **Wisconsin** Conservation Congress, was another small sign suggesting a more inclusive democracy was perhaps brewing in the Midwest in 2018.

The 2018 general election gave indications that not all Midwest voters opposed meaningful change in the political landscape—but, as in other regions, change didn't seem to be particularly welcome at the federal or state level, where alternative candidates struggled in every race in which they ran. In key Midwestern races involving smaller-party or independent candidates, Chris Graveline, the independent who successfully challenged **Michigan**'s petition-signature requirement to get on the ballot for attorney general, received 1.7 percent of the vote; Ohio gubernatorial candidates, Libertarian Travis Irvine and the Green Party's Constance Gadell-Newton, both fell short of winning the 3 percent of the vote required to keep their parties on the state ballot through 2022; and **Kansas**' John Doll, a sitting state senator who left the Republicans in March of 2018 to become an independent ticket's nominee for Lieutenant Governor, won 6.5 percent of votes in the race (alongside gubernatorial running mate Greg Orman)—finishing a distant third but well ahead of a Libertarian and another independent—before sliding back into the comfort of his State Senate seat as an independent. By the summer of 2019 Doll would rejoin the Republican Party.

South Dakota, **Missouri**, and **Wisconsin** each had a small number of Libertarians, Greens, and/or independents occupying elective local offices—the majority of those offices officially nonpartisan—leading up to November 2018. **Minnesota**, **Indiana**, **Iowa**, and **Illinois** had slightly higher numbers of alternative officeholders in such positions heading into the 2018 elections. In most of those seven states, alternative candidates at the local level managed to pull off a few more victories before the year was over. **North Dakota**, meanwhile, seemed to show few signs that an increasingly inclusive brand of democracy was in the works on either side of the 2018 elections.

Southwest

The situation in the Southwest, coming out of the 2018 general election, closely mirrored the situation in most of the country. ... As far as **Texas** was concerned, the Green Party and the Libertarian Party—the latter, Texas' only official party in 2018 other than the obvious two—were "represented" in Texas elective politics by each having one openly affiliated officeholder serving in a local nonpartisan post heading into the general election. Several more Libertarians statewide were elected to local nonpartisan posts in November. ... While the Greens made no significant gains in Texas over the course of 2018, the Libertarians' greatest success was Mark Ash's 25 percent showing in his two-person race—with no Democrat on the ballot—for a judgeship on the Texas Court of Criminal Appeals. While Ash trailed Republican Michelle Slaughter by a three-to-one margin in a partisan race, the roughly 1.6 million votes he earned guaranteed the Libertarian Party would remain on the Texas ballot through 2020. Other Libertarians in federal or state races—the vast majority facing both

Republicans and Democrats—mainly scored in the 1 to 3 percent range. Meanwhile, showings for independent candidates of various persuasions in federal or state races seemed to offer little cause for optimism. ... As in other states, when it came to looking for "change" during the 2018 midterms, many voters in Texas stayed within familiar parameters, as Democrat Beto O'Rourke scored well especially in certain "progressive" urban areas around the state and came close to upsetting ultimate Washington insider and 2016 presidential wannabe Senator Ted Cruz. Even after O'Rourke's defeat at the hands of Cruz, many voters inside and outside Texas seemed to regard O'Rourke—a three-term Democratic U.S. Representative who'd be stepping down in January of 2019—as a possible challenger to President Trump in 2020 and a potential messenger of change in Washington, D.C., and around the nation.

In **Oklahoma**, every partisan elective office appeared to be in the hands of a Republican or a Democrat on both sides of the 2018 general election, and most races in the general election involved only the big parties. ... A smaller number of races involved three or four candidates. In such races, candidates representing the Libertarian Party—the only party other than the "big two" to have official status in Oklahoma—scored in the single digits, as did the relatively small number of candidates identified as "independent." ... In two statewide races—for State Treasurer and State Auditor and Inspector—independent Charles de Coune and Libertarian John Yeutter, each facing a Republican candidate and no other opposition, managed to earn percentages in the twenties. Somewhat mirroring the situation in Texas, probably the greatest "victory" for the Libertarian Party in Oklahoma's 2018 general election was Yeutter's 25 percent showing—still a three-to-one loss in his statewide race but one that guaranteed the Libertarian Party would remain on the state ballot until 2022.

In **New Mexico**, 2012 and 2016 Libertarian Party presidential candidate Gary Johnson's bid to get elected U.S. Senator in 2018 came to naught. While Johnson's 15 percent share of the vote—over 107,000 votes in total—may have seemed impressive for a third-party candidate, it represented a fraction of the support he received while running two successful campaigns, both as a Republican, for governor in 1994 and 1998. ... A key challenge to major-party domination across the board in New Mexico's 2018 general election was in the form of independent Jarratt Applewhite, a former Santa Fe school board trustee endorsed by Unite America and committed to helping independent and smaller-party voters get their voices heard in Santa Fe. Like Ann Diamond in Washington State, Applewhite ran a strong grassroots campaign, but his 41 percent showing in a two-man race in State House District 50 against two-term Democratic incumbent

Matthew McQueen left Applewhite short of being the first New Mexican ever to get elected to the legislature as an independent.

As for **Arizona**, in a November 2018 nonpartisan race, Libertarian Levi Tappan was elected mayor of Page, a Northern Arizona city of about 7,000. ... The Green Party fell short in its efforts to aim high as nominees Angel Torres and Angela Green both earned 2 percent in their 2018 general election races for governor and U.S. Senator. ... In a two-man race for U.S. Representative in Arizona's Congressional District 7, Green Party nominee Gary Swing trailed Democratic incumbent Ruben Gallego 86 percent to 14. ... In Legislative District 21, independent candidate Kathy Knecht, a strong advocate for public education, fell just short in her State Senate race against Republican incumbent Rick Gray. Had she been elected, Knecht, who trailed Gray 52 percent to 48, would have been the first independent candidate ever elected to either house of the Arizona State Legislature.

12

Coming Out of the 2018 Midterms (Northeast, Mid-Atlantic, Appalachia, and Southeast)

Northeast

Maine's incumbent "independent" U.S. Senator Angus King was elected to a second term in 2018, soundly defeating Republican challenger and sitting state senator Eric Brakey. Trailing King and Brakey was Democrat Zak Ringelstein, with whose party King had caucused during his first term as senator. ... Teresea "Terry" Hayes, an ex–Democratic state representative who, as an independent, was appointed State Treasurer in 2015, ran for governor as an independent in 2018. Backed by Unite America, she won 6 percent of the vote, with the victory going to Democrat and sitting Attorney General Janet Mills.

At the local and state levels, Maine saw little change regarding inclusion of alternative officeholders following the 2018 general election. At the local level, the Libertarians and Greens maintained a small electoral presence; and at the state level, Maine, with eight non–Republican/non–Democratic state representatives going into the election, would slip to five in its aftermath—four independents and Common Sense Independent Party incumbent State Representative Kent Ackley, who narrowly retained his seat, 2,155 votes to 2,139, over his lone challenger, a Republican. The biggest loser among alternative parties in the State House was the "Green Independent Party" of Maine, which lost both of the seats it held through 2018—one due to electoral defeat and the other as a result of term limits. The holders of both seats heading into the November 2018 general election had been elected to the State House as Democrats before joining the Maine Green Independent Party in 2017.

New Hampshire's 2018 general election resulted in a slight increase in the small number of Libertarian-affiliated officials holding local office. At the state level, where a trio of state representatives—all elected as major-party nominees—had publicly realigned as Libertarians in 2017, all three would be on the way out in 2018, one through resignation and the other two through defeat in their first election as Libertarians. One of the Libertarian state representatives who lost in 2018, Brandon Phinney, still in his early twenties, addressed his trouncing (Welch, quoting from Phinney's Facebook page) by "[t]he Democratic candidate, who barely campaigned ... and [t]he Republican, who did NOTHING but put out yard signs." Phinney continued, "[V]oters care more about party than literally anything else and that's the biggest problem in this country." Phinney's own electoral history appeared to back up that position, as he got elected to the State House of Representatives, in 2016, as a Republican, earning 51 percent of the vote. Two years later, when he ran for the same seat as a Libertarian, his support plunged to 10 percent. ... Libertarian gubernatorial candidate Jilletta Jarvis' 1 percent showing in the 2018 general election effectively removed the party from the state ballot in 2020.

In **Vermont**, "independent" United States Senator Bernie Sanders defeated one Republican challenger, no Democrat, six independents, and one small-party candidate (with the six independents and the small-party candidate combining to earn 5 percent of the vote) to win reelection in November 2018 and, seemingly, keep alive his chances of catching fire in 2020 and winning the Democratic Party nomination for president. ... At the state level, Democratic Party–endorsed Progressive Party incumbents David Zuckerman and Doug Hoffer were reelected as Lieutenant Governor and Auditor of Accounts, respectively; and nearly 20 similarly (dually) endorsed Progressives were set to resume or commence service in the state legislature following the general election, according to the Vermont Secretary of State website. Meanwhile, two of Vermont's seven independent state legislators lost their reelection bids to Democrats. ... At the municipal/county level, a relatively small contingent of Progressives and independents remained in power coming out of the 2018 general election, which also saw a Libertarian-affiliated candidate elected as a nonpartisan Justice of the Peace in Bennington.

New York State held fairly steady in 2018, as far as the fortunes of alternative candidates and officeholders were concerned. Libertarian- or Green-affiliated officials held a smattering of local elective positions both heading into and coming out of the 2018 general election. ... Incumbent State Assemblyman Fred Thiele, representing eastern Long Island's State Assembly District 1, won another term—his twelfth overall and fifth since switching from the Republican Party to the Independence Party in 2009. Thiele, who caucused with the Democrats and faced no Democratic opposition since splitting from the Republicans, doubled as a major-party candidate in 2018, as he received the Democratic endorsement (as well as endorsements from several other smaller parties). ... None of New York State's other alternative candidates—the majority arguably more deserving of the "alternative" label than Thiele came close to winning a race at the state or federal level in 2018.

Fortunes didn't change much for the Green and Libertarian parties in **Massachusetts**, where a small number of each party's affiliates held local nonpartisan elective offices both before and after the November 2018 general election. ... Massachusetts had two independent state representatives heading into the general election, each having been elected as a Democrat or Republican before becoming "independent" while serving in the State House. One—Solomon Israel Goldstein-Rose, a Democrat until February 2018—dropped his reelection bid in August but still won 25 percent of the vote in his 3rd Hampshire District race, which was won by a Democrat. The other, Susannah Whipps, a Republican until August 2017, defeated her Democratic challenger, 70 percent to 30, to claim victory in the 2018 general election and head into 2019 as Massachusetts' only remaining "alternative" elected state- or federal-level officeholder.

Despite a few respectable but unsuccessful showings by Libertarians in local and state legislative races, there was little, stemming from the 2018 **Rhode Island** general election, to suggest prospects were promising for anyone with visions of challenging the Democratic and Republican parties' lock on power in the Ocean State in the foreseeable future. The Compassion Party candidates for governor and attorney general didn't recover sufficiently from their high-profile arrests a month before the general election to make competitive runs—not that they had a chance anyway. ... The District 73 race for state representative, pitting Republican David A. Quiroa against his son and independent David A. Quiroa, Jr., saw both come up short against the Democratic incumbent.

While **Connecticut** had a small a small contingent of alternative—mostly Green-affiliated—officeholders serving in local elective positions in 2018, the general election did nothing to improve the outlook for alternative candidates or organizations hoping to break through at the state or federal level in the Nutmeg State. State and federal races went much as expected—resulting in a clean sweep for the major parties, with no alternative candidate able to mount a serious challenge, even if facing only a single opponent. ... The 2018 general election seemed to serve much the same purpose in **New Jersey** as in Connecticut—i.e., to highlight just how dim prospects looked, for the foreseeable future, for anyone hoping to loosen the Democrats' and Republicans' grip on power. About the only significant difference between Connecticut and New Jersey in that regard is that the latter didn't appear to have nearly the degree of alternative representation at the local level, relative to its population, that Connecticut did.

Pennsylvania was another story. Blessed with a large population—second among Northeast states behind New York—the Keystone State had an impressive number of Libertarians and Greens serving in municipal and township elective offices both before the 2018 general election and coming out of it. As in other states, however, relative success at the local level for alternative candidates didn't translate to similar success for the relatively small number of Libertarian, Green, or independent candidates vying for state or federal office in 2018. While dozens of victories by alternative candidates in municipal/township/county elections in recent years (fueled by grassroots acceptance in small-population areas) were certainly positive a sign, every indication seemed to be that the Democratic and Republican parties—and Pennsylvania voters—weren't likely to make room for other serious competitors at the state or federal level for some time.

Mid-Atlantic

There were few signs that a more inclusive, less duopolistic political structure was in the works in **Maryland** heading into the 2018 general election. Yet the Green Party, with minimal connection to power at any level of government in the state, had perhaps a small taste of "victory" when Shane Robinson—an outgoing state delegate (state representative) who'd completed nearly two four-year terms as a Democrat before losing in the 2018 Democratic primary—switched to the Green Party after the general election as he served out the final weeks of his second term in Maryland's House of Delegates. As a Democrat, Robinson—who the *Montgomery County Sentinel* reported had been a Green Party member in earlier years—stood in alignment with Green Party views on issues relating to the environment while serving on the Environment and Transportation Committee. While Robinson, an experienced energy consultant, didn't express any plans to run for office in the future after switching to the Green Party, he appeared committed to remaining a strong voice on environmental issues beyond the end of his term in the legislature and "[being] a part of getting the word out." As Robinson told reporter Nickolai Sukharev, "This [isn't] about ... trying to get a critical mass to go out and win elections ... but you can get enough people involved to be able to move the needle on public policy that affects Marylanders."

A Maryland Green of some note going into the 2018 general election was long-time activist Annie Chambers, whose work over the years focused largely on issues related to welfare and homelessness. In recent years Chambers had served on the Baltimore Housing Authority's Resident Advisory Board. In 2018 Chambers was on the general election ballot as the Green Party nominee for Lieutenant Governor alongside gubernatorial running mate and fellow Green Ian Schlakman. Despite an early start to campaigning and solid party support, the Schlakman-Chambers ticket managed to score only about half a percent in the general election—roughly the same level of support the Libertarian Party ticket managed pick up in the same race.

In other Mid-Atlantic states—specifically **Delaware**, **Virginia**, and **North Carolina**—every partisan elective office at the federal or state level was held by a Republican or Democrat heading into the 2018 general election. That wouldn't change in the aftermath of the election, as alternative parties and independent/unaffiliated candidates had minimal impact in state, federal, and, in most areas, local races. ... North Carolina's Libertarian Party, eager to get one of its candidates elected to something other than a local office for the first time, ran 34 party nominees for state legislative seats and another for a partisan position on the State Court of Appeals. None put up a serious challenge, and only two of the 35 earned better than 4 percent of the general election vote. ... Most successful activity in the Mid-Atlantic region, as far as opposition to the big-party duopoly was concerned, figured to be centered in the **District of Columbia**, where, heading into the 2018 general election, the DC Council had two sitting independents, with one up for reelection. In some races, smaller-party candidates—mainly affiliates of the DC Statehood Green Party—figured to represent the toughest challenge to Democratic incumbents' reelection chances. ... As the dust settled following the general election, Democrats came out far ahead in all of the district's partisan races. The independent DC Council member up for reelection, at-large councilor Elissa Silverman, finished a distant second to Democrat Anita Bonds but retained her council seat by virtue of her second-place finish. In 2014 both Bonds and Silverman had been elected at-large councilors following a similar one-two finish.

Appalachia

In **Tennessee**, **Kentucky**, and **West Virginia**, the 2018 general election and its aftermath played out much as expected. ... While every state or federal elective office in Tennessee, heading into November, was held by a Republican or Democrat, three months before the general election, in

August 2018, four Libertarian-affiliated candidates got elected to four-year terms in county or municipal governments. The three who got elected to partisan offices were on the ballot as independents, as Tennessee officially recognized only the two major parties. ... Unfortunately, what little momentum there seemed to be coming out of those county/municipal elections and heading into the general election was stifled when "independents" of various persuasions were roundly rejected by voters choosing elected officials to serve in Washington, D.C., and Nashville.

It was a very similar situation in Kentucky. A few Libertarians held local offices heading into the 2018 general election, and a few more got elected in November; but, as in Tennessee, every state- or federal-level elective office in Kentucky was and would remain in Republican or Democratic hands. ... As far as West Virginia was concerned, the situation looked bleak, both before and after the 2018 general election, for Libertarians and alternative candidates across the board hoping to loosen the Republicans' and Democrats' grip on power anytime soon, even in the smallest districts or jurisdictions.

Southeast

In **Arkansas**, Democrat-turned-independent Mark McElroy finished second in a three-way race in the 2018 general election and failed to retain his state representative seat in District 11. McElroy finished ahead of the Republican nominee but trailed Don Glover, like McElroy a former judge who would go on to represent District 11 as a Democrat in Little Rock. ... Libertarian David Dinwiddie took 28 percent of the vote—nearly 240,000 votes in total—in a two-person race against incumbent Auditor of State, Republican Andrea Lea. A week before the general election, the *Arkansas Democrat-Gazette* identified Dinwiddie as a Pine Bluff, Arkansas, auto mechanic who said he joined the race "because the state auditor's office is the best source of information on where the money is spent and potentially wasted" (Roberts). ... The Arkansas Libertarian Party nominated Elvis Presley for a U.S. congressional seat in 2018. According to Fort Smith/Fayetteville's KFSM/KXNW-TV, Presley had "previously run for Arkansas governor, land commission and the state legislature." By all accounts Presley, unsuccessful in his earlier runs for office, wasn't the singer of Graceland fame but an Elvis lookalike KFSM/KXNW said "performs shows as the late Elvis A. Presley." As for his 2018 run for Congress, Presley took home 2 percent of the vote.

While both the Libertarian and Green parties were officially recognized in **Louisiana** in 2018, neither party had any significant success to report before or after the general election. That was particularly true of the Greens, who didn't appear to have a party member holding any level of elective office in the Bayou State. ... A few months after the 2018 general election, Jackson, Louisiana, businessman Roy Daryl Adams would win election as an independent to the Louisiana State House after finishing ahead of three Democrats in a February 2019 primary and defeating a Republican with eight years' experience in parish (essentially, county) elective office in a March 2019 special election. With the victory Adams, a former Democrat himself, joined three other independents in the State House, all three serving four-year terms and facing reelection or term-limit prospects in 2019/2020. Adams would face his first reelection test as early as the fall of 2019, barely half a year after winning office, and would be successful.

In **Mississippi**, **Alabama**, and **Georgia**, election of known alternative candidates to office of any level in 2018 seemed—and proved—an unlikely prospect, as public attention appeared to focus more on partisan bickering and choosing sides than on finding common ground via nonpartisan or even bipartisan solutions. ... **South Carolina**, meanwhile, held steady with a minimal presence of verifiably alternative local officeholders both before and following the 2018 general election.

While **Florida** had a sprinkling of local offices occupied in 2018 by elected officials unaffiliated with the Republican and Democratic parties, the road to success in state or federal races seemed as impassable for alternative candidates in the Sunshine State as in most of the Southeast. Rancorous Republican-Democrat races—particularly for governor and U.S. Senator—dominated headlines as major-party candidates were elected by razor-thin margins amid accusations of dirty play aimed at the opposing major party. Despite those thin margins, unaffiliated or smaller-party candidates had little to no bearing on outcomes, with one possible exception. In State Senate District 8, independent Charles Goston won 4,319 votes—just over 2 percent of the total—compared to 100,690 (49.4 percent) for Republican Keith Perry and 98,692 (48.5 percent) for Democrat Kayser Enneking. While Goston finished far behind his opponents, his vote tally exceeded the difference between his opponents' vote counts and, at least theoretically, could have made a difference in the outcome.

Here is a general accounting of the division of power nationwide between the Republican and Democratic parties following the 2018 U.S. midterm general election:

> The presidency, while appearing in peril at times in recent months and years, was, of course, uncontested in 2018 and remained in Republican hands.
> In the U.S. Senate, Republicans were poised to hold 53 seats

12. Coming Out of the 2018 Midterms   107

compared to 45 for Democrats and two for Democrat-caucusing "independents."

The U.S. House of Representatives swung toward the Democrats, who would emerge from the dust of the 2018 midterms with 235 seats to 200 for the Republicans.

Republican governors outnumbered Democratic governors, 29–21.

There was a marked movement away from split party control of state legislatures—i.e., the two major parties each controlling one house. Coming out of the 2018 midterms, only Minnesota's legislature would be under split party control during the coming Congress. According to *Pacific Standard* magazine's Seth Masket, "The last time just one state legislature was under split party control was 1914."

While the Democrats made some gains in state legislative races nationwide, the Republican Party maintained control of both legislative houses in 29 states (plus Nebraska's officially non-partisan Unicameral), according to the National Conference of State Legislatures.

At the municipal level, Democrats seemed a more visible electoral presence nationwide than Republicans, reflecting the general perception of the Democratic/Republican urban/rural divide in present-day America.

It may be difficult to apply such figures and perceptions to the task of coming up with a scorecard illustrating the major parties' balance of power following the 2018 midterms and heading toward 2020—and not merely because of small fluctuations following the 2018 midterms. But whether an observer weaves the data into a 50–50 split or a 55–45 advantage in favor of either major party, the scorecard that should really matter to anyone with a will for shaping up an American democracy that seems to have grown fat and lazy is one that lumps both major parties together and identifies their adversary as democracy itself—the very democracy that spawned the Democratic and Republican parties.

True, there are capable and committed alternative officeholders across the United States—many dedicated to the principles or platforms of smaller parties representing a wide variety of ideologies or approaches. Yet, to argue that true "independents" or "alternatives" in the current age command even a one-percent share of power or influence would be a gross overstatement. On a pie graph, accurately rendered, that share might look more like a line than a segment. But for the sake of sticking to easy math and presenting a snapshot that aims to get a key point across with some clarity, the scorecard that matters most, with regard to illustrating just where the United States stands all these years into its once-ambitious experiment with democracy, is one that looks like this: *Duopoly 99* (rounded down)–*Democracy 1* (rounded up).

13

Playing a Field of Two

Imagine that the two participants in a Super Bowl or World Series were set and known to just about everyone before the season even got started. There'd certainly be some surprises and entertainment value along the way, but there'd be no surprise as to where things were ultimately heading. And while there might be some mystery as to the names of the players who'd be on the field during the big showdown, there'd be no mystery at all about what uniforms they'd be wearing.

Those two teams destined for the showdown—year after year after year—may overlook the other "competition" and spend the whole regular season trash-talking each other. They may even hate each other, and probably do. Yet, despite that hatred, and despite the two teams' tendency to disagree on just about everything, there seem to be a few matters on which both agree.

That's probably a fair characterization of American politics.

In his 2004 book *Running on Empty: How the Democratic and Republican Parties Are Bankrupting Our Future and What Americans Can Do About It*, Peter G. Peterson makes the point that "[t]he Democrats and the Republicans, with their lopsided and mutually irreconcilable worldviews, have found … one important way to compromise, and this is for both sides to take what they want (low taxing and high spending) and send the bill to our kids" (ch. 1).

While there's plenty of truth in Peterson's observation, he might have added one more thing on which the two major parties agree: American government, or political sport in general, is best left to two teams. No other players should be allowed in the "big game."

As Greg Orman puts it in *A Declaration of Independents*, "Together, Republicans and Democrats form a ruling duopoly that keeps itself in power by protecting the status quo. Although the two political parties are forever at each other's throats, they really work in tandem to divide the electorate along party lines and distract it from the failings of the ruling elite in Washington" (Orman, "Opening Argument").

That seems to be a view that the American public is beginning to share in larger numbers than historically, and the increase in Americans claiming to be "independent" seems to bear that out. Peterson, who was U.S. Commerce Secretary for about a year under President Nixon, writes, "[M]illions of Americans who once worked, led, and campaigned for our major political parties have severed—or are at least rethinking—their attachment to them. ... They no longer want to belong to either camp—or at least want to remove the insignia from their old uniforms" (ch. 1).

Peterson's qualifying statement at the end captures the reality of the situation. While many erstwhile major-party stalwarts are weary of partisan wrangling, see through the inefficiency and antidemocratic nature of the modern-day American political machine, and even, in increasing numbers, profess to be "independent," the majority are still leaners—leaners toward one major party or the other ... but, perhaps more significantly, leaners toward the two-party system that has caused them to cringe and to question their long-established loyalties and beliefs.

A 2016–2017 survey by the Voter Study Group (voterstudygroup.org), interviewing 8,000 Americans who'd been surveyed in 2011 and 2012, determined that "13 percent of partisans [had] switched their affiliation in the last five years" (Griffin). According to the survey, the majority of those switching from either major party identified themselves as "independent" after making the switch. What's open to speculation, though, is how many of those self-identifying "independents" saw themselves as being on the fence or "free agents" not automatically beholden to either major party but simply playing the field—a limited field in which only two teams were considered to be in the game.

Another sports analogy that seems to fit in this discussion is that of the home-field advantage—and one reason the Democratic and Republican parties share a perpetual home-field advantage over all others is a practice that used to be a dirty word to many observers of American politics but has since, over the course of two centuries, quietly slid into national acceptance ... or at least general indifference, even while it's faced some legal challenges in recent years.

Massachusetts governor and later U.S. Vice President Elbridge Gerry came under some fire in 1812 after signing into law a bill establishing newly configured electoral districts in his state—some likened to the shape of a salamander and all designed to boost the election prospects of his Democratic-Republican Party, which controlled the Massachusetts legislature at the time. While Gerry was voted out of office later that same year and some expected the odd manner of redistricting in Massachusetts to be corrected, what happened instead was that the practice of "gerrymandering" soon caught on nationwide.

In *Pacific Standard* magazine, Ginger Strand offers a succinct summary of how gerrymandering applies in the current age:

> Once a decade ... there's a national census, followed by a constitutionally mandated round of reapportionment to determine how many representatives each state will send to Congress. Congressional districts and state legislative districts must then be redrawn to reflect changes in population. In 34 states, the new congressional maps are generated by the state legislature or by some commissions under legislative control. Not surprisingly, legislators often make politically motivated district maps, or gerrymanders. Sometimes incumbents from both parties cooperate to protect their seats. Other times the party in power draws maps to lock down majorities and to disadvantage the opposition.

In most cases, the commissions—used by about a third of the states to advise legislators or make recommendations concerning redrawing boundaries—consist of political appointees or legislators themselves. According to the Brennan Center for Justice, heading into 2019, only four states—California, Nevada, Colorado, and Michigan—involved independent commissioners "made up of members who [were] neither public officials nor current lawmakers [and who were] selected with the help of a screening process that is conducted by an independent entity" in the process of redrawing congressional and state legislative districts. The reality, however, is that independent commissions are often dominated by members of the major political parties and aren't so independent at all. On top of that, governors often have a say when it comes to matters of redistricting. Clearly, neither major party—nor the duopoly to which it belongs—is content to sit on the sidelines while any of its privileges are at stake.

Some of those advantages seem to reflect what Gerzon likens to a "complete violation of what we learned in sports" (ch. 4). Gerzon isn't referring here to dirty partisan politics of the recent era but to a situation that has persisted, generally attracting little concern along the way, over the course of United States history—specifically, that "the person who is in charge of elections in each state is a member of one of the competing teams" (ch. 4).

Gerzon is referring to the secretary of state—not the official in the federal cabinet who oversees foreign affairs but the official in each state (except three) who keeps records, supervises business practices, and oversees elections. The majority of state secretaries of state are elected to four-year terms in partisan elections; others are appointed by governors or state legislatures—and all but one sitting state secretary of state in 2019 was either a Republican or a Democrat. The exception, North Dakota's Al Jaeger, who was elected secretary of state as an independent in 2018, held the office as a Republican for a quarter-century before losing the state Republican Party nomination in 2018 and announcing he wouldn't be seeking reelection. After the fallout from a peeping-tom incident 12 years earlier knocked Republican endorsee Will Gardner out of the race for secretary of state, Jaeger gathered more than the required 1,000 signatures to get on the ballot as an independent and defeated his Democratic-Nonpartisan League Party opponent and a fellow independent in the general election to win another term.

As far as the three states without secretaries of state—Hawaii, Alaska, and Utah—are concerned, appointments to positions or commissions overseeing elections are carried out in a generally partisan manner. As a result, it would be fair to say the major parties have an enormous say in how elections are carried out nationwide.

But while state officials and legislators wield plenty of influence and "authority" concerning elections for state legislatures and the U.S. House of Representatives, their reach is more limited when it comes to statewide federal races for U.S. president and the U.S. Senate. Though state officials have plenty of say in who gets on ballots—and under what party designation or affiliation—they're powerless to redraw boundaries when it comes to races for president and the U.S. Senate.

Charles Wheelan, an unsuccessful Democratic candidate for Congress in 2009, reconsidered his party allegiance and, in 2013, wrote the *Centrist Manifesto*, a key document in helping shape the philosophy of Unite America, which Wheelan founded that year. After noting how extremes have taken hold in the Democratic and Republican parties with inability to compromise and political paralysis being the result, Wheelan notes that, of the two federal offices whose election boundaries can't be gerrymandered, the presidency poses more difficulty—perhaps an impossible situation—when it comes to breaking the major-party grip on power: "Even if a third-party presidential candidate were to catch fire with voters—perhaps even winning the plurality of votes cast—the Electoral College is more hostile still. ... Americans like to focus their political attention on the White House, but the presidency is a dead end in terms of transforming the current political landscape" (Wheelan, 123–124).

What Wheelan proposes as a means of shaking up the two-party logjam in Washington, D.C., is to focus on the U.S. Senate—and, specifically, to aim efforts at getting a few "centrist" (i.e., not extreme) candidates elected to the Senate. Wheelan writes, "Congress has grown increasingly polarized and dysfunctional because we have built a system that elects extremists" (Wheelan, 20). The solution, he says, lies in setting what at first seems both a modest and an ambitious goal aimed at producing what could be interpreted as either an achievable or unlikely result: "With a mere four or five U.S. Senate seats, the Centrists can deny either traditional party a majority. At that point, the Centrists would be America's power brokers. *Nothing could happen without those swing votes*" (italics in original; 12–13).

By "centrist" Wheelan is referring not only to candidates and voters who shy away from the extreme positions of either side or at either end of the spectrum. Instead, he sees the solution to the partisan paralysis created by two major parties that "have outlived their usefulness" (18) as lying in the creation of another party, "a third political party that empowers the middle" (12)—a party "[t]aking the best from each [major] party, and discarding the nonsense of the extremes" (24).

While acknowledging that the American two-party system poses serious challenges to any entity aiming at getting elected from the "outside," Wheelan argues that success is possible for a third party in the current era: "Conventional wisdom suggests that the American political system is hostile to all third parties. *That is wrong. The system is hostile to third parties emerging from the political fringe*" (italics in original; 24–25). Citing the Green Party as an example of a fringe party, Wheelan continues:

> When the fringe parties appear, potential supporters must choose between making noise and making a difference. … A Centrist Party [no connection to Reisman's Centrist Party, according to Wheelan] is the opposite. The American political system makes it possible for the Centrists to make noise *and* to make a difference. *Every Centrist candidate begins in the political center, which is where most of the voters are* [italics in original; 25–26].

In the current age the notion of "centrism" usually seems to suggest staking out a fairly safe middle ground—at most a relatively small swing minority which, under ideal circumstances, can exert more influence than its pure numbers would suggest. Whether the best chance of finding that fertile middle ground is at the state legislative level, as some see it, or in the U.S. Senate, as Wheelan suggests, the goal is less to supplant either major party—thus leaving no center to occupy—than simply to find a place of some reason, hopefully with a good sounding board, right in the middle, between the two major parties. As Wheelan himself acknowledges, "The Republicans and the Democrats are institutionally trenched. Americans have their minds wrapped around a two-party system" (121).

Presumably, that sort of thinking—or recognition of the obvious—guided Wheelan's seemingly modest proposal that centrists try to make their mark by putting their energy toward getting a few "Centrist" candidates elected to the U.S. Senate. Since *The Centrist Manifesto* was published there have been a few developments. One is the quiet emergence of Reisman's Centrist Party, which, it seems fair to say, hasn't budged the needle on American politics. Another development is that Wheelan himself, serving on Unite America's board after founding the organization, has dropped talk of a "Centrist Party"—at least, of that name.

Even while calling, in *The Centrist Manifesto*, for the election of a few U.S. senators aligned with his proposed Centrist Party, Wheelan seemed content to accord retroactive "Centrist" status to one sitting senator whose position on the political spectrum seemed to place him close enough to the center to make it plausible to claim him as a Centrist—though he caucused with the Democrats. "Angus King was elected to the Senate from Maine in 2012 as a moderate independent," Wheelan writes. "Consider him Centrist number one."

Wheelan's plan, beyond coopting King for his "Centrist" cause, was "to give Angus

Like many prominent U.S. politicians before him, U.S. Senator from Maine Angus King prefers to wear an "independent" label despite maintaining significant ties to the major party he represented earlier in his political career. Despite being an independent Senator, King has caucused and generally voted with the Democrats, much in the manner of Vermont Senator Bernie Sanders (United States Congress).

some more Centrist buddies in the Senate" in order to bring the next step of Wheelan's plan to fruition. "Once the Centrists control four or five U.S. Senate seats," he writes, "the party will hold the swing votes necessary for either the Republicans or the Democrats (including the President) to do *anything* [which seems at odds with various Unite America statements highlighting the importance of bridge-building, cooperation, and responsible, effective government]. The Centrists would be the gatekeepers of the entire federal government" (122).

Contacted by phone in 2019, six years after publication of *The Centrist Manifesto*, and asked what he saw as the best route to breaking up the Republican–Democratic logjam in Washington, D.C., post–2018, Wheelan said, "Going forward, the tactic is trying to support moderate Republicans and Democrats who are willing to join forces with others across the aisle.

… Those are the people who are essential in building any effective political coalition that's going to govern."

To some who were more in agreement with Unite America's approach through the 2018 U.S. elections, however, that perhaps seems less a pragmatic call for improving efficiency in DC without doing anything drastic than a waving of the white flag and a recipe aimed at ensuring the "big game" remains a birthright exclusive to two political parties.

14

Stacking the Deck

Among the most brazen accomplices, in stacking the deck against people and forces committed to opening up opportunities for alternative voices in Washington, D.C., and around the country, are several agencies and institutions whose policies and actions over the years warrant serious concern from voters. One such accomplice is the very "independent regulatory agency" whose mission, according to the Federal Election Commission (FEC) website, is "to protect the integrity of the federal campaign finance process."

"Integrity" may be too strong a word to associate with the mission of the FEC, founded in the mid-1970s, supposedly as a tool for helping clean up American democracy. The reality is that the FEC, over the course of 40-plus years, has functioned mainly as a device for ensuring American democracy—as reflected in federal election campaigns—remains anything *but* truly democratic.

One week before the 1980 U.S. federal election, Mary Meehan wrote, in an article posted on the Cato Institute website, "The FEC is ... an agency created and controlled directly by many of the persons it is supposed to regulate. Through those persons, it is effectively controlled by the Democratic and Republican parties. Minor-party candidates, independent candidates, and nonincumbent candidates have little or no voice in the FEC."

Before the FEC was established, financing of federal political campaigns was largely a wide-open affair where campaign money was often hard to trace and donors were essentially permitted to fund candidates and sell influence at will. The FEC imposed much-needed limits on campaign donations from political action committees and on amounts political parties were eligible to receive. Also established were limits on what individual citizens could legally donate to candidates, campaigns, and parties.

But even though the FEC's mandatory campaign contribution limits put a check on what in many ways had been a Wild West–like approach to campaign financing, historical patterns would prove difficult to overcome.

In short order, the FEC—controlled by the two major parties that were most in need of regulation and oversight—soon became just one more instrument for institutionalizing or perpetuating the domination of two political juggernauts that saw room for only two real teams on the political playing field. As Orman puts it, "Washington policy makers were careful to protect the duopoly—giving themselves a limit [on contributions] that was five times as large as minor parties (and infinitely larger than Independents...)" (226).

The gist of Orman's argument seems beyond dispute. As for specifics, he points out that, in the early years of FEC limits, "[p]olitical action committees were limited to [contributions of] $5,000. But the political parties themselves could receive up to $25,000—provided they were a 'major' party. ... For minor parties, the limit was $5,000" (226). Similar disparity has persisted in the more than four decades since the FEC was established.

As for more recent years, Orman writes, "[I]n 2014, Senate Democrats met behind closed doors with House Republicans to forge a $1.1 trillion spending bill that was part CR [continuing resolutions] and part omnibus bill. ... The ensuing legislation ... had the dubious distinction of codifying the corrupt ethics of the duopoly into a brazen new campaign finance law so grotesque it would have embarrassed the political bagmen of my grandfather's generation" (227).

Orman continues, "No longer are U.S. citizens limited to contributing a mere $97,200 annually to the Republican Party and the Democratic Party. The new limit was set at $777,600 [rising to $834,000 in 2016, according to Orman]. ... This limit is in addition to the amounts they can give to a Democratic or Republican candidate" running for federal office (227).

After pointing out that the most an American can contribute to an independent candidate running for federal office is $5,400 every two years, Orman concludes, "Only a Washington politician could justify such a disparity" (227).

Other concerns about the FEC have included the simple numerical nature of its composition. As a 2016 *Los Angeles Times* editorial explains, "The first page in any handbook for creating a government regulatory commission would lay out something obvious: There has to be an odd number of members." The alternative, as the editorial continues, is to have "the worse-than-useless [six-member] Federal Election Commission." It continues,

> What if the regulatory commission's membership is effectively controlled by the two biggest political parties, with each faction holding half the seats? And what if the commission's job is to enforce campaign laws? Then it's not really a regulatory and enforcement commission at all.

14. Stacking the Deck

In recent years, the FEC's makeup has been even more problematic than usual, as the resignation of sitting commissioners in 2017 and 2018 left membership at just four. All four, according to Dave Levinthal of the Center for Public Integrity, "[were] on the commission for a total of 32 years longer than they should have been." FEC commissioners whose terms expire are permitted to remain on the commission until they're replaced, and the four commissioners serving in 2018 had overstayed the single six-year terms for which they were eligible by periods ranging from five to 11 years, according to Levinthal. Some observers attributed President Trump's apparent reluctance to replenish the FEC in 2018—though by no means was he the first president to demonstrate such reluctance—to a belief that it was in his best interests to keep the FEC stripped down as a strategy for reducing possible fallout related to his alleged 2016 "hush money" payment to Stormy Daniels. In any event, regardless of where the blame lay, the FEC term-limit requirement—"effective" since 1998—proved to be as big a joke as the FEC's "independent commission" designation was from the beginning.

On paper, the Federal Election Commission, even with only four sitting members, is able to conduct business, as the number four represents a quorum when it comes to FEC rulings. But the reality is that a bare-bones quorum alone is no guarantee that anything meaningful will get done, as four is not only the quorum for conducting meaningful business but also the number of votes required for the FEC to make any ruling or, in effect, take any action at all.

From February 2018 to August 2019, the FEC was composed of two Republicans, one Democrat, and one independent—Nevada attorney Steve Walther—all appointed and confirmed over a decade earlier. Given the usual partisan breakdown of the commission, it's generally difficult, even with a full six-member commission in place, to get four members to agree on rulings or actions. Requiring unanimity in the recent political climate, even among a commission of four, is a recipe for utter failure, as has proved to be the case.

If things could get even worse for the FEC, they did so on August 31, 2019, when one of the four sitting commissioners, Republican Matthew S. Petersen, stepped down, leaving behind one Republican, one Democrat, one independent, and one "independent regulatory agency" that lacked all ability "to protect the integrity of the federal campaign finance process" even if it had the will. Heading into the 2020 federal election, the FEC remained stalled with a membership of three, all of whose mandates had long expired.

Even when the FEC has been operational, the inclusion of an independent, at times, on the commission hasn't appreciably leveled the playing field for non–Republican and non–Democrats, who seem to face unfair challenges at every level of the electoral-political process. As Meehan pointed out in 1980, the FEC all but shuts out all voices except those of the Democratic and Republican parties: "It is as though two television networks had established the Federal Communications Commission and carefully excluded all other networks and all independent stations from any participation in that agency's activities."

Those words still ring true more than 40 years after they were written—and the television analogy is especially fitting because the major parties enjoy a decided, and decidedly entrenched, advantage in that realm as well.

It should be clear to any American with a television that the two-party bias that exists in the United States at large is reflected in the television news media. While some news outlets do little or nothing to hide their partisan agendas, Orman writes, "[T]he distinction between the mainstream media and partisan media is blurring. This especially disadvantages Independents, who are caught up in a partisan-driven media

Ralph Nader (pictured here during his height as a consumer advocate) ran several times for political office, sometimes as a Democrat and other times as a third-party candidate. While never running a competitive race, Nader perhaps played a pivotal role in the 2000 U.S. presidential election when he ran as the Green Party nominee. When the outcome of the 2000 Bush-Gore race came down to Florida, it was noted by many that Nader's modest vote total still greatly exceeded the margin of Bush's victory over Gore—and quite possibly cost Gore the presidency (Library of Congress, U.S. News & World Report collection).

environment that only reinforces the belief that politics is nothing more than a contest between two tired old political parties" (194). This trend, he says, has resulted in "mainstream media's adoption of the blue/red paradigm" (201)—a result that, in reality, has been evident for decades.

While there have been plenty of opportunities on national or regional television for the likes of Ross Perot, Jesse Ventura, or Ralph Nader— the latter a four-time alternative presidential candidate who played a possible spoiler role in Florida in the 2000 presidential election—such has hardly been the case for the vast majority of alternative candidates for high-profile offices, most of them largely relegated to spots on public access TV or pricey paid ads and denied the opportunity to make their case to voters in televised debates.

Televised presidential debates, of course, made their debut in the United States in 1960, when then–Vice President Richard Nixon and U.S. Senator from Massachusetts John F. Kennedy accepted the invitation to face off in a two-man series of four debates, beginning in late September and set to conclude two and a half weeks before the November 8 election, with all three major television networks at the time participating. Several other candidates ran for president in 1960, but none had any semblance of a national campaign or national support. Yet the Federal Communications Commission (FCC) equal-time rule, established as a component of the Communications Act of 1934, would have required the networks to let all the presidential candidates participate in the debates—had a two-party Congress not voted to suspend the equal-time rule so that the upcoming debates could be limited to the two major parties' candidates. According to an article posted on the Purdue University College of Liberal Arts "History of Presidential Debate" webpage, the networks had lobbied Congress in 1960 to waive the equal-time provision for the presidential debates.

The Kennedy-Nixon debates were the first-ever presidential general election campaign debates between party nominees for president. While casual followers of politics sometimes "remember" the first such debates to have been the marathon series of exchanges between Democrat Stephen Douglas and Republican Abraham Lincoln, opposing candidates for president in 1860, those debates had taken place two years earlier, when Douglas and Lincoln were opposing major-party candidates for U.S. Senator from Illinois in an election that Douglas won, not by popular vote but by election by the state legislature. Lincoln and Douglas didn't have a debate rematch when both were running for president in 1860.

The American landscape had changed radically in the intervening hundred years leading to the Nixon-Kennedy showdown, and television— barely out of its teens as a broadcast medium of any significance—had played a major role, to say the least, in that transformation. The strength of an argument now was viewed by many to lie more within its packaging than in matters of greater substance, and clearly that was something Kennedy understood far better than Nixon did.

Nixon's failings before the television camera in 1960—his initial refusal to wear makeup, his failure to dress to the standards viewers had come to associate with television, his apparent unfamiliarity with the TV debate format, and his tendency to fidget or sweat on-camera—quickly put him behind the eight ball even though many observers, judging on the basis of spoken content alone, believed Nixon outdebated Kennedy. Not quite able to mount a comeback after his rocky start on television, and with Kennedy projecting greater poise, confidence, and energy, Nixon went on to lose the tightest U.S. presidential election in decades. As to the importance of the debates—especially the initial one in which an unwitting Nixon failed to make his best impression on well over 60 million viewers (over a third of the U.S. population at the time)—*Time* reported, in a September 24, 2010, article by Kayla Webley, half a century after the Nixon-Kennedy debates kicked off, "It's now common knowledge that without the nation's first televised debate ... Kennedy would never have been president."

In the aftermath of his awkward self-presentation to the nation under the bright lights of the televised 1960 U.S. presidential debates, Nixon shied away from debating during his presidential election and reelection campaigns in 1968 and 1972. In 1964 President Lyndon B. Johnson, campaigning for his first full term, made a similar call, likely figuring—with a healthy lead and, like Nixon, perhaps a look or demeanor better suited to radio than TV—he had more to lose than to gain by getting into a nationally televised exchange with the fiery Barry Goldwater. Whatever the motivations, it wasn't until 1976 that the second series of party nominees' U.S. presidential election debates would take place.

Those debates took place in September and October 1976 between Republican incumbent Gerald Ford, seeking his first full term as president, and Jimmy Carter, a little-known candidate nationally before besting the field in the majority of state primaries en route to winning the Democratic nomination. As far as the 1976 debates were concerned, they probably helped erase some of the damage from Carter's ill-advised "lust in my heart" *Playboy* interview, which started appearing in September of 1976, and helped reestablish the down-home ex-governor of Georgia with a thick Southern accent as what he most sought to have voters see in him: the antithesis of a Washington insider. Ford, meanwhile, stumbled a bit, lost the incumbent's home-field advantage at least partly as a result, and, just two weeks after the third and final debate, ended up losing a close election that showed a serious partisan division in the country along geographic lines.

14. Stacking the Deck

As in 1960, the major-party presidential nominees didn't have to share the stage with any third-party or independent outliers in 1976. The same was true of the 1976 major-party vice-presidential nominees, Republican Bob Dole and Democrat Walter Mondale, who faced off in a single one-on-one debate. This time the FCC equal-time rule wasn't a factor because sponsorship of the debates had been transferred from the television networks themselves—beholden to FCC rulings regarding equal accessibility to all candidates—to an outside organization, the League of Women Voters. The change allowed the networks simply to carry the debates as newsworthy events without having to be concerned about who would or wouldn't be allowed to participate.

The League of Women Voters had been established in the final months of the women's suffrage movement leading to passage of the 19th Amendment in 1920. In 1952 the League sponsored a presidential primary debate televised nationally on NBC, but the organization had no involvement in the 1960 presidential election debates. Nearly a quarter-century after sponsoring 1952's televised primary debate, the League of Women Voters, an officially nonpartisan organization having final say as to which candidates ought to be invited to participate in its debates, "worked on behalf of the public by openly pushing for lively debate formats and the inclusion of third-party and independent candidates," according to PBS.org. The League of Women Voters website (lwv.org) adds, "[T]he League[-]sponsored ... first televised presidential debates since 1960 ... won an Emmy award for Outstanding Achievement in Broadcast Journalism" (PBS.org, "The History of Presidential Debates: The Televised Years").

Despite what may have been the League's best intentions, the organization's sponsorship of three series of presidential election debates beginning in 1976 did little to level the playing field for candidates aiming to challenge the major-party grip on the presidential election process. The only "alternative" presidential candidate to benefit over the course of a dozen years of League of Women Voters' sponsorship of presidential debates was ex–Republican and 1980 independent candidate John Anderson, who was invited to go one-on-one with Ronald Reagan in the first of a pair of debates when Carter refused to participate in any debate that included Anderson. The second debate in 1980 was another one-on-one meeting, with Carter facing off against Reagan, who was generally seen as coming out of the debate looking better than Carter—not only because of his ease in front of a camera but, in the view of some, because of his insistence that Anderson be allowed to participate in the debates.

The League-sponsored presidential debates in 1984 consisted of a pair of one-on-one Reagan-Mondale debates, each with a moderator and a panel of three questioners. PBS.org reports, "The Reagan and Mondale campaigns asked for an unprecedented degree of control over the debates—going so far as to veto nearly a hundred proposed panelists"—much in the manner opposing legal teams will vet potential jurors they fear may be biased (or fear may be so *un*biased or judicious as not to pose any advantage to one side or the other). As a result of the major parties' shenanigans prior to the first debate, PBS.org reports, "The League of Women Voters blasted both campaigns publicly" (PBS.org, "The History of Presidential Debates...").

Both parties, mindful of how lackluster performances, in particular by Nixon and Ford, had seemingly turned elections around, essentially caved in to the League's demand in 1984 to lay off the gamesmanship and get down to debating. But then, in 1988, the Democratic and Republican parties decided *they* should be the ones to lay down the law. PBS.org reports,

Independent presidential candidate John Anderson was a rare example of an "outsider" given a place on the televised presidential debate stage alongside a major-party nominee when he debated Republican Ronald Reagan on Sept. 21, 1980. Then-president and Democratic Party nominee Jimmy Carter debated Reagan the following month but refused to share the stage with Anderson (photograph by Warren K. Leffler, Library of Congress).

> ...the political parties wanted more control over the debates. ... The Democratic and Republican parties signed a secretly negotiated "memorandum of understanding" that dictated everything from the selection of the panelists, to the makeup of the audience, to banning follow-up questions [which would increase the likelihood of errors or embarrassing gaffes]. When they had agreed on all the details, the campaigns presented the document to the League. ... The struggle ended with the League of Women Voters withdrawing as a sponsor of the general election debates.

14. Stacking the Deck

In over three decades since ending its sponsorship of presidential debates less than two weeks before a scheduled debate in October 1988, the League of Women Voters has remained active in providing a platform to candidates, without regard to party affiliation, in local, state, and federal election campaigns across the country. While the League, though nonpartisan, holds well-known positions on a variety of issues and probably attracts mainly candidates and audiences leaning in the same direction, the organization nonetheless does a service to many alternative candidates who are eager to speak to any gathering of engaged voters they may be able to sway.

Since 1988, presidential debates have been in the hands of the Commission on Presidential Debates (CPD), an organization effectively controlled by the Democratic and Republican parties—although the CPD website maintains that "[i]t is not controlled by any political party ... and it does not endorse, support, or oppose political candidates for parties." That may be true, but almost every independent observer has concluded that the CPD—based on its leadership, its rules, and its practices—has served predominantly to ensure participation in presidential debates in recent decades has remained a privilege exclusive to the Republican and Democratic parties.

After independent candidate Ross Perot's strong showing in the 1992 presidential debates significantly increased his support nationwide, the CPD made sure not to invite him for a return performance in 1996. In 2000 the CPD took the "precaution" of issuing invitations only to candidates with multiple poll showings of 15 percent or better among voters—a requirement that hasn't changed since—"[locking] out anyone but the nominees of the two major parties" (Orman, 230). While other organizations have stepped in to sponsor smaller-scale debates involving alternative presidential (or vice-presidential) candidates, the CPD hasn't included an alternative candidate in any of its presidential (or vice-presidential) debates since Perot took part in 1992—this despite the fact that many alternative candidates over the past 30 years have fought, if not *clawed*, their way onto enough state ballots as to have at least a mathematical chance of winning the Electoral College ... at least, on a more even playing field.

With the CPD, the FEC, and statewide election organizations or overseers across the country firmly in support of maintaining a duopoly that has eaten away at American democracy for many decades, it probably goes without saying that anyone intent on running for office against major-party nominees had better get plenty of practice running uphill. Not only do the media, as a whole, reinforce the system of two-party dominance, but so do the high rollers intent on offering donations along with a few policy suggestions to candidates judged most likely to be in a

Despite performing strongly on the presidential debate stage in 1992, independent presidential candidate Ross Perot (pictured at right with fellow debaters Bill Clinton, left, and George H.W. Bush, center) wasn't invited back to the debate stage in 1996, when he was the Reform Party nominee for president. In fact, Perot's participation in 1992 marks the last time anyone other than a Republican or Democrat has been invited to take part in a televised presidential debate (George H.W. Bush Presidential Library & Museum).

position to ensure a return on the investment—i.e., Republicans or Democrats. Another obvious challenge are the party primaries—whether open or closed—held during election years in most states. While open primaries—generally allowing any voter, regardless of affiliation or nonaffiliation, to vote in a party's primary—may seem democratic in principle, they only reinforce the position that the party holding the primary is a favored entity. Even though outsiders theoretically can collude and try to get a weak and beatable major-party nominee selected in a primary, that's not a course of action that appears likely to result in improved prospects for any entities or individuals proposing meaningful alternatives to the major parties.

Open, closed, or semi-open primaries (the latter allowing any voter, regardless of affiliation, to vote in any *one* party's primary) don't provide potential to level the playing field for candidates lacking the (D) or (R) brand designation. The same can be said of major-party primaries that bar participation by registered members of the other major party but allow unaffiliated or independent voters to participate. In effect, this "concession" to unaffiliated/independent voters—inviting them "in" to where it matters—only reinforces the perception that they're on the "outside" and can be relevant only when the good graces of a major party accommodate them. As a result, it seems reasonable to say that such primaries essentially amount to recruitment drives.

Clearly, one road to equal opportunity—even a bumpy, uphill road where that goal of equal opportunity is barely perceptible in the distance—seems to lie in the top-two primary system currently employed in Washington, California, and, to some degree, Nebraska and Louisiana. Of course, the "top two" selected in most races are openly affiliated with, or identify with, the two major parties, and it's rare for any alternative candidate opposing candidates allied with both major parties in a top-two primary to advance to a general election. Yet a top-two "jungle primary" seems the likeliest setting in which lightning may strike.

Meanwhile, the blanket primary system still employed in most states ups the challenge for smaller-party candidates by often forcing them to jump through hoops in order to get their party affiliations across to voters and onto ballots. The vast majority of smaller parties in the United States aren't even close to gaining official recognition as "major parties" eligible to hold primaries and at least "earn" the right to dine on scraps at the table shared by the Republicans and Democrats. Even "minor" or "official" party status is unlikely for the majority of smaller parties, often out chasing signatures in hope of satisfying election commissions that seem designed to muscle out would-be competitors to the two-party system. Orman describes a duopoly, in the private sector, as "two all-encompassing, competitive entities [working] together to erect barriers that protect the duopoly" (219). He writes, "They define the parameters of the game—and then rig the rules to keep others out" (219). Clearly, the same applies to duopolies in the political sphere, where, according to a 2017 report funded by Harvard Business School, "[t]he [Democratic and Republican] parties have taken major steps to increase and widen the barriers to entry" (Gehl and Porter, 36).

Yet, as daunting as the institutional challenges and disadvantages facing alternative candidates may be, they probably pale in comparison to another hurdle. Early on in *A Declaration of Independents*, Orman says, "voters want a real alternative to the ruling duopoly and the establishment forces that control both major parties" (9). But later Orman—who, four years before his unsuccessful 2018 independent run for governor of Kansas, had fallen short in an independent bid for the U.S. Senate—reports that a poll taken early in his 2014 Senate run revealed "35 percent of respondents said they wouldn't consider my candidacy because they viewed a vote for an Independent candidate as a wasted vote" (48). Clearly, polls touting the rising number of "independent" voters in the United States don't tell whole story as much as election results do. Those results show the biggest challenge and most vital test for alternative candidates and parties nationwide is to convince the rising number of "independent" voters—often exceeding 40 percent in recent years, according to Gallup figures—to stay the course and not to default to their major-party leanings, as many "independent" voters have been shown to do, election after election, when it really matters—i.e., when it comes time to cast their votes.

15

Missed Opportunity
The Kavanaugh Hearing

As much an embarrassment to the nation as the July 2018 House Judiciary Committee Peter Strzok hearing was, the Senate Judiciary Committee's Brett Kavanaugh Supreme Court confirmation hearing that got underway two months later clearly revealed to millions of American TV viewers just what sort of animal the two-party system had become: an utterly dysfunctional and dangerous beast that voters had every right to put out of its misery in the 2018 midterm elections. If ever Americans had good reason to take steps toward overturning a failed and embarrassing political duopoly, it was in the aftermath of the Kavanaugh debacle in the late summer and early fall of 2018.

Following Justice Anthony Kennedy's announcement in June 2018 that he'd be retiring from the United States Supreme Court the following month, President Trump nominated Kavanaugh as Kennedy's replacement. Kavanaugh was the second Trump nominee to the Supreme Court. The first, Neil Gorsuch, had been confirmed by the Senate in April of 2017—a full 14 months after the death of Justice Anton Scalia, whose seat Gorsuch would assume. The reason for the lengthy delay was that Senate Republicans, who had the majority, were hell-bent on thwarting any effort by President Obama, during the final year of his presidency, to replace Scalia. As precedent, Senate Republicans cited a June 1992 speech by Joe Biden—then a member of the Democratic majority in the U.S. Senate during the final year of George H.W. Bush's Republican presidency—in which Biden expressed the opinion that "Senate consideration of a nominee under these circumstances [would not be] fair to the president, the nominee or to the Senate itself" (Wheaton). Further, Biden said, "[I]t is my view that if a Supreme Court Justice resigns tomorrow or within the next several weeks, or resigns at the end of the summer, President Bush should consider following the practice of the majority of his predecessors and not—and not—name a nominee until after the November election is completed."

Republicans retained their Senate majority in the 2016 elections, and Trump nominated Gorsuch for the Supreme Court shortly after taking office in January 2017. Of course, Senate Democrats were seething as a result of the Republicans' filibustering tactics during the previous year, and the Gorsuch nomination hearing, which took place in March, was an exercise in partisan bickering and gamesmanship that could have come to naught had the Republican Senate not voted to end the filibuster rule and, in essence, forced a vote on the Gorsuch nomination, with a simple majority required for confirmation. The vote, which went mainly along party lines, capped off a Senate hearing that never seemed to come close to putting the major parties or the two-party system in a good light—and there seemed to be no reason to expect anything better of the Kavanaugh confirmation hearing, which got underway on September 4, 2018.

Partisanship played heavily in the confirmation "debate" from the moment Kavanaugh was announced by President Trump as the nominee to replace Justice Kennedy on the Supreme Court—if not before that. According to Maine Republican U.S. Senator Susan Collins, quoted at PBS.org, "[W]e're so polarized right now that we had outside ideologically driven interest groups putting out press releases in opposition to President Trump's nominee before they even knew who the nominee was. One press release actually says, Oppose Judge XXX. They forgot to fill in the judge's name" (Trautwein).

From the outset, Kavanaugh seemed to spur knee-jerk reactions and partisan jabs from two uncompromising camps that viewed him through opposing lenses. While Kavanaugh, in a September 4, 2018, National Public Radio (NPR) report by Scott Horsley, opined that "[t]he justices on the Supreme Court do not sit on opposite sides of an aisle," Kavanaugh did serve for five years as a White House counsel and staff secretary to Republican President George W. Bush. But what particularly raised partisan suspicions on the Democratic side concerning the Kavanaugh nomination was the Trump administration's decision to block the release of the vast majority of documents that might have shed light on the full nature of Kavanaugh's opinions, decisions, and actions in the Bush White House.

Democratic Senator Dick Durbin of Illinois, quoted by Horsley, told Kavanaugh early in his confirmation hearing, "There's a 35-month black hole in your White House career where we've been denied access to any and all documents"—an allusion, perhaps, to Republican comments or concerns about Hillary Clinton's enormous cache of deleted emails in 2016. "During that period of time," Durbin continued, "President Bush was considering same-sex marriage—an amendment to ban it—abortion, executive power, detainees, torture, Supreme Court nominees, warrantless wiretapping."

15. Missed Opportunity

"[Y]ou were a political operative, involved in the most political and partisan controversies of our time," Vermont Democratic Senator Patrick Leahy told Kavanaugh (Horsley). While it can certainly be argued that the Democrats' railing against cover-ups and partisanship on the other side was a case of the pot calling the kettle black, it seems safe to say there were valid grounds for calls to release documents relating to a nominee for a lifetime appointment to the U.S. Supreme Court. But it's probably just as safe to assume that the further release of documents would have had little or no bearing on where senators—or the most vocal protesters on both sides—stood with regard to the Kavanaugh confirmation. A far greater factor than information that might have been released in any further documents, it seems clear, was political party affiliation.

On September 12, 2018—a week after the hearing was thought to be over and a week before the Judiciary Committee was expected to vote—*The Intercept* led off with a headline advising readers, "Dianne Feinstein Withholding Brett Kavanaugh Document from Fellow Judiciary Democrats." The article, by Ryan Grim, indicated Democratic members of the Judiciary Committee, on which Feinstein was the highest-ranking Democrat, knew of a letter from a California resident that had been delivered to Feinstein. Her Democratic colleagues' requests to see the letter, according to Grim, were met by "Feinstein's refusal to share" it. The article didn't identify the writer or address the exact nature of the letter but indicated "the one consistent theme" brought up by Grim's sources "was that [the letter] describes an incident involving Kavanaugh and a woman while they were in high school."

The following day, September 13, Feinstein released a statement confirming the existence of the letter, whose writer, Feinstein wrote, "strongly requested confidentiality." Feinstein added, "I have honored that decision. I have, however, referred the matter to federal investigative authorities." The following day, September 14, *The New York Times* published an updated report about a "secretive letter" alleging that Kavanaugh, when he attended Georgetown Preparatory School as a teenager, took part in an attempt to assault a teenage girl at a party. According to Nicholas Fandos and Michael S. Schmidt, who wrote the report, information about the allegations against Kavanaugh had been placed in the background file that would factor into his confirmation decision.

Two days later, in a September 16 *Washington Post* interview, Christine Blasey Ford, a California psychology professor and researcher, identified herself as the letter writer and Kavanaugh accuser.

When word of the Ford letter put the brakes to the Kavanaugh confirmation process, the hearing was extended to give senators time to weigh allegations that a drunken Kavanaugh had assaulted 15-year-old student Christine Blasey 36 years earlier, in the summer of 1982. A deal was reached for Blasey Ford to testify, and she and Kavanaugh were called to give their testimony before the Senate Judiciary Committee on September 27, 2018.

The hearing resumed when Ford delivered an opening statement accusing Kavanaugh of sexual assault in the summer of 1982, when both were students attending different schools in the Washington, D.C., area. Speaking of "a small gathering at a house in the Chevy Chase/Bethesda [Maryland] area" when she was 15, Blasey Ford admitted, of the gathering she said both she and then-17-year-old Kavanaugh attended, "I do not remember all of the details of how that gathering came together." She said she didn't recall how she got to the party and "don't remember as much as I would like to. But the details about that night that brings me here are ones I will never forget."

Among the key details Ford presented were that "I was pushed onto [a] bed and Brett got on top of me. He began running his hands over my body and grinding his hips into me. I yelled, hoping someone downstairs might hear me, and tried to get away from him, but his weight was heavy. Brett groped me and tried to take off my clothes. ... I believed he was going to rape me. I tried to yell for help. When I did, Brett put his hand over my mouth to stop me from screaming. This was what terrified me the most, and has had the most lasting impact on my life."

Ford's Q&A testimony to Republican-appointed hearing interviewer Rachel Mitchell showed some uncertainty as to certain details surrounding the alleged attack. Following a question by Mitchell, Ford's recollection of "a day of swimming at the [Columbia Country Club]" on the day of the alleged attack became a "best estimate" of her activity prior to the alleged attack. Despite recounting details of her exit, following the alleged attack, from the house she was in, Ford testified that she didn't recall how she got to her own home immediately afterward, other than that "I did not drive home," which, according to her testimony, seemed to be several miles away. While Ford testified that it was possible someone drove her home, no one had come forward to identify himself or herself as the driver.

Mitchell's low-key questioning of Ford pointed out that Ford had told *The Washington Post*, in a July 6, 2018, text, that the alleged attack had taken place in the mid–1980s; but Ford's letter to Feinstein, written 24 days later, indicated the incident had occurred in the early 1980s. By the time Ford was interviewed by the *Post* for her interview published on September 16, Ford, as Mitchell pointed out, had settled on the summer of 1982 as the time of the attack.

Ford's repeated responses of "I don't remember" concerning specifics of the summer of 1982 and more recent times—including as recently as during her *Post* interview—seemed in stark contrast to the certainty with which she claimed to recall details of the alleged attack by Kavanaugh 36 years earlier. While experts may point out that such is the nature of the mind's reaction to an experience of the sort Ford recounted, it seems fair to point out that there was no corroborating evidence of the alleged attack in 1982 and that Blasey Ford, by her own testimony, "had never told the details [of the alleged attack] to anyone until May 2012," when she was seeing a therapist. She said she'd discussed the incident in general terms with her husband and some close friends, "[b]ut until July 2018, I had never named Mr. Kavanaugh as my attacker outside of therapy."

Free from the pressure of answering questions before Mitchell, senators, and a national and international television audience, Ford had presented a straightforward account in her July 30, 2018, letter to Feinstein marked "CONFIDENTIAL." In the letter of under 400 words, Ford briefly told about her alleged attack by Kavanaugh "in the early 1980s ... in a suburban Maryland home at a gathering that included me and four others." During the Mitchell questioning Ford would testify that there were at least five people, besides herself, in the home. Ford indicated in her letter to Feinstein that her motivation for writing the letter was to provide "information relevant in evaluating the current nominee to the Supreme Court." Ford indicated she was "available to speak further should you wish to discuss" the matter but cautioned that "I expect that you will maintain this as confidential until we have further opportunity to speak."

Kavanaugh's response to the Ford allegations, despite the admission in the prepared statement he submitted to the Senate Judiciary Committee that "I was not perfect in those days, just as I am not perfect today," was to insist on the opportunity to clear his name of alleged "misconduct ... completely inconsistent with the rest of my life." While some observers who were inclined to believe the gist of Kavanaugh's flat denial thought he wasn't completely forthcoming in his follow-up testimony and was perhaps a little less than the more saintly figure he painted for the committee, there seemed to be nothing in his words or reaction inconsistent with the self-defense of a man wrongly accused of a serious misdeed that would cast a shadow on his name and could well cost him the opportunity of a lifetime. Without corroborating evidence to shore up Ford's allegations against Kavanaugh, there seemed to be ample grounds—at least in a nonpartisan world—for presumption of innocence.

A widely cited Quinnipiac University poll of 1,111 respondents, divided fairly equally among people who identified themselves—"generally speaking," according to the party identification question they were asked—as Republican, Democrat, or Independent, led numerous media outlets to conclude that the American electorate believed Ford's version of events over Kavanaugh's and leaned—to the extent a plurality but not a majority could lean—toward opposing the Kavanaugh confirmation. As Matthew Zeitlin put it, at slate.com, on October 1, 2018, "Brett Kavanaugh's unpopularity has surged since he and Christine Blasey Ford gave testimony on Thursday, a Quinnipiac poll released Monday showed."

But Mitchell, rising above concerns about "unpopularity" in her analysis, reached probably the only conclusion a serious analyst could when it came to judging the merits of the Ford testimony based on legal or judicial criteria and not gut reactions or political gamesmanship. Mitchell, with a long history of prosecuting sex crimes, made note of numerous inconsistencies, changes, and omissions in Ford's account of events and in her testimony and even presented the damning opinion near the end of her report that "[t]he activities of congressional Democrats and Dr. Ford's attorneys likely affected Dr. Ford's account."

Mitchell's report, dated September 30, 2018, was addressed to "All Republican Senators," as it was the Judiciary Committee chairman, Iowa Republican Charles Grassley, who'd hired Mitchell to question the accuser and the accused as part of the reconvened Kavanaugh hearing on September 27. Of course, that detail wasn't lost on Democrats, many of whom objected to the choice of Mitchell, a registered Republican, to question Ford and Kavanaugh and to provide an independent assessment. For her part, Mitchell states up front in her report, "While I am a registered Republican, I am not a political or partisan person."

She goes further in establishing her boundaries or limits as to politics: "[T]he world in which I work is the legal world, not the political world. Thus, I can only provide my assessment of Dr. Ford's allegations in that legal context." One would hope legal standards would apply at least generally in the political arena—i.e., that a person's character or opportunity would be subject to similar protections and that the accused would be afforded a fair opportunity to clear his or her name against allegations that couldn't be corroborated.

To be sure, there were plenty of components to the case: Democrats' determination to stymie the second Supreme Court nomination of the Trump presidency, whether it was for Kavanaugh or, apparently, anybody else; Feinstein's decision, according to James W. Rushford in a 3 October 2018 "My Turn" column for calmatters.org, to "[sit] on the letter from Ford for 60 days," never mentioning the letter when meeting Kavanaugh afterward and then "[using] it to ambush Judge Kavanaugh"; and the hiring of a Republican to conduct key questioning and, in many ways, orchestrate the dynamics that would leave a lasting impression on a severely divided TV viewership and electorate. But despite all that, Mitchell's report arrived

15. Missed Opportunity

at probably the only conclusion it could, if it adhered to any semblance of legal standards. Mitchell's bottom-line statement concludes:

> A "he said, she said" case is incredibly difficult to prove. But this case is even weaker than that. Dr. Ford identified other witnesses to the event, and those witnesses either refuted her allegations or failed to corroborate them. ... I do not think that a reasonable prosecutor would bring this case based on the evidence before the Committee. Nor do I believe that the evidence is sufficient to satisfy the preponderance-of-the-evidence standard.

While the Quinnipiac poll took the too-common pollsters' (and marketers') approach of breaking American society into easy-to-label component parts (most notably, white/black/Hispanic) and focusing more on what divides or differentiates Americans than on what unifies or unites them, a few items coming out of the poll were particularly compelling. First, a greater percentage of respondents (48–41) indicated they believed Ford's testimony over Kavanaugh's. Not surprisingly, views on whether Kavanaugh should be confirmed followed the same pattern almost exactly: 48 percent saying no, and 42 percent saying yes. The remainder, rounded to 9 percent, were unsure.

Yet more respondents—46 percent to 43—said they believed Kavanaugh, in general, was honest rather than dishonest. Presumably, many simply believed Ford was *more* honest—which may be difficult to jive with the fact their testimonies were at odds (i.e., one or the other was clearly deceptive or, to say the least, confused). More respondents disapproved than approved of the way *both* parties handled the accusations of sexual misconduct against Kavanaugh—which was a bit surprising, considering how polarized Republican and Democratic responses were to other questions in the poll. A greater percentage of respondents—48 compared to 43—believed Ford had been treated fairly since coming forward with her allegations than believed Kavanaugh had been treated fairly. Perhaps most tellingly, more respondents—49 percent to 45—said yes than said no to the final question in the poll, which asked whether they thought Kavanaugh was "the target of a politically motivated smear campaign."

It could be construed, then, that while millions of Americans—maybe even a majority—are suspicious of the major parties and their death grip on political power at almost every level in the United States, the vast majority stick to their leanings because, in their view, one devil seems "less worse" than the other. In that light it seems utterly safe to say that most of the 34 percent of Quinnipiac pollees identifying themselves as independent viewed their serious electoral options in partisan races as being either/or—i.e., within the strict confines of the two-party framework.

As far as Kavanaugh was concerned, a plurality found him generally honest and believed he was "the target of a politically motivated smear campaign." But the perceptions of pollees identifying with one major party were at odds with perceptions of those aligned with the opposing major party. To illustrate, while opinions on Kavanaugh's general honesty were divided fairly evenly (46 percent yes, 43 percent no, 11 percent unsure), by *major party* the differences were stark (Republicans, 87 percent yes, 8 no, 5 unsure; Democrats 77 percent no, 11 yes, 12 unsure). To the question of whether Kavanaugh had been the victim of a politically motivated smear campaign, the breakdown by party was 83 percent yes, 12 no, 4 unsure for Republicans and 81 percent no, 15 yes, 4 unsure for Democrats. Overall, it wouldn't be much of a stretch to suggest Democrats and Republicans had been watching entirely different hearings.

What an optimist could perhaps draw out of the Quinnipiac poll is that responses from the 34 percent of participants who identified themselves as "independent" suggested a degree of moderation not evident in responses from pollees in the Democratic and Republican camps. While it may be possible that "independents" were as biased or divided in their views as the Republican and Democratic groups were and simply averaged out in a way that suggested moderation or a middle-of-the-road approach, it seems likely that self-professed independents—even if the majority are major-party leaners—often identify themselves as independents largely because they oppose or at least question extreme views of one or both major parties. It would be reasonable, then, for an optimist to suggest, based on the Quinnipiac poll, that a significant segment of the American electorate—in this case, the 34 percent of self-identified independents—represents a huge potential swing vote in coming elections.

Unfortunately, a realist will quickly point out that there's little likelihood the votes of the majority of people in that large "independent" bloc representing about a third of voters will swing anywhere but from one major party to the other ... or back.

Kavanaugh faced further accusations of sexual assault or misbehavior dating back to the 1980s—including allegations, published in *The New Yorker* just four days before his appearance before Mitchell and the Senate Judiciary Committee, that he exposed himself to an ex-classmate at Yale—but maintained his innocence throughout. There seemed to be nothing to corroborate any of the allegations against him.

Apparently thinking better of taking the high road, President Trump mocked Ford at an early October campaign rally in Mississippi. Three Republican senators responded by openly criticizing the president's behavior—which hardly stood out from previous behavior many prominent Republicans, at least publicly, had been turning a blind eye to ever since it became apparent Trump was going to be the party's nominee for

15. Missed Opportunity

president in 2016. One of the three criticizing Trump's mocking of Ford was Arizona's Jeff Flake, who'd announced in October 2017—trailing his Republican challenger in polls at the time—that he wouldn't seek reelection in 2018. Earlier in 2017, Flake had summoned the spirit of Barry Goldwater and released a book called *Conscience of a Conservative* in which Flake lamented that his Republican Party had "given in to the politics of anger—the belief that riling up the base can make up for failed attempts to broaden the electorate. These are the spasms of a dying party" (Flake, 8).

After a brief and limited FBI investigation into allegations against Kavanaugh, a slim Republican majority in both the Judiciary Committee and in the Senate assured Kavanaugh's confirmation to the high court. Three accusers, according to foxnews.com, ended up getting referred by Senate Republicans to the Justice Department for investigation (Schallhorn). As far as the confirmation vote itself went, neither Flake nor any of his Republican peers present in the Senate voted against Kavanaugh's confirmation. One Republican, Alaska's Lisa Murkowski—another of the senators who'd criticized Trump for mocking Ford in Mississippi—apparently opposed rushing the vote and issued a tepid objection to proceedings by voting "present," reportedly as a courtesy to fellow Republican senator Steve Daines of Montana, who'd intended to vote "yes" but wasn't in attendance.

Nearly as lopsided as the Republican vote on the Kavanaugh confirmation was the vote of Democrats on the full Senate floor. While a September 28, 2018, headline posted at vox.com ("Senate Judiciary Committee votes along party lines to advance Kavanaugh") requires no explanation, the final Senate confirmation vote eight days later saw West Virginia Democratic Senator and former governor Joe Manchin—identified at factcheck.org as having "voted with Trump more than any Democratic senator"—vote yes, the only Democrat to do so.

Manchin voted for the Kavanaugh confirmation despite being, essentially, a blue dot in a state that had gone deep red—and in a reelection year, no less. But Manchin was used to speaking his mind and occasionally stirring up controversy while generally remaining popular at home and coming out on top. Often rumored to be a candidate for defection to the Republicans or for a position in the Trump cabinet, Manchin instead chose to remain a Democrat and seemed content to continue steering his own course through challenging waters in the nation's capital. Sizing up his 2018 reelection bid, Manchin said, as reported by Michael Kruse and Burgess Everett in the March/April 2017 issue of *Politico* magazine, "What really pisses me off is all anybody thinks is I'm going to vote the way I vote or think the way I think because of getting elected. ... They don't understand. I don't give a shit about getting elected."

At the time of the Kavanaugh confirmation vote, Republicans held the thinnest possible majority—51 seats—in the Senate. With Daines absent from the vote and Murkowski voting "present," that meant the Republicans needed one defection from the Democrats (or Democrat-caucusing "independents") to get the 50 votes needed for confirmation. Manchin provided that vote.

While Manchin's yes vote on the confirmation may have played well with some voters at home, it should be noted that he was facing a Republican opponent in the 2018 election who ran largely on a platform of being the antithesis to Manchin. As Joe Perticone wrote in an October 22, 2018, article at BusinessInsider.com, "[Manchin's opponent Patrick] Morrisey is running on being the anti–Joe Manchin in West Virginia, railing against the incumbent Democratic senator's record of bipartisanship and often contentious voting choices." As it turned out, Manchin's victory in 2018 would be the closest of his three general election races for the U.S. Senate. He won with a plurality, finishing three points ahead of his Republican challenger in a race in which the Libertarian candidate's 4 percent showing, at least theoretically, may have swung the result.

But—at least, according to polls and reporters in the recent era—the swing vote that matters, when it comes to improving the fortunes of alternative political organizations or candidates, is represented by the growing mass of voters identifying themselves as independent. The problem, however, is that such a swing vote—comprising about a third of the U.S. electorate identifying itself as independent, as suggested by the 2018 Quinnipiac poll—doesn't exist for the most part, as most self-identifying "independents" lean toward one of the major parties and lean *heavily* toward the two-party system. If it were otherwise, results of the 2018 U.S. midterm elections, on the heels of such a debacle as the Kavanaugh hearing, would have shown some movement in the American electorate's readiness to "step outside the box" and give a fair hearing to a greater number of alternative candidates who were eager to pump up an electoral system gone flat. Clearly, major-party leaners dominated Quinnipiac's large "independent" bloc, and "independents" who broke ranks with the party they'd leaned toward, *if* they switched, very often switched to the other major party. True, there were a few alternative candidate/alternative party successes sprinkled around the country—though none beyond the state level … except in the cases of "independent" U.S. senators Sanders and King.

In the end, as reported in an earlier chapter, the Democratic and Republican parties retained their shared vise-like grip on power, and the political scorecard that mattered most seemed to read *Duopoly 99* (rounded down)–*Democracy 1* (rounded up). Despite some hope being placed in a large potential swing vote supposedly hungry for change, results of the 2018 midterms pointed right at the obvious reality—yet another lost opportunity for voters to reclaim their voice and at least start the process of resuscitating American democracy. In the aftermath of one of the most embarrassing partisan spectacles in the history of the United States, the nation would emerge perhaps more partisan—and more committed to a dysfunctional two-party system—than ever.

16

Three Walls

Following the Kavanaugh confirmation debacle and the 2018 midterms, democracy's drubbing at the hands of the duopoly continued into the 2020 election cycle. The 116th United States Congress convened on January 3, 2019, 13 days into a federal government shutdown that perhaps should have been taken as another clear signal that polarized two-party politics was more of a cause than a solution to much of what was wrong in America.

While some observers made much of the diversity of the incoming class of members of Congress and were heartened by what they saw as the ideal balance of power—with each major party controlling one house of Congress—the reality was that the 116th Congress' "diversity" didn't extend much at all to political affiliations. The balance of power in Congress remained, more than anything, a practice in two-party control, and the only non–Republicans/non–Democrats at the start of the 116th Congress were "independent" senators Sanders and King, who caucused with the Democrats.

The two sides battled it out for three weeks into the new Congress, until both houses and President Trump agreed, on January 25, to a measure that would reopen and fund government services until February 15. The temporary measure was passed without agreement on a solution to what had emerged as the key sticking point between Republicans and Democrats hoping to hammer out a more lasting appropriations bill to fund the government during the 2019 fiscal year: inclusion of over $5 billion to help pay for the border wall Trump had promised voters during the 2016 presidential campaign—and which he'd promised that Mexico, and not U.S. taxpayers, would fund.

The shutdown of late 2018/early 2019—which, although partial, adversely affected millions of people depending on federal services, payments, and salaries—had been over a year in the making. In September 2017 Trump announced his intention to end the Deferred Action for Childhood Arrivals (DACA) program, established during the Obama administration and aimed at protecting the right of young, undocumented immigrants (or Dreamers) to remain in the United States and to receive the same sort of services and privileges enjoyed by documented immigrants.

As Russell Berman reports in *The Atlantic*, "Prospects for a quick [bipartisan] agreement brightened briefly in September [2017] after Trump appeared to sign off on a framework with Democratic leaders Nancy Pelosi and Charles Schumer; that plan would have traded the Dream Act for additional security at the border. But under pressure from immigration hard-liners, Trump backed away and added a whole new set of demands for a DACA deal, including funding for his border wall...."

According to MSNBC's Steve Benen, in January 2018 Trump worked out a deal with Senate Minority Leader Schumer for wall funding—to the tune of $25 billion—in exchange for DACA protections, including a path to citizenship for children of immigrants who were brought to the United States when they were young. But then, as Benen reports, "After Trump negotiated the terms, the White House balked" and Trump "declared that he'd need far more in any deal, including significant cuts to legal immigration." Further negotiations over the course of 2018 were unsuccessful, with one key impasse in the form of the major parties' inability to reach a compromise before the year and the 115th U.S. Congress were over that would have allocated necessary funding for several key federal departments and agencies to continue operating throughout the 2019 fiscal year. According to *Business Insider*'s Bob Bryan, departments denied the necessary funding included agriculture, commerce, justice, homeland security, the interior, state, and HUD—and starting on December 22, 2018, a significant shutdown of U.S. government operations and services went into effect, bringing the prospect of impending hardship to millions of people providing or needing such services just days before Christmas.

It was exactly a month after Christmas when the 116th Congress and President Trump agreed on a temporary measure to end the longest U.S. government shutdown in history. Without reaching agreement on substantial immigration issues, including funding for the border wall, both parties—Republicans controlling the Senate, and Democrats the House—and the president managed to agree on a measure to fund the government for three weeks, allowing furloughed employees to return to work and to try to get things back to normal in their respective departments and agencies while the political partisans in Washington, D.C., tried to reach a more lasting solution.

Given the tone of things in Washington, there was no guarantee, of course, that such a solution would be reached anytime soon. But the temporary solution—borne more out of desperation than any perceptible search for common ground—enabled Trump to deliver his 2019 State of the Union address, which had been scheduled for January 29 before getting delayed when House Speaker Pelosi withdrew her invitation for Trump to address the nation from the House of Representatives during the shutdown. Trump finally got to deliver his address on February 5, 10 days before the temporary government funding measure was set to expire.

Starting by reminding Americans that the nation was standing "at a moment of unlimited potential," Trump assured his audience, despite a wave of recent history that suggested otherwise, "The agenda I will lay out this evening is not a Republican agenda or a Democrat agenda. It is the agenda of the American people" (CNN, "State of the Union 2019").

Striking a conciliatory tone, Trump continued, "Together, we can bridge old divisions, heal old wounds, build new coalitions, forge new solutions, and unlock the extraordinary promise of America's future. The decision is ours to make. ... Now is the time for bipartisan action."

Trump went on to describe successes of his administration's first two years, including "an unprecedented economic boom," tax reform, massive regulation-cutting, increased energy production, and job creation. He then lauded bipartisan efforts during the previous Congress, when "both parties came together to pass unprecedented legislation to confront the opioid crisis, a sweeping new Farm Bill, historic VA reforms [and] groundbreaking criminal justice reform" (CNN, "State of the Union 2019").

But when he got around to expounding issues lying before the 116th Congress, Trump drove hard on the issue of border protection. "Now is the time," he said, "for the Congress to show the world that America is committed to ending illegal immigration and putting the ruthless coyotes, cartels, drug dealers, and human traffickers out of business. As we speak, large, organized caravans are on the march to the United States."

Though declaring "Republicans and Democrats must join forces" to ensure border security, Trump made the case that "[w]ealthy politicians and donors push for open borders while living their lives behind walls and gates and guards." Meanwhile, he said, sex traffickers "[took] advantage of the wide open area between our points of entry to smuggle thousands of young girls and women into the United States and to sell them into prostitution and modern-day slavery. Tens of thousands of innocent Americans are killed by lethal drugs that cross our border and flood into our cities." Gang activity, Trump said, had flooded into many American states "through our southern border."

Among key measures needed to stop the flow of illegal activity from Latin America, Trump said, were "plans for a new physical barrier, or wall, to secure the vast areas between our ports of entry. In the past," he said, "most of the people in this room [the U.S. House] voted for a wall—but

16. Three Walls 141

the proper wall never got built. I'll get it built" (CNN, "State of the Union 2019").

Trump's call for bipartisan action on immigration, the wall, and other issues perhaps rang hollow to millions of Americans who, several weeks earlier, had heard Trump say he was prepared to keep the government shut down for "months or even longer" if Democrats didn't come around to funding his border wall (Pramuk). Presumably, many of the doubters based their skepticism on what must have been clear to millions: The American two-party system wasn't a well-oiled machine at all. Instead, having separated from the track it had been bouncing on for decades, the two-party system—in the wake of the Kavanaugh hearing, the 2018 midterms, and the longest shutdown in U.S. government history—seemed to be bouncing harder than ever even as the track was fading from view.

Mindful of public repercussions that might ensue if government services weren't funded beyond the three-week period agreed to on January 25, Congress, on February 14, 2019, one day before the temporary funding measure was set to expire, passed a measure described in *The Guardian* as "a sweeping, 1,159-page spending bill" containing a "border security

President Trump's border wall (a stretch of it pictured here) was intended as a barrier to block the flow of drugs and undocumented travelers from Mexico to the U.S., but it could also be seen to represent the seemingly impenetrable barrier separating the Republican and Democratic parties during the Trump administration (Carol M. Highsmith Archive, Library of Congress, Prints and Photographs Division).

compromise [that] would appropriate $1.375 [billion] for 55 miles of new fencing along the border with Mexico, which is far less than the $5.7 [billion] Trump sought for a concrete or steel wall" (Canon).

Needless to say, Trump, who saw dozens of his fellow Republicans vote alongside Democrats in support of the bill, wasn't happy about how things had transpired. Nonetheless, he appeared to soften his stance and signed the compromise funding bill just in time to avert a resumption of the shutdown. By then he had plenty of other concerns and didn't need to complicate matters by having to explain inflexibility and a further standstill even to people who normally supported his positions and bought into his persona as an iconoclastic anti-politician.

Others, of course, saw Trump as something entirely different—more as a person of questionable character who didn't have nearly the track record he claimed to have had in the business world and who'd hoodwinked his way to the presidency only to find himself in well over his head after getting there. By the time another government shutdown was averted on February 15, 2019, there were plenty of rumblings in Washington and around the nation about some high-profile firings by Trump, the roguish manner in which he seemed to conduct foreign policy, high-profile arrests of Trump colleagues and staffers, and the manner in which Trump denied Speaker Pelosi the use of a military aircraft for a planned visit to an Afghan war zone during the shutdown. Many critics of Trump were biding their time as the release of the Mueller report seemed to be within sight; and some Democrats made no secret that they were ready to pounce into impeachment proceedings as soon as Mueller delivered the goods to confirm Trump's collusion with Russia during the 2016 presidential campaign. Trump and his cohorts, meanwhile—with William Barr newly appointed as an attorney general who, over time, would seem to confirm suspicions that his loyalties lay more with Trump than with genuine and impartial justice—appeared to make sport of twisting the truth and seemed to be banking almost entirely on the loyalty of Republican stalwarts committed to building a wall … not just a wall on the southern border but a wall between themselves and the despicable Democrats.

On that matter—the building of a wall between the two parties—the Democratic camp seemed just as agreeable. In fact, after the two parties, in mid–February 2019, came together momentarily to avert a government shutdown that would have come at great cost to both parties' public images, about the only thing the major parties seemed to agree on was the placement of the wall separating them—and the retention of that other wall *around* them, both of them, that kept other players out of the game and reduced politics in the United States to a two-party comedy of errors that clearly had great potential to turn tragic.

17

Spinning the Mueller Report

Following Trump's photo-op summit in late February 2019 with North Korea's Kim Jong Un, reports in early March about alleged Trump hush-money payments to "adult film" actress Stormy Daniels, and a public-image smearing—if such was still possible—over comments Trump made in mid-March about the late Senator John McCain caused minor uproars among many Democrats (and a few Republicans), on March 22, 2019, the Democrats got the news they'd been eagerly awaiting for 22 months: Special Counsel Robert Mueller had completed his investigation of Trump and released it to Attorney General Barr.

That same day, Barr released a letter to U.S. Senators Lindsey Graham and Diane Feinstein and U.S. Representatives Jerrold Nadler and Doug Collins, the highest-ranking Republicans and Democrats on the Senate and House Judiciary Committees. In the letter Barr voiced his intent to release information from Mueller's report on the Trump investigation in a manner "consistent with the law ... and the [Justice] Department's long-standing practices and policies" (Associated Press). Barr assured the Congressional leaders to whom the letter was addressed—and the public, to whom the letter was also released—that "I remain committed to as much transparency as possible" (Associated Press).

Two days later, Barr released another letter to Graham, Feinstein, Nadler, and Collins—a four-page document "to advise [them] of the principal conclusions reached by Special Counsel Robert S Mueller III" in his "Report on the Investigation into Russian Interference in the 2016 Presidential Election," based on Barr's first review of the report (Kruzel).

After emphasizing the exhaustiveness of Mueller's investigation—involving 19 lawyers, about 40 FBI agents and other professionals, and hundreds of warrants and witnesses—Barr stated, correctly, that "[t]he Special Counsel's investigation did not find [or conclude] that the Trump campaign or anyone associated with it conspired or coordinated with Russia in its efforts to influence the 2016 U.S. presidential election" (Kruzel).

Barr was also accurate in portraying what Mueller had to say about conduct by Trump that Mueller investigated "as potentially raising obstruction-of-justice concerns." According to Barr, "The Special Counsel ... did not draw a conclusion—one way or the other—as to whether the examined conduct constituted obstruction." Barr then quoted from the report: "[W]hile this report does not conclude that the President committed a crime, it also does not exonerate him" (Kruzel).

Barr continued, "The Special Counsel's decision to describe the facts of his obstruction investigation without reaching any legal conclusions leaves it to the Attorney General to determine whether the conduct described in the report constitutes a crime. ... Deputy Attorney General Rod Rosenstein and I have concluded that the evidence developed during the Special Counsel's investigation is not sufficient to establish that the President committed an obstruction-of-justice offense."

As in his March 22 letter, Barr emphasized his commitment to transparency and his intent "to release [publicly] as much of the Special Counsel's report as I can consistent with applicable law, regulations, and Departmental policies." Such a release, Barr indicated, would take place after redactions were made to material relevant to ongoing legal and criminal investigations—no minor consideration during the Trump administration—along with "any information that could impact other ongoing matters, including those that the Special Counsel has referred to other offices. As soon as that process is complete, I will be in a position to move forward expeditiously in determining what can be released in light of applicable law, regulations, and Departmental policies" (Kruzel).

As it turned out, the full Mueller report, minus hundreds of redactions of varying length, was released to the public on April 18, 2019, just short of four weeks after it was received by Barr. Despite the blacking-out of substantial material in the 448-page document and the replacement of much material with notes indicating why each redaction was necessary—ranging from "Personal Privacy" to "Investigative Technique" to potential "Harm to Ongoing Matter"—it didn't take long for a curious reader, let alone an army of angry Democrats, to determine that Barr had jumped the gun with his March 24 declaration that, based on his initial reading of the report, Trump hadn't done anything worthy of further investigation.

Although declining to state directly that Trump had done anything illegal, Mueller, a registered Republican and former FBI chief, clearly laid out numerous instances that at least gave the appearance that improprieties had occurred and that the wrong lines had been crossed. But while Barr—capitalizing on Mueller's neutrality regarding whether Trump had engaged in improper collusion or obstruction—apparently didn't hesitate to declare the case against Trump closed, others saw things differently.

Following the release of the redacted Mueller report, the American

17. Spinning the Mueller Report

Constitution Society (ACS), a legal organization widely characterized as "progressive" or "liberal," posted on its website an article listing and discussing "Stark Contrasts between the Mueller Report and Attorney General Barr's Summary." Leading off the ACS's list of key points from the report that Barr left out of his summary was Mueller's statement, regarding the question of whether Trump had obstructed justice, that "if we had confidence after a thorough investigation of the facts that the President clearly did not commit obstruction of justice, we would so state. Based on the facts and the applicable legal standards, we are unable to reach that judgment." The ACS article goes on to say, "The report presents facts regarding eleven episodes of potentially obstructive conduct. ... In addition, the report emphasizes that 'it is important to view the President's pattern of conduct as a whole' including 'multiple acts by the President that were capable of exerting undue influence over law enforcement investigations, including the Russian-interference and obstruction investigations.'" The ACS article also notes that, in Mueller's report, "the Special Counsel's office described considerations guiding its obstruction of justice review [and, presumably, its caution, regardless of findings, to declare legal wrongdoing on the part of the president], highlighting as the first item the fact that the Department of Justice has a policy against indicting a sitting president." The ACS article continues, "The Attorney General omitted any reference to the role that the indictment policy played for the Special Counsel in his obstruction of justice case."

Charlie Savage takes this further in the April 20, 2019, *New York Times*. He writes, "[W]hile the O.L.C. [the Justice Department's Office of Legal Counsel] opinion concludes that a sitting president may not be prosecuted, it recognizes that a criminal investigation during the president's term is permissible. The O.L.C. opinion also recognizes that a president does not have immunity after he leaves office. ... Mr. Barr did not explain that Mr. Mueller was trying to leave open the possibility that prosecutors in the future, after Mr. Trump leaves office, could look at the evidence he gathered and decide then whether to indict Mr. Trump."

As for Mueller himself, in a letter to Barr dated March 27, 2019, he wrote, "The summary letter the Department [of Justice] sent to Congress and released to the public late in the afternoon of March 24 did not fully capture the context, nature, and substance of this Office's work and conclusions. We communicated that concern to the Department on the morning of March 25. There is now public confusion about critical aspects of the results of our investigation" (*The Hill*).

At a Senate Judiciary Committee hearing on May 1, 2019, two weeks after the release of the reacted Mueller report, Barr, asked about Mueller's letter of March 27, described it as "a bit snitty ... probably written by one of his staff people" and added that "he had spoken with Mueller by phone after receiving his letter, and the special counsel told him he did not think Barr's description of the report's findings were inaccurate" (Shabad). Predictably, following Barr's May 1 testimony, there were calls from Democrats for the attorney general's resignation. Also in the aftermath of Barr's Senate committee hearing was the Trump Justice Department's refusal to allow Barr to testify, as planned, before the House Judiciary Committee the following day.

As some saw it, there wasn't any need for Barr to testify a second time because, in their view, the battle was over as a result of the attorney general's spinning of the Mueller report. As David A. Graham reported in *The Atlantic* on May 1, 2019, "When William Barr was appointed attorney general, his critics warned that Barr would do everything he could to either interfere with Special Counsel Robert Mueller's work or suppress his report." But Barr did little or none of that, instead biding his time, issuing his summary of the Mueller report on March 24 and then springing into action on April 18, the day the redacted report was released, giving his selective and tilted view of what was stated in the report, and probably banking on the likelihood that few people—especially on Trump's side of what had become American society's Great Divide—would ever bother digging through the 448-page report for themselves.

Closing out his *Atlantic* piece titled "Barr Misled the Public—And It Worked," Graham wrote, "Rather than clumsily suppress the report, Barr did something much subtler—and far more effective." The predictable result was that two warring parties hunkered down in their respective camps, arming themselves with whatever they could spin from the Mueller investigation and report. Both sides were also armed with unmitigated anger—on one side, over a perceived upending of democracy and a hatred-driven challenge to the legitimacy of a duly elected president; and on the other, over the actions of a president who saw himself as above the law and a cadre of enablers, led by the attorney general, who sought to protect that rogue president's interests, but not the country's, at any cost. Needless to say, all the firing of verbal missiles or threats from each camp at the other effectively drowned out any chance of other voices being heard or having any effect at all on the battle that was raging.

Every other political party in the country was effectively excluded from the "debate" raging in Washington, D.C., and around the country over what to do about a president who seemed content to put the old political rulebook—if not the Constitution—through a shredder. One major party seemed to be inching its camp further from the American mainstream, dissociating itself from historical precedent or tradition, and shutting down debate among those on the inside or outside who had questions or concerns about where the party was heading; and the other seemed to be represented by what often came across as a cult of dangerously unstable personality. Meanwhile, millions of Americans who saw the danger of aligning with either camp seemed to view their best option as biting their lips, looking the other way, and simply trying to get through the next few—*hopefully*, just a few—years as unscathed as possible.

18

Justin Amash
A Bold Statement

The remainder of the spring of 2019 saw little chance of a ceasefire, particularly after Trump invoked executive privilege in early May and, a month later, the Democratic-controlled House voted to hold Barr in civil contempt of Congress for refusing to turn over the unredacted version of the Mueller report.

On July 17 another House vote found Barr in criminal contempt of Congress—a rare charge for a sitting member of the Cabinet—for his part in refusing to testify or turn over documents related to the addition of a citizenship question to the 2020 census. The vote, as expected, went almost entirely along party lines, with Republicans voting 198–0 against finding Barr guilty of contempt and Democrats voting 229–4 in favor of finding him guilty.

There was one other vote, on the "yea" side, cast by a congressman from Michigan's 3rd congressional district serving several counties in western Michigan and the metropolitan centers of Grand Rapids and Battle Creek. Throughout its history, Michigan's 3rd congressional district had largely seen voters favor the Republican Party.

In 2008 Justin Amash, a Grand Rapids lawyer and the son of Middle eastern immigrants to the United States, was elected, as a Republican, to the Michigan House of Representatives, where he quickly earned a reputation for supporting limited government and transparency in politics. In 2010, backed by major Republican connections and over $1 million in contributions, Amash ran a successful campaign to represent voters from Michigan's 3rd district in the U.S. House of Representatives on a platform calling for fiscal restraint, smaller government, and a libertarian approach to governing. In 2012 Amash—again raising well over $1 million—was reelected to the U.S. House handily, defeating a Democrat and a Libertarian in the general election. In 2014 and 2016 Amash was reelected with about half again as many votes as his Democratic challengers.

But the difference between Amash's 2014 and 2016 campaigns, at least on the surface, was that Amash, in 2014, was regarded as a rising star in the Republican Party—and one whose differences with the party's mainstream didn't seem to threaten his standing in the party or his patience to work for change within the party; while, in 2016, Amash clearly positioned himself as an independent voice within the Republican Party—one who was deeply concerned about aspects of the Trump agenda and approach but probably more concerned about how the party, with few dissenting voices above a whisper, had hitched itself to Trump.

As Mark Tower reported on the Michigan news website mlive.com on December 15, 2016, following Amash's—and Trump's—general election victory, "Many congressional Republicans who once criticized Donald Trump the candidate have hurried to get in line behind the president-elect, seeing benefits of GOP control over the House, Senate and White House. But not U.S. Rep. Justin Amash." Pointing out that "Amash said he was not elected to fight for 'Team Republican,' but to directly represent the interest of his constituents," Tower quoted Amash: "I view my job as being the representative for everyone in the district, regardless of political party. ... I will take positions that sometimes the political establishment—my own party—won't like. I will take positions that sometimes the Trump administration won't like. ... My job is to be fair."

As Tower concluded the article, "Amash [said] he does not believe he has been elected to serve a political party, but to serve as 'an independent voice for constituents'"—nothing short of fighting words to Trump loyalists and, particularly, Trump himself, long known for prioritizing loyalty—not to the country but to *him*—above competence in his underlings. To Trump and his loyalists, Amash's backing of other candidates for the 2016 Republican presidential nomination was bad enough, but far worse was Amash's refusal to fall in line *after* Trump won the nomination—not to mention his comments about being a watchdog or "an independent voice" from within the Republican Party as the 115th Congress prepared to unfold.

Nearly three months into the 115th Congress, Todd Spangler led off an article about Amash in the April 15, 2017, *Detroit Free Press* by writing, "When Donald Trump became the first Republican presidential nominee to win Michigan in 28 years, any number of Democrats seemed poised to become his regional rival-in-chief. Who would have guessed it would be a Republican instead?"

Although Trump certainly had a long list of vocal Democratic critics, in Michigan and nationwide, raising the alarm over his apparent dictatorial leanings, his refusal to release his tax returns, his dismissal of tradition or science when it didn't suit his aims, and a variety of other concerns, those critics seldom seemed to find receptive ears outside their own camp. Someone like Amash, however—coming across as a reasonable voice who could be taken seriously by people across the political spectrum who were willing to listen—seemed to set a different type of example with his reasoned criticism of policies and what he saw as abuses, intrusions, or missteps on both sides of the political divide.

Yet, on the hyperpartisan battlefield in which he emerged as a national name, Amash seemed to be regarded less as "an independent voice for constituents" or a potential bridge between warring camps than a traitor to the Republican Party.

Spangler, maintaining an objective tone but perhaps not telling the whole story, wrote, "Since before Trump took office, [Amash] has been sniping at the new president. He has belittled him on Twitter for criticizing civil rights legend John Lewis of Georgia, blasted a decision to bomb a Syrian air base without congressional approval and—most notably—successfully led a charge to derail a hastily drawn Republican plan to replace the Affordable Care Act, aka Obamacare. ... Since joining Congress in 2011, he has been part of the rump in the Republican Party and battled openly with the leadership. And when GOP leaders in Michigan's delegation have tried to bring him into line on party initiatives, they've had little success."

Many of Amash's critics failed to point out that Amash was probably less a gadfly by nature than a conscientious person who'd joined the ranks of the major political party whose platform aligned more closely with his own. Expecting that his voice would be heard in policy debates, he learned instead that real debate was as discouraged in his own party as it was in the Democratic Party—especially since Trump took over the presidency. Certainly by the 115th U.S. Congress, there was little appetite for real debate between the warring camps in Washington, D.C., or *within* either camp, as conditions instead seemed suited to quiet consensus or silent disagreement within either warring camp and to blaring insults, accusations, and attacks across the political divide.

It wouldn't be until the 116th Congress, after winning election to a fifth term as a Republican, that Amash took a step—some would say off a cliff—to separate his voice from the din of partisan bickering and quarreling prevalent in Washington and, to an ever-growing degree, around the nation. As Jeff Jacoby reported in the July 12, 2019, *Boston Globe*, "On July 4, Representative Justin Amash of Michigan announced that he was leaving the Republican Party to which he had long belonged, and would henceforth represent his constituents as an independent. He condemned the 'partisan death spiral' in which American politics is caught, and urged others to join him in 'rejecting the partisan loyalties and rhetoric that divide and humanize us.'

"With that move," Jacoby continued, "Amash became the only one of the House of Representatives' 435 members who does not belong to a political party"—one of two political parties, to be exact.

Jacoby added, "The 'people's house' was designed to reflect the public's loyalties, preferences, and passions. In a nation where more than 1 of every 4 registered voters explicitly rejects a party affiliation, there ought to be scores of independents serving in the House. ... Yet it's still virtually unheard-of for candidates who don't belong to a political party to win public office."

Whether or not harsh reality played into Amash's decision to run for a fifth term as a Republican and to delay his departure from the party until half a year into the 116th Congress, his announcement, in a July 4, 2019, *Washington Post* op-ed, that "I am declaring my independence and leaving the Republican Party" was a bold statement. He continued, "I'm asking you to believe that we can do better than this two-party system—and to work toward it. If we continue to take America for granted, we will lose it."

Thirteen days later Amash added an exclamation mark to his departure from the Republican Party by casting his vote in the House of Representatives to declare Barr guilty of criminal contempt of Congress.

19

July–September 2019
Embarrassing Developments

Despite Justin Amash's well-chronicled departure from the Republican Party on Independence Day, the summer of 2019, politically speaking, was characterized primarily by the two sides maintaining their positions along the political divide. On one side, Republicans circled around Trump and berated Democrats for being driven by hatred and refusing to accept the will of an Electoral College majority that had elected an outsider and a proven businessman to the presidency. On the other side, many Democrats dismissed Trump's acumen for running a business or a country, pointing out that he'd gone bankrupt several times and, in two and a half years at the nation's helm, had shown the potential to lead the country down that same road, at least morally. "Debates" raged about Trump's refusal to come clean by releasing his tax returns and about his periodic get-togethers with Kim Jong Un and his readiness to scrap international deals cobbled together by his predecessors. Even more contentious were the findings of the Mueller report, which one side saw as a ticket for exoneration of the president and the other side saw as a ticket for impeachment … if only a smoking gun would turn up to help set things in motion.

Clearly, the opposing camps were in wartime mode, stifling dissent among their own troops with regard to the issues driving the war. Failure to line up behind Trump, regardless of how preposterous numerous claims and positions he put forth appeared to be, seemed to be seen by many Republicans—most of all, Trump—as an act of treason. Indiscretion could perhaps be overlooked at the more regional or local levels of government, but even there, the highly polarized, hyperpartisan atmosphere evident throughout the country clearly put dissenters with any visibility or discernible voice at risk. As far as those with any national presence were concerned, the Amash situation had demonstrated how conscientious dissenters could be hounded, belittled, and driven out.

When Amash went public with his view that the president had

apparently engaged in impeachable conduct, he suggested many of his fellow congressmen, despite their readiness to line up in battle and toe the party line, hadn't bothered to read the Mueller report. To that effect, Amash tweeted on May 18, 2019, "[T]heir minds were made up based on partisan affiliation."

Regardless of how many U.S. Representatives read the report, Amash's assessment seems fair. Clearly, especially in recent times, partisan affiliation is the prime motivator when it comes to determining how a Republican or Democrat will vote.

The day after Amash tweeted his view that Trump had obstructed justice, House Minority Leader Kevin McCarthy went on Fox News to deliver a scathing attack on Amash.

"This is exactly what he wants[;] he wants to have attention," Ron Blitzer quotes McCarthy as saying at foxnews.com. "You've got to understand Justin Amash. He's been in Congress for quite some time. I think he's asked one question in all the committees that he's been in. He votes more with Nancy Pelosi than he ever votes with me. It's a question whether he's even in our Republican conference as a whole."

Amash took plenty of other flak—most notably, from Trump, who tweeted, "Never a fan of @justinamash, a total lightweight who opposes me and some of our great Republican ideas and policies just for the sake of getting his name out there through controversy. ... Justin is a loser who sadly plays right into our opponents['] hands!" (Burke).

The "loser" label—a favorite "debating point" of Trump's—resurfaced when Trump tweeted several weeks later in response to Amash's announcement that he was leaving the Republican Party. Responding to Amash's plea for others, "[n]o matter your circumstances, ... to join me in rejecting the partisan loyalties and rhetoric that divide and dehumanize us" (Amash), Trump tweeted, "Great news for the Republican Party as one of the dumbest & most disloyal men in Congress is 'quitting' the Party. ... A total loser!" (BBC.com).

It's fair to say the Democratic Party, as a unit, was every bit as averse to true debate on issues constituting the core of where the party stood in 2019 as the Republicans were. Issues such as Roe v. Wade, "heartbeat bills" that surfaced in some states with Republican legislatures, global warming, healthcare costs, and same-sex marriage seemed to galvanize the Democratic Party as a unit, even if a significant number of registered or self-identifying Democrats nationwide weren't entirely comfortable with the direction in which, or the distance, the party had moved in recent years. By 2019, however, the party position on those issues—at least, as determined by party leaders and trumpeted by Democrats serving in Washington, D.C., including members of the 116th Congress' freshman class—seemed to reflect party custom and tradition much less than the will of some of Congress' most vocal members to mimic Trump in attempting to remake an outdated major party in their image.

While there was little patience among Democrats for voices on the wrong side of issues the party wrapped itself around in 2019, there certainly was discussion regarding the finer points consistent with positions the party had adopted or considered settled. Matters such as how to ensure abortion access, racial or gender equality, "better" education or healthcare, or cleaner energy were acceptable and even encouraged—as long as certain lines weren't crossed.

It was in that context that more than two dozen contenders vied for the party's 2020 presidential nomination—and by the summer of 2019, the Democratic presidential primary debates were underway, with one highlight coming in the form of Kamala Harris taking Joe Biden to task for his opposition to court-ordered school busing in the 1970s and his association in past years with Southern segregationists. To some observers, Biden seemed to show surprising spryness by dancing his way out of those accusations—which Harris apparently forgot or overlooked by the time she joined the Biden team the following year.

Another issue that was fair game within the Democratic Party following the release of the redacted Mueller report was a matter some Democrats had been calling for since 2017—the impeachment of President Trump.

Back on June 7, 2017, Democratic Congressmen Brad Sherman (California) and Al Green (Texas) announced plans to draft documents supporting Trump's impeachment. Five days later, they released a draft asserting that Trump had obstructed justice in the investigation of his alleged collusion with Russian nationals during the 2016 campaign. A key part of their assertion rested on testimony by former FBI director James Comey—fired by Trump in May 2017—that Trump had pressured him to end an investigation of Michael Flynn, Trump's former national security advisor and one of an alarming number of Trump associates to face legal challenges over the course of his presidency. Flynn, a retired lieutenant general in the U.S. Army, was accused of lying to the FBI about the nature of his communication with the Russian ambassador to the United States while Flynn was a top staffer on the Trump campaign team—a charge that ended his tenure as national security advisor after just three weeks and to which Flynn would later plead guilty.

The following month, on July 12, 2017, Green and Sherman went a step further and filed an article of impeachment against Trump. Their resolution, House Resolution 438, cited a "pattern of behavior" evident in Trump's manner of obstructing the Flynn investigation and creating circumstances under which "[FBI] Director Comey might be terminated" if he failed to end the investigation. The resolution went on to assert that only after deciding to fire Comey "[did Trump request] that the Deputy Attorney General provide him with a memorandum detailing inadequacies in the Director's performance of his duties." The resolution continued, "Despite offering different rationales for the termination of the Director of Federal Bureau of Investigation, [Trump] admitted subsequently that the main reason for the termination was that the Director would not close or alter the investigation of matters related to the involvement of Russia in the 2016 campaign for President of the United States." As a result, House Resolution 438 concluded, "Donald John Trump, by such conduct, warrants impeachment and trial, and removal from office."

It probably goes without saying that, with Republicans holding a majority in the House, Sherman and Green's call for impeachment didn't get much consideration by U.S. Representatives following the filing of House Resolution 438. Even House Democrats were overwhelmingly hesitant to push for impeachment at that time, realizing that, given the divide in Washington and around the nation, their best efforts were unlikely to result in anything but a stalemate—which millions of Americans would perceive as a loss for the Democrats.

Many Democrats, however, saw reason for hope in a development that had taken place the day before the filing of Resolution 438 in the House. On July 11, 2017, Donald Trump, Jr., tweeted images of emails from the 2016 campaign that observers across the spectrum generally viewed as anywhere from alarming to unconscionable or incriminating. As CNN's Jeremy Diamond reported on July 11, "President Donald Trump's eldest son, Donald Trump Jr., agreed to meet with someone he believed to be a 'Russian government attorney' last summer after receiving an email offering him 'very high level and sensitive information' that would 'incriminate' Democratic presidential nominee Hillary Clinton, according to emails the younger Trump publicly released [today]"—in effect, heading off the imminent publication of the emails by *The New York Times*.

After a year of outright denial by the Trump campaign that any such meetings had ever taken place, *The New York Times* reported on July 8, 2017, that Trump Jr.—accompanied by brother-in-law Jared Kushner and Paul Manafort (one of several Trump associates who would do jail time)—had met Russian businessman Aras Agolarov, with whom Donald Trump had had business ties, and Russian attorney Natalia Veselnitskaya, who, like Agolarov, was believed to have connections to the Kremlin (Becker). Following the July 8, 2017, *Times* report—by which time Donald Trump had wrapped up the Republican presidential nomination—Trump Jr. issued a statement widely reported as having been dictated by his father:

"It was a short introductory meeting. ... We primarily discussed a program about the adoption of Russian children that was active and popular with American families years ago and was since ended by the Russian government, but it was not a campaign issue at the time and there was no follow up."

That account, of course, seemed inconsistent with the emails released by Trump Jr. later that same week, on July 11. On top of that, on July 9 the *Times* "[cited] three advisers to the White House who told the *Times* that Trump Jr. had agreed to meet with [Russian attorney] Veselnitskaya [in June 2016] after he was promised she would provide damaging information about Hillary Clinton" (CBS News), Trump Jr. did himself no favors by tweeting, on July 10, "Obviously, I'm the first person on a campaign to ever take a meeting to hear info about an opponent ... [it] went nowhere but [I] had to listen."

Despite at least the appearance of some impropriety on the part of the Trump campaign leading up to the 2016 election, Democratic calls for Trump's impeachment, even after details of the Trump Jr.–Veselnitskaya meeting went public in mid-2017, were muted as a result of Republican control of the executive and legislative branches and the acutely partisan nature of the American public. Mindful of how the Republican-embracing and Republican-leaning segment of the public would view any serious effort on their part to proceed toward impeachment of the president, Democrats exercised some restraint and seemed to place their hopes for impeachment in two possible developments on the horizon: a better outcome for the party in the 2018 midterm elections, and the revelation of a smoking gun when the Mueller investigation was over and the report released.

With the Republicans' loss of 35 seats in the House following the 2018 midterms, the Democrats did gain a solid majority that could at least get the ball rolling on the presidential impeachment. A key complicating factor, however, was that the Republican gain of two seats in the U.S. Senate, allowing the party to retain a slim majority, virtually eliminated any hope of following up an impeachment by the House with a conviction (and removal of the president from office) by the Senate—all the more impossible given the requirement of a two-thirds majority in the Senate to convict the president.

The Mueller report, redacted or not, didn't change many minds, and the Democrats appeared destined to put aside serious hopes of impeachment and to focus on surviving the Trump term and hoping for better things in 2020—at least, until word got out regarding the supposed nature of a phone call Trump made to Ukrainian president Volodymyr Zelenskiy in the summer of 2019.

Trump's July 25 call to Zelenskiy followed the announcement, in June, of a major military aid package for Ukraine, which had weathered a Russian invasion five years earlier. As vox.com reported, "The $391 million in military aid to Ukraine had already been approved in the 2019 federal budget. It was meant to bolster Ukrainian forces in their ongoing conflict against Russian invaders in the country's east and included money for arms and radar systems as well as funding for naval forces and NATO aid" (Collins).

But then, a few weeks later, the aid package was held up for reasons that never seemed to be explained by the president or his allies in clear and convincing fashion. Whatever the real cause of the delay may have been, the Ukrainian package was disbursed on September 11, 2019.

One month earlier, on August 12, 2019—about three weeks after Trump's call to Zelenskiy—an anonymous whistleblower filed a complaint with intelligence inspector general Michael Atkinson outlining matters of concern over the nature of the call. On August 26 Atkinson, "[a]fter two weeks of independent investigation ... determined the whistleblower complaint viable and of 'urgent concern,'" and passed the complaint on to new director of national intelligence Joseph Maguire (Pecorin). Maguire determined that the whistleblower complaint wasn't serious enough to warrant his reporting it to Congress within the week Maguire had to make such a determination. But then, as Allison Pecorin reported for ABC News, one week after the intelligence director's deadline, "[a]fter Maguire did not disclose the information to Congress, Atkinson did. In a letter to the top Democrat and Republican on the House Intelligence Committee, Atkinson wrote that he had 'received a disclosure [from] an individual regarding an alleged "urgent concern."'"

Adam Schiff, lead Democrat on the House Intelligence Committee, responded the next day by requesting, unsuccessfully, that the full text of the whistleblower's complaint be turned over to the committee. Two days later, Schiff filed a subpoena to get the document.

The following week, on September 18, 2019, *The Washington Post* indicated that the subject of the whistleblower's complaint was President Trump (Miller). The complaint focused on Trump's July 25 call to Zelenskiy and, specifically, the nature of his "suggestion" that the military aid package that had been approved by the U.S. Congress and then held up could be facilitated if Ukrainian authorities took a harder line in combating corruption—specifically, by digging deeper into the case of Hunter Biden, Joe Biden's son, who'd worked for five years as a highly paid consultant for a Ukrainian energy firm in a manner that seemed to defy all qualifications except the one linking him by blood to the man serving much of that time as vice president of the United States.

Even without a copy of the whistleblower's complaint turned over to Congress, things moved quickly in the wake of the September 18 *Washington Post* report. Within three days, *The Wall Street Journal* led off an article by declaring, "President Trump in a July phone call repeatedly pressured the president of Ukraine to investigate Joe Biden's son, according to people familiar with the matter, urging Volodymyr [Zelenskiy] about eight times to work on a probe that would hamper Mr. Trump's potential 2020 opponent" (Cullison). To some observers, unattributed comments by "people familiar with the matter" didn't carry any more weight than comments or concerns by the whistleblower hiding behind anonymity. Yet sentiments among key Democrats seemed to be moving toward hitting the switch on impeachment—even though conviction by the Senate seemed a pipe dream. But as far as the House was concerned, it was clear that Schiff, Pelosi, and others saw their opportunity to go on the offensive.

On September 25, the day after Speaker Pelosi announced that the House would investigate Trump's "betrayal of his oath of office and betrayal of our national security and betrayal of the integrity of our elections" (Kirby)—which seemed to put the cart before the horse as far as Pelosi's call for an investigation was concerned—the White House responded by releasing what was characterized as a "rough" transcript of Trump's call to Zelenskiy. The unclassified transcript referred to an anti-corruption campaign in Ukraine and to reports that Trump commented on a "[Ukrainian] prosecutor who was very good and he was shut down and that's really unfair. ... There's a lot of talk about Biden's son, that [Joe] Biden stopped the prosecution. ... Biden went around bragging that he stopped the prosecution so if you can look into it ... It sounds horrible to me" (CNN, "Read Trump's phone conversation..."). The released transcript went on to indicate that Zelenskiy assured Trump, "Since we have won the absolute majority in our Parliament, the next prosecutor general will be 100 percent my person.... He or she will look into the situation.... The issue of the investigation of the case is actually the issue of making sure to restore the honesty so we will take care of that and will work on the investigation of the case" (CNN, "Read Trump's phone conversation...").

By most accounts, the firing of the Ukrainian prosecutor in question, Viktor Shokin, was less the brainchild of Joe Biden than the will of others in the international community before Biden applied pressure. The *Financial Times* reported, "EU diplomats working on Ukraine at the time ... have told the FT that they were looking for ways to pursue Kiev to remove Mr Shokin well before Mr Biden entered the picture" (Politi).

The *Financial Times* quotes an EU diplomat familiar with the situation: "All of us were really pushing [former Ukrainian president Petro]

Poroshenko that he needs to do something, because the prosecutor was not following any of the corruption issues. He was really bad news. ... It was Biden who finally came in [and triggered it]. Biden was the most vocal, as the U.S. usually is. But we were all literally complaining about the prosecutor" (Politi).

The theory that Shokin was removed preemptively because he planned to investigate Burisma, the Ukrainian gas company that employed Hunter Biden, has roundly been dismissed—and is characterized as one of many lies in the Trump arsenal over the course of his presidency. While there are serious grounds for questioning Hunter Biden's lucrative arrangement with Burisma during his father's tenure as vice president, it's difficult to give credence to Trump's account of why Shokin was fired as a prosecutor, given more credible accounts and Trump's track record with the truth.

As for the issue of whether Trump, in his phone call with Zelenskiy, had committed an impeachable offense, Pelosi wasn't the only one to jump the gun. On September 25, 2019, the day the rough transcript of the Trump-Zelenskiy call was released by the White House and the day be*fore* the House of Representatives Intelligence Committee would launch an inquiry into impeachment proceedings against the president, Adam Schiff made a mockery of his position as committee chairman by joining other Democratic voices in Washington and around the country and, essentially, pronouncing Trump guilty before the investigation got underway.

Commenting on the phone call transcript shortly after it was released on September 25, Schiff said, "It is shocking ... that the White House would release these notes and felt that this would help the president's case or cause because what those notes reflect is a classic mafia-like shakedown of a foreign leader. ... The president communicates to his Ukrainian counterpart that the United States has done a lot for Ukraine ... more than the Europeans or anyone else has done for Ukraine, but there's not much reciprocity here. This is how a mafia boss talks. ... 'I have a favor I want to ask you.' ... Of course the favor is to investigate his political rival ... and it's clear that the Ukrainian president understands exactly what is expected of him, and he's making every effort to mollify the president. ... Like any mafia boss, the president didn't need to say, 'That's a nice country you have. It would be a shame if something happened to it'" (PBS.org, "Watch...").

The same day that Schiff made his comments, Zelenskiy was in New York for a meeting with Trump. Asked by a reporter whether he felt Trump had pressured him to investigate Joe and Hunter Biden, Zelenskiy said, "We had, I think, a good phone call. It was normal. We spoke about many things. And so, I think, and you read it, that nobody pushed—pushed me" (Yuhas).

Schiff was well within his rights to find Zelenskiy's response—with

Trump sitting beside the Ukrainian president—less than convincing and to read anything he wanted into the transcript of the phone call between the two presidents. At long last the Democrats saw their opportunity to push forward with impeachment without losing face, even though failure seemed inevitable once proceedings made it to the Republican-controlled Senate, where a two-thirds vote was needed for conviction. Yet the outrage among Democrats was such that simply getting the stain of impeachment by the House on the record of a reviled president seemed a desirable enough consolation prize to go after at full throttle—and the Democrats had the majority they needed to do that. By that point, going for the president's throat even in a battle nearly everyone knew the Democrats were destined to lose wasn't likely to cost the party any votes—so divided was the country, and so decisively were the battle lines drawn.

What the Democrats—at least the vocal ones—seemed to miss, however, was that Schiff's tirade and his declaration of Trump's guilt even before the House Intelligence Committee investigation got underway seemed to make it clear where the investigation was heading—i.e., to the low road associated with kangaroo courts. In short, Schiff may have been fortunate that U.S. representatives aren't liable to impeachment proceedings, because it could easily be argued that his behavior—his inability to maintain any semblance of justice and professionalism and to hold his tongue even for a day or two—was about as impeachable an act as anything he or his party accused Trump of doing.

But it shouldn't have been too surprising that a leading Democrat seemed to join a Republican president on the wrong side of the line separating appropriate and responsible behavior from what was unbecoming and—at least morally—impeachable. If anything, that was only a reflection of the sad reality that, in the long, deliberate process of crippling American democracy, one major party was as guilty as the other.

20

Impeachment and Acquittal
A Foregone Conclusion

The day after publicly likening Trump to a mafia don and, in effect, declaring him guilty of impeachable behavior, Rep. Adam Schiff took his place in the House chamber amid a barrage of clicking cameras and essentially repeated his account of the president's shakedown of Ukrainian counterpart Zelenskiy and his declaration of Trump's guilt. By any reasonable measure, Schiff's monologue to kick off the House Intelligence Committee's impeachment inquiry was more akin to a summation by a prosecutor wrapping up arguments *after* evidence was presented in a trial than any indication—before the first shred of evidence was presented—that any semblance of an impartial inquiry was about to get underway. To an impartial listener determined enough to sit through Schiff's opening comments, the eventual outcome of the inquiry was as predictable as the gist of Schiff's monologue.

A few minutes into his opening comments on September 26, 2019, Schiff declared, "This matter would not have come to the attention of our committee or the nation's attention without the courage of a single person, the whistle-blower" (C-SPAN, Video and transcript of proceedings…). Then, addressing intelligence director Joseph Maguire, who was on hand to explain his decision not to report the whistleblower's complaint to Congress, Schiff said, "[T]he intelligence committee is dependent on whistle-blowers to reveal wrongdoing when it occurs, when the agencies do not self-report because outside parties are not allowed to scrutinize your work and to guide us. If that system is allowed to break down, as it did here, if whistle-blowers come to understand that they will not be protected, one of two things happen[:] serious wrongdoing goes unreported or whistle-blower[s] take matters into their own hands and divulge classified information to the press in violation of the law and placing our national security at risk. This is why the whistle-blower system is so vital to us and why your handling of this urgent complaint is also so troubling" (C-SPAN, Video and transcript of proceedings...).

Schiff roundly scolded Maguire for his decision not to report the whistleblower's complaint—and, in particular, "why you stand silent when an intelligence professional under your care and protection was ridiculed by the president, was accused of potentially betraying his or her country, when that whistleblower, by that very act of coming forward, has shown more dedication to country, more of an understanding of the president's oath of office, than the president himself" (C-SPAN, Video and transcript of proceedings...).

The ranking Republican on the House Intelligence Committee, California's Devin Nunes, seated beside Schiff, took over the floor and proceeded to "congratulate the Democrats on the rollout of their latest information warfare operation against the president and their extraordinary ability to once again [enlist] the mainstream media in their campaign" (C-SPAN, Video and transcript of proceedings...). Although Nunes went on to deliver an opening statement every bit as partisan and self-serving as Schiff's, it seems fair to say that Nunes won the opening-statement "debate" by pointing out a key detail Schiff had conveniently overlooked: "[T]he complaint relied on hearsay evidence provided by the whistle-blower."

Nunes' point was confirmed that same day when the whistleblower's complaint was released. While appearing to make a confident case that "the President of the United States is using the power of his office to solicit interference from a foreign country in the 2020 U.S. election" (CNN, "Read":), early on the whistleblower concedes, "I was not a direct witness to most of the events described" in the complaint. If anything, that's an understatement, as a reading of the whistleblower's nine-page letter and appendix doesn't seem to turn up a single case of where the whistleblower's thesis that "the President of the United States is using the power of his office to solicit interference from a foreign country in the 2020 U.S. election" is based on anything but hearsay. Sprinkled throughout the complaint and appendix are the following potentially undermining statements or phrases (all at CNN, "Read":):

- "Over the past four months, more than half a dozen U.S. officials have informed me..."
- "Multiple White House officials with direct knowledge of the call informed me..."
- "The White House officials who told me this information were deeply disturbed..."
- "I was told by White House officials..."

- "Based on my understanding…"
- "The officials I spoke with told me…"
- "I was told that…"
- "In the days following the phone call, I learned from multiple U.S. officials…"
- "White House officials told me…"
- "One White House official described…"
- "Based on multiple readouts of these meetings recounted to me by various U.S. officials…"
- "I also learned from multiple U.S. officials…"
- "The U.S. officials characterized this…"
- "Separately, multiple U.S. officials told me…"
- "On or about 29 April, I learned from U.S. officials with direct knowledge of the situation…"
- "Around the same time, I also learned from a U.S. official…"
- "However, several U.S. officials told me…"
- "Starting in mid–May, I heard from multiple U.S. officials…"
- "These officials also told me…"
- "During this same time frame, multiple U.S. officials told me…"
- "This was the general understanding of the state of affairs as conveyed to me by U.S. officials…"
- "According to multiple White House officials I spoke with…"
- "According to White House officials I spoke with…"
- "I learned from U.S. officials…"
- "According to these officials…"
- "As of early August, I heard from U.S. officials…"

In other words, every damning detail the whistleblower professed to "know" seemed to be based on hearsay and, as a result, fell short of the normal minimum legal standard for determination of guilt—the same standard to which the Democrats had seemed oblivious during the Kavanaugh proceedings.

Although it was entirely reasonable for the Democrats to launch an investigation and to question officials and others who could shed light on the whistleblower's concern, it was inexcusable for Schiff, Pelosi, and others, right out of the gate, to conclude that Trump had committed an impeachable offense. As far as Schiff was concerned, his utter disregard for process and fairness may well have caused a few observers to wonder what insights he'd gotten out of his law degree from Harvard before getting into a career in politics.

In October 2019, the month after the Trump impeachment inquiry was kicked off in the House, Republicans predictably didn't get anywhere in an effort to censure Schiff for his part in the inquiry. After House Democrats voted down a Republican resolution to discipline the House Intelligence Committee chairman, Schiff tweeted, "It will be said of House Republicans, [w]hen they found they lacked the courage to confront the most dangerous and unethical president in American history, [t]hey consoled themselves by attacking those who did" (Shabad and Moe).

That same month, the majority of participants in the fifth debate for Democrats vying for the party's 2020 presidential nomination managed to make their case for the Trump impeachment—an issue that was continuing to expand division in the country. While plenty of reports and polls suggested a significant number of Republicans shared the view that Trump ought to be impeached, it's hard to locate a single poll that tracked or presented such findings in a clear and convincing matter. For example, an October 1, 2019, "analysis" by Harry Enten indicating that Trump ought to be concerned about "a part of the Republican Party that gets less notoriety: the more moderate part" and an October 8, 2019, *Guardian* report by Martin Pengelly declaring that "[n]early 30 percent of Republicans support the impeachment inquiry, with nearly 20 percent favouring formal impeachment" failed to provide

Democrat Adam Schiff was chairman of the House Intelligence Committee "investigating" whether President Trump had committed impeachable behavior. Rather than waiting for testimony and allowing an impartial investigation to play out, Chairman Schiff seemed to make a public announcement of Trump's guilt before the committee investigation even got underway (United States Congress).

much insight—in the articles themselves or in the polls the articles linked to—on how those conclusions were reached. Far more convincing, and better supported by the data it presented, was an NPR/PBS NewsHour/Marist poll released in October 2019.

The NPR/PBS poll of 1,123 adults (Maristpoll.marist.edu), conducted from October 3–8, found that slightly over half of respondents approved of the House of Representatives impeachment inquiry into Trump's activity, compared to slightly under half who'd felt that way the previous month. The poll indicated that while 87 percent of Democrats supported a Trump impeachment, a higher percentage of Republicans—93 percent—opposed it. "Independents," comprising 39 percent in this poll, were right in the middle, with 47 percent supporting impeachment—hardly surprising since the majority of those "independents" could more accurately be described as Democratic and Republican leaners. As for the perception that a growing number of Republicans were fed up with Trump's behavior and wanted him impeached, a whopping 93 percent of Republicans in the NPR/PBS NewsHour/Marist poll said "the future of Donald Trump's presidency" should be decided "at the ballot box" and not "by the impeachment process."

Meanwhile, a Pew poll (Pew Research Center, "Partisan Antipathy") released in October 2019 drew from the responses of nearly 10,000 "panelists" or participants. While more Democrats than Republicans participated, both groups far outnumbered the total of participants in the NPR/PBS NewsHour/Marist poll released the same month. Questions of impeachment didn't come up in the Pew poll. Instead, the poll focused more generally on partisanship and division in the United States during the Trump era. Among the poll's findings were that:

- a large majority of both Republicans and Democrats agreed that partisan divisions were growing
- a large majority in both parties said there was "a great deal" of difference between the two parties
- a large majority in both parties said most Republican and Democratic voters "not only disagree over plans and policies, but also cannot agree on basic facts"
- a large majority in both parties gave "'cold' ratings to those in [the] opposing party"
- a large majority in both parties considered members of the other party more closed-minded than other Americans

Those sentiments were exacerbated by the obvious spillover of hyperpartisanship from the political to the social realm, resulting in broken friendships, strained family relations, pent-up anger let off at inopportune times, and, in many cases, an era of mini–Cold Wars in the office, gym, church, or home. All too often, the goal in social settings had simply become a workable détente based primarily on an agreement to refrain from launching the first missile or bringing up a topic that didn't seem to lend itself well to civilized debate.

It was in that sad context—and with the prospect of another federal government shutdown looming—that the House Intelligence Committee, after hearing testimony from various U.S. government officials and releasing transcripts over the course of several weeks, brought live cameras into the impeachment inquiry and, in effect, opened up its partisan presidential impeachment hearing to what had become a largely polarized partisan public. Among witnesses called to testify during the first week of public testimony in mid–November was former U.S. ambassador to Ukraine Marie Yovanovitch, ousted as ambassador by the Trump administration six months earlier amid allegations by Trump supporters that she opposed the president's push for an investigation into the Bidens' actions and affairs in Ukraine. Or, as *Time* reported on November 15, 2019, the day Yovanovitch testified, "Ambassador Marie 'Masha' Yovanovitch … was ousted in May after what her former colleagues describe as a 'smear campaign' by Trump's allies, led by his personal lawyer Rudy Giuliani" (Bergengruen).

Yovanovitch opened her testimony with a powerful statement acknowledging her parents' escape from the Soviet Union, her "gratitude for all that this country has given to me and to my family," and her "great empathy for others, like the Ukrainian people who want to be free." She went on to discuss personal dangers she'd faced over the course of her 33-year diplomatic career. Regarding her work in Ukraine, she testified, "I worked to advance U.S. policy, fully embraced by Democrats and Republicans alike, to help Ukraine become a stable and independent democratic state with a market economy integrated into Europe." Key to that, she said, was helping to protect Ukraine from Russian domination and "battling the Soviet legacy of corruption which has pervaded Ukraine's Government" (C-SPAN, "Video and transcript of testimony by Marie Yovanovitch…").

As to allegations by Trump supporters that she took measures to protect the Bidens from an anticorruption investigation by Ukrainian authorities, Yovanovitch testified, "[T]he allegation that I disseminated a do-not-prosecute list was a fabrication. … I did not tell [former Ukrainian prosecutor general] Lutsenko or other Ukrainian officials who they should or should not prosecute. … Also untrue are unsourced allegations that I told unidentified embassy employees or Ukrainian officials that President Trump's orders should be ignored because he was going to be impeached, or for any other reason. I did not and I would not say such a thing. Such statements would be inconsistent with my training as a Foreign Service officer and my role as an ambassador" (C-SPAN, "Video and transcript of testimony by Marie Yovanovitch...").

Yovanovitch testified that, after a smear campaign against her got underway, she was to be relieved of her duties in July but then got called back to the United States in late April. Back in Washington, she testified, "Deputy Secretary of State Sullivan told me there had been a concerted campaign against me, that the president no longer wished me to serve as ambassador to Ukraine, and that, in fact, the president had been pushing for my removal since the prior summer."

After delivering a forceful account of her innocence and impartiality, Yovanovitch said, "I obviously don't dispute that the president has the right to withdraw an ambassador at any time for any reason. But what I do wonder is why it was necessary to smear my reputation" (C-SPAN, "Video and transcript of testimony by Marie Yovanovitch..."). Even during Yovanovitch's testimony, Trump couldn't resist tweeting, "Everywhere Marie Yovanovitch went turned bad. She started off in Somalia, how did that go?" (Berengruen).

Belittling and smearing had long been favored weapons of Trump's, and by 2019—as predictable as they were transparent—they hardly raised an eyebrow. Next in line for smearing was National Security Council staffer Alexander Vindman, an army lieutenant colonel who, with his family, fled the Soviet Union at age three and landed in New York City. In a closed-door deposition before the House Intelligence Committee on October 29, 2019, Vindman testified, "I have a deep appreciation for American values and ideals and the power of freedom. I am a patriot. It is my sacred duty and honor to advance and defend our country irrespective of party or politics." That sense of duty and honor had caused Vindman to raise concerns internally about the July 25 call from Trump to Zelenskiy. As Vindman testified to the committee:

> I listened to the call in the Situation Room with colleagues from the NSC [National Security Council] and Office of the Vice President. ... I was concerned by the call. I did not think it was proper to demand that a foreign government investigate a U.S. citizen, and I was worried about the implications to the U.S. Government's support of Ukraine. ... I realized that if Ukraine pursued an investigation into the Bidens and Burisma, it would likely be interpreted as a partisan play, which would undoubtedly result in Ukraine losing the bipartisan support it has thus far maintained. This would all undermine U.S. national security. Following the call, I again reported my concerns to NSC's legal counsel (NPR, "Alexander Vindman Testimony").

During the three weeks between his closed-door deposition to the intelligence committee and his return appearance during the public phase of the inquiry, Vindman came under vicious personal attack from supporters of Trump who questioned his patriotism, suggested his loyalties lay more with Ukraine than the United States, and even likened him to a spy. Trump didn't go that far, at least publicly, instead referring to Vindman—without any apparent grounds—as a Never Trumper following Vindman's closed-door deposition (Grenoble). But then, during Vindman's public testimony on November 19, the official White House Twitter account—"a social media account maintained at taxpayer expense, and not [President Trump's] personal one" (Wilkie)—said, "Tim Morrison, Alexander Vindman's former boss, testified in his deposition that he had concerns about Vindman's judgment" (Wilkie). Morrison, Vindman's NSC supervisor at the time of the Trump-Zelenskiy call and at the time Vindman gave his closed-door testimony, faced questions from "Republican members of the House Intelligence Committee [who] focused much of their attention on undercutting the credibility of Lt Col Alexander Vindman" (Subramanian). While Morrison acknowledged that he'd heard or entertained concerns about Vindman's professional judgment—including the possibility that Vindman had leaked information, an allegation Vindman strongly denied—nothing in Morrison's testimony seemed to suggest it was Vindman's character and not simply a few instances of judgment that had raised concern.

Clearly, both sides in the impeachment "debate" were satisfied to lay out their "evidence," or dogma, with little attention to what debate is usually believed to be about; i.e., convincing the other side, or at least those in the middle, to see things in a new light. The reason, of course, is that the majority of minds were already made up. As a headline on ABC News' fivethirtyeight.com website said on December 4, 2019, the day after the House Intelligence Committee approved the majority Democrats' 298-page impeachment inquiry report and voted, entirely along party lines, to adopt the report, "The Impeachment Hearings Just Confirmed Voters' Preexisting Opinions." Citing a FiveThirtyEight/Ipsos tracking poll released the same day, the fivethirtyeight.com article, by Amelia Thomson-DeVeaux and Laura Bronner, went on to say, "Overall ... opinion on impeachment seems to have hardened as a result of the public testimony instead of persuading people to change their position."

It was almost a humorous afterthought when the House Intelligence Committee chairman, Adam Schiff, decided to put up an impartial front after the intelligence committee voted on December 3, 2019, to move into the next phase of impeachment hearings. As C-SPAN reported on December 3, 2019, "Adam Schiff says he will, for the time being, reserve judgment on whether President Trump actually should be impeached and removed from office"—as if Schiff had any judgment left to reserve after likening Trump to a mafia boss over two months earlier, before the impeachment inquiry had even gotten underway.

It was surely no surprise to Schiff, or to virtually anyone else, when the House Judiciary Committee—active in the next phase of the impeachment hearing—voted, also entirely along party lines, to approve articles of impeachment against the president. Equally predictable was the full House vote on December 18, 2019, in favor of impeaching Trump for abusing power and obstructing justice. Perhaps the only related matter that *wasn't* predictable were the votes of two (of 233) Democratic representatives who didn't approve both articles of impeachment against Trump. It's worth noting, of the two "renegade" Democrats who didn't approve both articles of impeachment, that one, Minnesota's Collin Peterson, would get voted out of his "Democratic district" in 2020 after a 30-year run in Congress (Gunderson); and the other, New Jersey's Jefferson Van Drew, announced, on December 19, 2019, the day after voting against impeachment, that he was leaving the Democratic Party to become a Republican (Breuninger).

Following her party's House vote victory, Speaker Pelosi was reluctant to turn over the articles of impeachment to Senate majority leader Mitch McConnell, every bit the knee-jerk partisan that Pelosi and Schiff were. Given McConnell's apparent determination to get impeachment proceedings in the Senate over with as quickly as possible without doing anything to rile his Republican Party base and, particularly, Trump, it seems almost reasonable that it took Pelosi nearly a month to hand over the keys on impeachment to McConnell, whose view on presidential guilt or innocence, heading into the Senate's impeachment trial, was as transparent as Schiff's verdict had been before his House committee's inquiry had gotten underway.

McConnell had set an apparently dangerous precedent—and, to many outside his party, one deserving of serious sanction—by telling reporters on December 17, 2019, "I'm not an impartial juror." As the nonprofit Public Citizen, founded by Ralph Nader, pointed out, McConnell's words were in direct violation of his oath "that in all things appertaining to the trial of the impeachment of President Donald Trump, now pending, I will do impartial justice according to the Constitution and laws" (Holman).

The Senate impeachment trial officially convened on January 16, 2020, and five days later senators met to agree on rules to govern the trial. According to the rules, each party would present its arguments over several days, and findings from the House inquiry would be entered as evidence in the trial. Senate Democrats, led by minority leader Chuck Schumer, hoped to issue subpoenas for testimony and/or documents from key figures close to the Trump presidency—most notably, former National

Security Advisor John Bolton, who'd left the Trump administration on bad terms in September 2019 and become a vocal critic of the president. Bolton made it clear that he'd testify only if subpoenaed, a position some observers attributed to a desire to save any dirt he had on the Trump presidency for the book he was working on, which would see its release in mid-2020, several months after the impeachment trial.

After several days of partisan bickering among senators and opposing legal teams, on January 31 Senate Republicans won a 51–49 vote—with Utah's Mitt Romney and Maine's Susan Collins dissenting—to turn back the Democrats' attempt to call new witnesses to the trial. After closing arguments were made by both sides on February 3, the Senate held its vote on whether to convict Trump on February 5. While Mitt Romney may have surprised some observers by becoming the first senator in U.S. history to register a vote in favor of convicting a president representing the same party, the result of the Senate vote was every bit as predictable as the result of the previous month's vote in the House. As John Turley reported at BBC.com on February 6, 2020, "The trial was like watching a movie where the audience heard only the lines that they came to hear."

It came as no surprise to anyone when Trump launched a Twitter attack on Romney after getting acquitted. The morning after Romney voted for Trump's conviction and removal from office, Trump tweeted, "Had failed presidential candidate @Mitt Romney devoted the same energy and anger to defeating a faltering Barack Obama (in the 2012 presidential campaign) as he sanctimoniously does to me, he could have won the election" (Forgey). As Rishika Dugyala reported at politico.com, the president followed that up by retweeting "assertions that Romney 'stabbed Trump in the back' by joining Democrats in attempts to overturn the 2016 election, and that the Utah senator was connected to ... claims that Hunter Biden, the son of former Vice President Joe Biden, was corruptly involved with the Burisma Holdings energy company in Ukraine." According to Dugyala, Trump retweeted that "Mitt Romney is tied to Hunter Biden's Burisma corruption. That's why he's bent over backwards for the media with this show 'guilty' vote[.] ... He doesn't want this story EXPOSED!" The accusation, of course, seemed totally unfounded.

Trump couldn't help lashing out at others as well in what Dugyala calls "a weekend tweetstorm against the [impeachment trial] proceedings and his perceived foes." Targets included not only members of Congress who'd called for his impeachment but also a key witness from the House inquiry—Lt. Col Vindman, who was promptly relieved by the White House of his duties as the National Security Director for European Affairs following the Trump acquittal in the Senate.

"He was very insubordinate, reported contents of my 'perfect' calls incorrectly, & was given a horrendous report by his superior, the man he reported to, who publicly stated that Vindman had problems with judgement, adhering to the chain of command and leaking information," Trump tweeted the day after dismissing Vindman from his duties (Choi).

People who knew Vindman came to his defense, pointing out the obvious political and retaliatory nature of his dismissal while acknowledging the at-will status of political appointees, who, for the most part, could legally be fired on the spot for any reason or for no reason. But to many observers, "for no reason" didn't apply to the dismissal of Vindman or the dismissal of Gordon Sondland, U.S. ambassador to the European Union, another appointee who'd voiced concern over Trump's call to Zelenskiy during the House inquiry and was fired from his post in the wake of the president's Senate acquittal. To many, the reason for Vindman's and Sondland's firings by an emboldened, "exonerated" Trump couldn't have been more obvious.

Just as obvious, coming out of yet another embarrassing charade in the practice of two-party politics, was that neither of the warring sides, as intent on shoring up a failed duopoly as on sticking up for its own interests, appeared to have learned anything of benefit outside the distorted world of partisan politics. Both warring sides—ever careful not to go so far as to upend the system they'd colluded for so long to implement and maintain as a self-serving substitute for true democracy—came out of the 2019–2020 impeachment debacle as hardened versions of what they'd been going *in*, with no stomach for meaningful debate or any vision for putting the nation's interests before their own. Individuals on either side of the aisle in Washington who'd entertained notions of listening to the other side were rendered insignificant—mere curiosities, within their major parties, who were driven to the sidelines or, like Romney, berated simply for making an effort to put country before party.

But just as obvious—and even sadder—was that Americans *outside* Washington, D.C., hadn't appeared to learn much coming out of the 2019–2020 Trump impeachment inquiry and trial. Even more than the 2018 Kavanaugh hearing, the Trump impeachment process represented a lost opportunity of epic proportions—the opportunity, coming out of a series of events that magnified the obvious flaws and failings of a two-party death grip on power in the oldest "democracy" in the world, to try to make something better of the American political system. As in previous years, polls in 2020 identified a significant percentage of "independent" voters across the nation—a number generally ranging from a quarter to more than two-fifths—and a Gallup, Inc., survey tracking the percentage of Americans identifying as independent, Democratic, and Republican over a 17-year period from 2004 to 2021 revealed little change in the percentage share of those camps as a result of the impeachment proceedings.

While "independents" in the Gallup survey were tracking slightly above 40 percent during the impeachment inquiry and hearing—as had often been the case in previous years—that number in fact dropped slightly, into the high thirties, after the Trump acquittal. But, of course, as had been well established previously, "independents" in the surveys and polls, for the most part, didn't translate to true independents looking for alternatives to the two major parties but to "free agent" voters who saw their options limited to one major party or the other. There was nothing in the aftermath of the Trump acquittal to suggest anything was different this time around—and, in a sense, in the view of American citizens and voters, it appeared that the American political duopoly, as much as the American president, had emerged from the Trump impeachment trial with an acquittal of its own.

21

Covid-19

Division Trumps Unity

The major parties' polar views on everything Trump—including the Trump-ordered killing of top Iranian military commander Qasem Soleimani in early January 2020—and on the manner in which society was evolving or degenerating, depending on which party made the call, seemed to undermine a nation that took notice of a mysterious virus, apparently coming out of central China, that made its first confirmed appearance in the United States through a traveler who returned from China on January 15, 2020.

On January 21, 2020, the same day the Trump Senate impeachment trial established its rules, that traveler was confirmed to have the novel coronavirus later identified as Covid-19.

On February 9, following Trump's acquittal—and with 15 confirmed cases of Covid-19 in the United States—Trump seemed to compare the new illness favorably with the flu, which, as he pointed out, killed thousands of Americans every year. Continuing to understate the danger facing Americans and to put forth hollow assurances that his administration was on top of things and that the virus could be expected to fizzle out when the weather got warmer, Trump presented a compelling image of everything a leader *shouldn't* be when facing a possible national crisis. It would be confirmed about seven months later, through the release of a conversation with reporter and author Bob Woodward recorded on February 7, 2020—two days before Trump's comments on February 9—that Trump had an altogether different private view of the coronavirus than the one he shared with the public two days later, and would continue to express publicly for weeks afterward. On February 7 Trump described the coronavirus to Woodward as "more deadly than even your strenuous flus" (Woodward, Prologue). The following month, interviewed again by Woodward, Trump accounted for the discrepancy between his public statements on the coronavirus and his private views by explaining, "I want to always play it down. I still like playing it down because I don't want to create a panic" (NPR, "Trump Tells Woodward…").

NPR host Rachel Martin put it another way on September 10, 2020: "Several times during the Trump administration, a whistleblower has accused the president of wrongdoing. This time, in effect, the whistleblower is the president himself. Recordings show he said one thing on TV and another off camera. He made misleading claims about the pandemic, a life-or-death matter affecting almost every American" (NPR, "Trump Tells Woodward…").

Trump wasn't the first U.S. official to declare the risk of coronavirus transmission low to Americans, as key medical officials, all the way up to National Institute of Allergy and Infectious Diseases director Anthony Fauci, made similar statements during the early days or weeks after the virus' arrival in the United States. The difference, of course, is that Trump was the one who blew the whistle on himself—and the one, after seemingly countless instances of fudging facts and promises, whose word seemed to mean absolutely nothing to anyone who wasn't a card-carrying member of the cult that his party, as some observers saw it, seemed to have become.

By March, with testing and confirmed cases rising steeply in the United States, there was little doubt in anyone's mind—with the exception of religiously committed naysayers—that Covid-19, as far as pandemics were concerned, was the real deal. On March 13 Trump declared a national emergency, and three days later he put up a serious front in urging Americans to dedicate the next 15 days to slowing the spread of the virus by avoiding unnecessary travel, avoiding gatherings of more than 10 people, and staying home as much as possible. "If everyone makes this change, or these critical changes, and sacrifices now, we will rally together as one nation and we will defeat the virus," Trump said (NPR, "How 15 Days…"). On March 27 Trump signed a $2 trillion stimulus package designed to help individuals, families, businesses, and health care providers hit by the pandemic and a reeling economy.

On March 29, 2020, as the United States approached 200,000 confirmed cases of Covid-19, Trump extended the guidelines he declared on March 16 for another month. A Morning Consult/Politico poll released four days before Trump's March 29 extension of Covid guidelines determined that a large majority of Republicans, Democrats, and "independents" strongly or somewhat supported "a national quarantine in which only essential travel, such as trips to the grocery store and pharmacy, are permitted to control the spread of the coronavirus" (Murad). While the schism in Washington, D.C., and the nation at large clearly remained, at that point there at least seemed to be a heightened sense that putting nation before party was the right thing to do.

However, the federal guidelines introduced on March 16 and extended nearly two weeks later were just that: *guidelines*. There was no federal order for states or municipalities to adhere to the guidelines, and many didn't. While every U.S. state or territory made some concession to the obvious reality that a pandemic was raging, there were varying levels of compliance with the federal guidelines when it came to such matters as stay-at-home orders, travel restrictions, quarantining, closing of restaurants and most retail businesses, and so forth. Even so, the vast majority of schools nationwide halted in-person instruction, every state or territory made some move to slow the spread of coronavirus by limiting the size of gatherings, and the majority of Americans—with a few noisy exceptions—seemed to be on the same page when it came to combating the virus and getting life back at least to some semblance of normality. While some voices warned that a few more weeks of caution wouldn't be enough to make a dent in the challenge Americans were facing, the majority—regardless of political affiliation—seemed to agree that playing it safe for a limited time was the wise and patriotic thing to do.

After several weeks of mixed messaging, the federal government introduced masking guidelines on April 3, 2020. The masking issue seemed to hit a nerve with many Americans who saw any attempt to impose masking as an infringement of personal rights and, in many cases, a measure they weren't convinced would make any difference. While the majority of states followed federal recommendations and began—at least, in theory—to require mask-wearing in public, other states, the majority represented primarily by Republicans in state-level office, refused to go further than echoing the federal government's recommendation to mask up in public.

Anti-mask sentiments and protests, coupled with impatience and growing weariness when it came to staying at home or limiting socializing, sprang up in April, especially as it became obvious that the federal guidelines, at least as practiced, weren't as effective as hoped. Covid cases and deaths rose dramatically in most of the country in April, and many Americans clearly viewed orders to mask up or stay home as one more effort to lull—or beat—them into submission. Many simply viewed government recommendations to sit on the sidelines as something more dangerous than a virus that some saw more as a conspiracy than a physical threat.

With rising protests and calls in certain media for an end to government-imposed restrictions on personal liberty, and with a declining economy and fast-rising unemployment unlikely to have any positive effect on Republican election prospects later in the year, the White House issued reopening guidelines to the states on April 16, 2020. But those guidelines, calling for a three-phase lifting of pandemic restrictions, were to be based on state recommendations and left to the states to impose as they saw fit—a recipe that seemed to guarantee failure as far as a speedy national recovery from Covid was concerned.

Within days states began to announce plans for opening up or lifting restrictions, and clearly the federal government had no stomach for leading a unified national effort to halt the spread of a virus that seemed to have rendered the legislative branch nearly useless and the executive branch—led by a president who made himself a laughingstock by making ridiculous "medical" suggestions about how to combat the virus—perhaps *worse* than useless when it came to leading the citizenry through what seemed a dire time in U.S. history. Things took a positive turn, however, when Trump, on May 15, 2020, announced Operation Warp Speed, a concerted effort to develop a coronavirus vaccine in record time. "We'd love to see if we could do it prior to the end of the year," Trump announced. Unfortunately, perhaps defaulting to his more customary manner of "facing down" the virus that had killed nearly 90,000 Americans at the time of his Warp Speed announcement, Trump went on to say, "We think we're going to have a vaccine in the pretty near future. And if we do, we're going to be a big step ahead. And if we don't, we're going to be like so many other cases where you had a problem come in[;] it'll go away. At some point, it'll go away. It may flare up and it may not flare[;] up we'll have to see what happens" (Rev.com, "Donald Trump Speech Transcript on Vaccine Development…").

In the aftermath of the Warp Speed announcement, many states announced plans to ease or lift Covid restrictions in an effort to stimulate economies, lift spirits, and at least begin the "return to normalcy" after two months or more of coronavirus measures. By that point, clearly, the party on each side of the political divide had reassumed its war footing, and Democrats and Republicans were back on familiar ground, facing not the common enemy and threat that had barged into the picture in recent months but the enemy each side had been programmed to disdain for decades—especially recent ones. Once again, the other side was to blame for the predicament the nation was in, whether the perceived predicament centered on the spread of a deadly virus, the violation of personal freedom, or simply the overblown inconvenience of masking up. And once again, participation in the "conversation"—in a presidential election year—was limited to two angry sides with little will to listen to each other and even less will to listen to any other voices struggling to be heard above the clamor of a donkey's and an elephant's "debate."

22

Law and Disorder

Less than two weeks after President Trump announced Operation Warp Speed, America's partisan dysfunction was largely diverted from the pandemic by a sad incident in Minneapolis that led to protests in that city that quickly spread across the nation and beyond.

The killing of George Floyd at the hands of Minneapolis police on Memorial Day—May 25, 2020—horrified many people across the political spectrum. While some commentators and observers suggested or argued that there was more to the incident than the public was aware of, there seemed to be plenty of evidence to confirm that Floyd had been the victim of a horrendous chain of events that could and should have been avoided.

On Memorial Day 2020 police were summoned to a South Minneapolis market when a clerk called 911 and reported that a black male customer had paid for a purchase with a counterfeit $20 bill. According to the *St. Cloud Times*, counterfeit bills had been circulating in the neighborhood prior to Memorial Day (Hertel). A transcript of the 911 call published by CBS Minnesota indicates the clerk went out to the customer's van, which was parked across the street, and asked him to return the items he'd purchased "so he can go home." As the clerk reported to the 911 dispatcher, it was after the customer refused that request that the clerk called 911.

Sadly, as reported by Aymann Ismail at slate.com, a more horrific phone call took place shortly afterward, when one of owners of the market "got a panicked call from a teenage employee" indicating that "[a] police officer had pinned a customer to the ground outside the store, and that man was saying he couldn't breathe. … The man was named George Floyd, and … a cop was kneeling on his neck."

Video evidence—seen by much of the world—bears out that description of events, and the world knows what happened as a result. The police officers at the scene while Floyd was being brutalized were dismissed from the Minneapolis Police Department the day after the incident, and Derek Chauvin, the officer whose knee was on or near Floyd's neck for nine minutes—a third of that time after Floyd stopped being responsive—was charged with third-degree murder.

While the Minneapolis police chief—who made the call to fire the officers—and an owner of the market were quick to express alarm or sadness over the killing of Floyd, thousands of Minneapolitans took to the streets in the aftermath of the incident, expressing outrage over the incident and what many viewed as the systemic racism leading to it. Given the nature of Floyd's treatment at the hands of police and legitimate concerns about the bigger picture surrounding his killing, emotions boiled over to the point where there were heated protests on the streets of Minneapolis, neighboring St. Paul, and, in short order, cities and towns across the country and beyond U.S. borders.

Although the majority of protesters and protests were peaceful, images of apparently opportunistic or mindless violence by protesters—often identified or described as outsiders with an agenda extending beyond mere racial equality or peaceful coexistence—raised alarms among observers who viewed the Floyd killing as an unfortunate event stemming from factors beyond the control of the officers who'd taken Floyd into custody. Some attributed the killing to Floyd's noncompliance with police—which video evidence seemed to attribute far more to fear than willfulness—and pointed out that he had a fairly long criminal record, which included acts of violence. A counterargument was that there seemed to be absolutely nothing in the video evidence that made that relevant. As to arguments that Floyd was "high" at the time of his arrest and killing, while a county coroner's report released afterward confirmed the presence of fentanyl and methamphetamine in Floyd's system, the cause of Floyd's death was ruled not to be the result of drug use but police force meeting the standard of murder.

In the hostile, choose-your-side environment in which the Floyd killing took place—an environment in which political party affiliation seemed the surest predictor of one's beliefs and course of action—many observers who may have been more sympathetic to Floyd and the peaceful protesters were so aghast at the violence perpetrated in the name of George Floyd and calls from protesters to "defund the police" that they lined up staunchly on the other side to defend law and order.

To many on the protesters' side—including the peaceful majority—the "law and order" embraced by those across the social and political divide was based on inequality, injustice, and conditions that had directly contributed to the killing of George Floyd and numerous other victims of institutional brutality before him. While there clearly was plenty of middle ground for fruitful discussion among members on both sides of 2020's Great Divide, the warring sides in Washington, D.C., and on the airwaves didn't seem to have any more interest in building bridges in the aftermath of the Floyd killing that they'd exhibited in recent months or years—and the public largely had followed suit.

Supporters of "law and order"—clearly aligned with the Republican Party—seemed to view the other side as a monolith, making little distinction between peaceful protesters and any violent or riotous "infiltrators" among them. Fostering that view were the actions—or the inaction—of elected Democratic leaders at the municipal or state level who allowed protesters to run rampant, in some cases for months, declaring "autonomous zones," vandalizing private and public property including police precincts, and exercising an ill-gotten "right" to decide where police should or shouldn't be allowed to go. Clearly, it was argued by the other side, such Democratic "leaders" were playing to a political base that had gone out of control, posed a direct danger to fundamental values on which American democracy was based, and weren't in any way worthy of a place at a negotiation table.

Conversely, many Americans who supported peaceful protests seemed to view the violent "infiltrators" on their side as less objectionable than the peaceful majority on the other side. Promises by police forces to address issues of concern were largely viewed as hollow by many on the protesters' side who were distrustful of police or saw police as an enemy, despite evidence suggesting that many others on the same side were hesitant to limit police presence in their areas of residence. As for the other side's view that the protests endangered values on which the country had been based, the protesting side was quick to respond that the values the other side was so bent on protecting were based on institutional racial injustice that had persisted to the present.

Once again, with an election campaign of monumental significance playing out in the background—amid a pandemic that only got worse over the course of months as protesters crowded together and clearly had other things on their minds than "social distancing" and wearing masks—the major parties, and the nation at large, were at an impasse, with little indication that things were likely to get better anytime soon.

23

Flipping (and Flopping) the High Court

Bipolar reactions to incidents involving police violence or force, irrepressible protest and rioting in some cities, and an equally irrepressible pandemic were still the order of the day when Trump found himself with an opportunity to pack the Supreme Court a little further in his favor.

The death of Justice Ruth Bader Ginsburg on September 18, 2020—just seven weeks before Election Day 2020—provided an opportunity for Trump to complete a flip of the Supreme Court from what was generally perceived as a 6–3 disadvantage when he took office to a 6–3 *advantage*, if things went right, before the nation weighed in on his reelection.

The first of Trump's Supreme Court appointees—Justice Gorsuch, nominated by Trump shortly after he was sworn in as president—was the result of Republicans in the U.S. Senate, including Majority Leader McConnell, putting their feet to the brakes and using every means possible to prevent an Obama nominee from ascending to the high court during a presidential election year. Republicans defended their action of thwarting Obama's appointment of Merrick Garland to the high court by arguing that a president in a presidential election year shouldn't make any Supreme Court appointments but should instead allow voters to cast their ballots before a nominee is named. Democrats at that time—perhaps most prominently then–Vice President Joe Biden—contended that a president in the final year of a term had every right to fill a vacancy in the Supreme Court without delay.

But in 2020, with a Republican filling the presidency, Biden, McConnell, and others in their respective camps flipped positions and put forth arguments they would have found loathsome four years earlier, when those same arguments were made by the other side.

Justice Ginsburg had worked through difficult health conditions during much of her tenure on the high court, and several weeks after the recurrence of pancreatic cancer in the spring of 2020, she released a

23. Flipping (and Flopping) the High Court

statement saying, "I am tolerating chemotherapy well and am encouraged by the success of my current treatment. I will continue bi-weekly chemotherapy to keep my cancer at bay, and am able to maintain an active daily routine. Throughout, I have kept up with opinion writing and all other Court work. I have often said I would remain a member of the Court as long as I can do the job full steam. I remain able to do that" (Supreme Court).

It's unclear whether Ginsburg—a giant in American judicial history, regardless of how one views her rulings or opinions—would have been so firmly committed to remaining on the high court had she seen any prospect of being replaced by a nominee with views halfway compatible with her own. Surely, it was clear to her that any nomination put forth by President Trump would be a threat to her legacy and would likely undermine much of what Ginsburg had devoted her career to establishing.

After Ginsburg's death, it was reported that, days earlier, she'd dictated a statement to her granddaughter: "My most fervent wish is that I will not be replaced until a new president is installed" (Totenberg, "Justice Ruth Bader Ginsburg...").

While it's difficult to ascertain from that statement alone whether Ginsburg disagreed in principle with the practice of putting forth a Supreme Court nominee during the waning weeks of a presidential term or was simply fearful of what a third Trump appointee would bring to the high court, there's evidence to suggest her concern lay more in the latter. Almost exactly four years before sharing her dying wish with her granddaughter, Ginsburg, speaking at Georgetown University's School of Law, weighed in on whether hearings to confirm Obama Supreme Court appointee Garland should be delayed until after the 2016 presidential election.

"I hope [it happens] sooner rather than later," Ginsburg said (Hurley). About two months earlier, in a *New York Times* interview, she'd pointed out, "There's nothing in the Constitution that says the president stops being president in his last year" (Liptak).

While the 2016 high court vacancy—effected by the death of Justice Antonin Scalia—occurred much earlier in the year than the 2020 vacancy would occur, simple timing seemed to be much less on Ginsburg's mind than other circumstances. In 2016, when she seemed to oppose a politically motivated delay in restoring the Supreme Court to its full membership of nine, she gave a strong hint of *why* she opposed delay when she spoke about 2016 Republican presidential nominee Donald Trump in her *Times* interview: "I can't imagine what this place would be—I can't imagine what the country would be—with Donald Trump as our president. ... For the country, it could be four years. For the court, it could be—I don't even want to contemplate that" (Liptak).

That seemed to be precisely the sentiment that caused Ginsburg to reconsider her view of how the U.S. Senate should proceed with a Supreme Court nomination during the final year of a presidential term. Ginsburg, of course, wasn't the only one to reconsider the matter, as Biden, McConnell, and numerous other elected "leaders" in Washington flip-flopped right along with her and once again revealed their true colors to a hyperpartisan public that had flipped and flopped right along with *them*. In any case, it probably surprised few observers when the Trump administration and a generally cooperative Republican Senate majority were able to orchestrate the confirmation of Amy Coney Barrett, without the help of a single Democratic vote in support, on October 26, 2020, just one month after Barrett was nominated to the Supreme Court by Trump—and, as many saw it, just in time for Trump to have a solid majority of his own in place on the high court in case things didn't go quite his way on Election Day, by then a mere two weeks away.

The death of Supreme Court Justice Ruth Bader Ginsburg (pictured) in September 2020 gave President Trump an opportunity to tilt the high court in his party's favor during the final months of his presidency. As had become the norm in Washington, the confirmation process went overwhelmingly along party lines (photograph by Michael Jenkins, Library of Congress).

24

The Year 2020 in Review

A Step Back

With the clamor of partisanship often rising to a crescendo amid unprecedented conditions and events throughout 2020, it was hardly surprising that alternative political voices failed to attract or hold much attention in the United States that year.

At the national level, a few high-profile voices threatened, at least momentarily, to break through the partisan yelling and the growing sounds of malfunction from a two-party machine that was making its best case ever for obsolescence. Names that came up at some point as possible third-party or independent 2020 presidential candidates included Jesse Ventura, Mark Cuban, and Michigan's Justin Amash, but all three—no doubt mindful of how the nation was more split than ever into two warring camps—declined to run. A high-profile figure who *did* run for president in 2020 was rapper Kanye West, whose pop-culture standing could be expected to earn him some support but some of whose philosophies and principles seemed hard to figure out. In 2020 West, who'd supported Trump's candidacy in 2016, qualified, as an independent, for the ballot in 12 states.

According to Jane Coaston at vox.com, while nine people other than Trump and Biden were "technically" running for president in 2020, only two—Libertarian nominee Jo Jorgensen and Green Party nominee Howie Hawkins—were on enough state ballots to "hypothetically receive the 270 votes required to win the Electoral College and thus the White House.... [In] comparison to 2016," Coaston continued, "third-party candidates like Jorgenson and Hawkins—and even rapper Kanye West ...—are generating far less interest, and consequently, drawing far fewer votes."

Although third-party and independent candidates for president in 2016 hadn't scored competitively at the national or statewide level, there were instances where their modest vote totals played a pivotal role in determining which of the big-party presidential candidates ended up winning all the electoral votes in particular states.

As Susan Milligan reported in the September 15, 2020, edition of *U.S. News & World Report*, "The excruciating closeness of several individual state results in 2016 meant that third-party candidates—mainly Libertarian Gary Johnson and Green Party candidate Jill Stein—could be blamed (or credited) with handing a win to Trump or Democrat Hillary Clinton, in states where neither got more than 50 percent of the vote." Regarding the situation in 2016, Milligan wrote:

- "In Wisconsin, a state Trump won [by] less than 1 percent of the vote, third-party candidates won 6.4 percent of the ballots"
- "In Michigan, another state won in 2016 [by] less than 1 percent of the votes, 5.8 percent of voters went for a third-party choice"
- "In Pennsylvania, where Trump had a whisper-thin victory in 2016, 4.4 percent of voters went for a third party"
- "[A] state Clinton won—Minnesota—might have gone differently had there been no appealing third party offer. In 2016, a startling 8.6 percent of voters in Minnesota went with third-party candidates. Clinton won the state with 46.9 percent of the votes—less than two percentage points more than Trump"
- In Florida, "4.4 percent of the electorate voted third party in 2016. Trump won the state by 1.2 percent"

As for 2020, with the U.S. electorate more holed up than ever in warring camps, Milligan said voters, "with a heightened sense of the dramatic consequences of giving a vote to someone with no chance of winning the presidency, ... aren't taking the chance" on voting for anyone other than the Democratic or Republican candidate. A look back at 2020 U.S. presidential vote totals from the present moment largely bears that out. While FEC.gov reports that votes nationally for other than the two major-party candidates for president in 2016 totaled 5.7 percent, the Cook Political Report's 2020 National Popular Vote Tracker notes that, despite record participation in the 2020 presidential election, only 1.8 percent of voters cast a ballot for anyone other than the Republican incumbent or the Democratic challenger—less than one-third of the percentage of "other" or alternative voters in 2016.

As far as U.S. Senate races in 2020 were concerned, there were few surprises or strong finishes among candidates other than Democrats or Republicans—especially those facing more than a single opponent. In Alaska, physician Al Gross, touted as an independent, finished second to incumbent U.S. Senator Dan Sullivan. Gross, however, wasn't independent enough not to have accepted the Democratic Party nomination—à la Bernie Sanders—en route to winning 41 percent of the vote compared to 54 percent for Republican Sullivan. In Arkansas, meanwhile, Libertarian

Ricky Harrington, facing a single major-party nominee in Republican incumbent U.S. Senator Tom Cotton, won 33 percent of the vote in his race.

In Georgia, taking only 2.3 percent in his race for a U.S. Senate seat but making a disproportionate impact was podcast host and Libertarian Shane Hazel. Hazel's major-party opponents for the U.S. Senate, Republican incumbent David Perdue and Democrat Jon Ossoff, finished less than 90,000 votes apart out of nearly five million votes cast. Hazel's modest vote total of about 115,000 in the tight one-two race was enough to prevent either major-party nominee from winning 50 percent of the vote, the threshold in Georgia for being certified the winner in a U.S. Senate election. As a result, Hazel, an ex–Marine and ex–Republican, was a bona fide spoiler, forcing one of the two runoffs in Georgia that would determine the balance of power in the U.S. Senate in 2021.

As for the U.S. House of Representatives, while a few alternative candidates—individually or clustered with other alternative candidates—scored well enough to prevent major-party candidates from winning an outright majority of votes in their races, none posed any threat to the two-party system or came anywhere close to claiming victory. One of the few alternative candidates who may have played a spoiler role in the 2020 U.S. House elections was Adam Weeks, who represented the Legal Marijuana Now Party in Minnesota's 2nd congressional district. Although Weeks passed away in September 2020 as a result of a reported accidental fentanyl overdose, his name remained on the ballot, and Weeks won 5.8 percent of the vote, which was far more than the 2.3 percent that separated the winning candidate, Democrat Angie Craig, from runner-up and Republican Tyler Kistner. Following Weeks' death, and weeks before the election, the Minneapolis *Star Tribune* reported that Weeks, in a voicemail recording, had said "Republicans in the Second District approached him two weeks before the filing deadline to run for Congress in the hopes he'd 'pull votes away' from incumbent [Craig] and give an advantage to [Kistner], the Republican-endorsed candidate" (Bierschbach). The *Star Tribune* went on to quote Weeks in the voicemail: "I swear to God … I'm not kidding, this is no joke. … They want me to run as a third-party, liberal candidate" to help defeat Craig, who ended up getting reelected with 48 percent of the vote.

Following a predictable string of losses by alternative candidates in the 2020 U.S. House elections, the only non–Democratic/non–Republican presence in the House of Representatives in the wake of the 2020 elections was in the form of the endgame of Michigan's Justin Amash, by Election Day 2020 a Libertarian for about seven months whose tenure in the House would end three days into 2021.

Little changed nationally with regard to alternative representation in state, county, and municipal offices coming out of the 2020 U.S. elections. No alternative candidate came close to contending for a state executive office. A smattering of true independents and small-party elected officials, however, held on to their partisan offices and were joined in office by a small wave—largely spurred by the growing tumult, division, and hostility in recent years—of major-party officeholders in a few state legislative bodies who decided it was time to leave one major party or the other. Unfortunately, that already-small wave would be significantly reduced by the choice of some newly converted "independents" to caucus with the major party opposing the one they'd decided to leave.

While 2020 saw the reelection of legitimately alternative state legislators such as Massachusetts' Susannah Whipps, Vermont's Laura Sibilia, and Maine's William Pluecker, there seemed to be few additions to their ranks coming out of the 2020 elections. Falling just short of getting reelected in Maine was small-party incumbent Kent Ackley, who'd won his race over a former Republican state representative in 2016 and 2018 but lost by a few dozen votes to that same Republican ex-legislator in 2020. In Wyoming, meanwhile, Ernie Chambers, a true independent and the longest-serving legislator in Nebraska's history, fell victim to consecutive-term-limit requirements and was forced to sit out a state legislative election for the second time in a dozen years.

As for the Green and Libertarian parties, little seemed to go in the former's favor at the state level in the 2020 elections. The Libertarians did a little better, as Bob Johnson reported on the party's website, on November 11, 2020, that Wyoming's Marshall Burt won election to the State House. According to Johnson, Burt was the first candidate "running only on the LP label," to win election to a state legislature in 20 years. Reporting on another of the party's rising stars, however, Johnson wrote, "Bethany Baldes, who lost her race for the Wyoming state house 55th district by 53 votes two years ago, lost by only 32 votes" in 2020.

In the author's home state of Washington, a shared victory by the "big two" in 2020's partisan elections seemed as sure a bet as one could find in uncertain times. As it turned out, the four alternative candidates on the ballot in Washington State's U.S. presidential voting in 2020 combined to take about three percent of the popular vote—the majority of that going to Jo Jorgensen and Libertarian running mate Jeremy Cohen.

With Washington's U.S. Senate seats not on the line in 2020, plenty of attention was turned to races in the state's 10 U.S. House districts—nine of which had some small number of candidates identifying themselves on the primary ballot as other than Republican or Democratic. Yet it came as no surprise when none of those alternative candidates made it to the general election in November.

As for state-level races in Washington, while some form of alternative opposition was on the primary ballot in most executive partisan contests, every such race in the general election came down to a battle between major-party candidates—either Republican vs. Democrat or, in the race for lieutenant governor, Democrat vs. Democrat. The gubernatorial race saw well over a dozen alternative candidates file for the primary, but each one ended up winning less than one percent of the primary vote— the majority *far* less. Also scoring in that neighborhood was Washington State's perennial candidate Goodspaceguy, who ran for the governorship in 2020 as a "Trump Republican" committed to raising the standard of living and opposing Covid-related government shutdowns.

Meanwhile, the Washington State Public Disclosure Commission website and voter.votewa.gov indicated, following the May 15, 2020, candidate filing deadline, that 28 alternative candidates (not counting a few who'd withdrawn early) had filed to participate in Washington State's 125 legislative races in 2020. Exactly half, or 14, had filed as independents or nonpartisans—down from 29 in 2018—and five as Libertarians, down from 12 in 2018. The remaining nine alternative candidates who'd filed for legislative runs in 2020 represented entities or names such as The Alliance, the Education Party, the Socialist Party, the Seattle People's Party, the Unity Restoration Party, the Progressive Party, and the Shortstop Party. Also listed as legislative candidates were several "Independent Republicans" and one "Classical Democrat."

While there were a few familiar names on the list of alternative candidates vying for legislative posts in Washington's 2020 primary, the majority of names represented relative newcomers to elective politics ... most at a serious disadvantage, right out of the gate, in terms of funding—or of simply being heard—compared to their Democratic and Republican counterparts. As far as independents/nonpartisans were concerned, 2018 had offered at least a glimmer of hope in the form of Washington Independents, the organization that financially got behind a few candidates— particularly Ann Diamond, who made a good run at becoming the first independent since 1889 to get elected to the state legislature. But in 2020 there was no such source of support for independents/nonpartisans aiming for the Washington Legislature, as Washington Independents had suspended operations in May 2019. As for Diamond, after declaring early as an independent candidate for the legislature in 2020, she suspended her campaign in March 2020 amid Covid concerns. Explaining in May why she ultimately decided against running in 2020, Diamond wrote, in an email reported in the May 20, 2020, *Methow Valley News*, "Hyper-polarization makes an Independent run more difficult. ... And then there is COVID-19. No knocking on doors, no meet-and-greets—both of which limit my ability to reach people who might not otherwise consider me. ... Social media will not sustain an independent campaign."

Washington Independents cofounder Chris Vance goes a step further, saying by phone, "The idea of electing independents ... in my mind, if it isn't dead, it should be dead. It just doesn't work."

Of the 28 alternative candidates on the primary ballot for state legislative races in Washington in 2020, nine advanced to the general election—none having to overcome the challenge of facing opposition from both major parties on the primary ballot. All nine, of course, appeared to have virtually no chance of victory in the general election; and as events played out in November, all nine were buried in general-election landslides that nearly every serious observer saw coming.

25

A Sad Ending

Things didn't quite go Trump's way in the election of 2020, though the outgoing president, both before ballots were all counted and for weeks afterward, did just about everything humanly possible to deny it. But while Trump did democracy no favors by assuming the demeanor of a pouting dictator, refusing to face the music, and burdening the legal system with dubious lawsuits seeking to overturn election results, he found no allies on the high court, even among those he'd nominated. Half the country, it seemed—or even a little more, as election results suggested—seemed delighted that, following an exceedingly tough year and an election that appeared to confirm the obvious as far as Donald Trump was concerned, change was just around the corner.

Unfortunately, in at least one important regard, that perception was as far removed from reality as Trump's view of the election result appeared to be. Despite ample opportunity to own up to the failings of a broken duopoly that had never been more obvious than in 2020, American voters, once more, had looked the other way and given another vote of confidence to an off-the-rails two-party system that didn't seem to have any chance of ever getting back on track.

The aftermath of the 2020 U.S. presidential election brought back memories of what had transpired in 2000—as some observers had suggested it would. In 2020, as in 2000, states were required to certify their presidential election results by mid-December. In 2000, with a legal ping-pong match ensuing in Florida in the aftermath of the presidential vote on November 7—blamed by some on the presence on the ballot of Green Party nominee Ralph Nader and Reform Party nominee Pat Buchanan—states were required to certify their vote count for each presidential candidate by December 12. On that same day—December 12, 2000—the U.S. Supreme Court effectively put a stop to Democratic nominee Al Gore's efforts to get clarity regarding a statewide vote count that seemed less than clear. Florida quickly certified its vote count, which had Republican candidate George W. Bush slightly ahead, and Gore—who'd won a preliminary vote count after the election—quickly conceded an election that many people thought had been stolen from him.

"I say to President-elect Bush that what remains of partisan rancor must now be put aside, and may God bless his stewardship of this country," Gore said in his concession speech. He continued, "Now the U.S. Supreme Court has spoken. Let there be no doubt, while I strongly disagree with the court's decision, I accept it. I accept the finality of this outcome which will be ratified in the Electoral College. And tonight, for the sake of our unity of the people and the strength of our democracy, I offer my concession. ... President-elect Bush inherits a nation whose citizens will be ready to assist him in the conduct of his large responsibilities. I personally will be at his disposal, and I call on all Americans—I particularly urge all who stood with us—to work behind our next president" (*The Washington Post*).

The words and actions of President Trump in the aftermath of the 2020 U.S. presidential election couldn't have been in starker contrast to the words and actions of Gore in late 2000.

Though occupying a very different place on the political spectrum than fellow 2000 third-party presidential candidate Ralph Nader, Reform Party candidate Pat Buchanan (pictured here), like Nader, is widely believed to have played a key role in denying Democratic Party nominee Al Gore the presidency in 2000. In Buchanan's case, it's believed that the "butterfly" ballots used in Palm Beach County, Florida, confused voters and resulted in many votes going to Buchanan that were intended for Gore. Since George W. Bush's eventual margin of victory in Florida—the state that decided the election—was only about 500 votes, a popular theory has held that Buchanan, despite winning only 0.3 percent of Florida's vote, inadvertently helped Bush win the presidency (photograph by Kyle Cassidy, CC BY-SA 3.0: https://creativecommons.org/licenses/by-sa/3.0/deed.en).

In July 2020 Trump gave a hint of things to come in a rambling interview with Chris Wallace of Fox News. Asked by Wallace whether, in the event he was declared the loser in November, he'd adhere to the American tradition of a "peaceful transition of power [dictating] that no matter how hard fought a campaign is, that at the end of the campaign ... the loser concedes to the winner," Trump replied, "I will tell you at that time. I'll keep you in suspense" (Fox News, "Transcript...").

While the 2020 presidential election itself kept Americans in suspense for a few days as vote-counting was getting completed in a few key states with close races, there wasn't much suspense immediately before, during, or following the election with regard to where Trump stood on the issue of conceding. Heading into the election, Trump, energized by the large, largely unmasked, and fervid crowds he was drawing at rallies in those same key states, seemed unable to grasp—or at least acknowledge— the prospect of losing to Democratic nominee Biden, who did most of his campaigning from home. Yet, while kindling the fire as he preached to his choir, Trump seemingly failed to recognize, as Milligan wrote in an October 28, 2020, report at usnews.com, that "voters in battleground states do not approve of Trump's largely maskless, packed rallies." Citing a Priorities USA poll of 4,800 likely voters in six key battleground states released that same day—October 28, 2020—at Priorities.org, Milligan continued, "[V]oters in those states [Arizona, Florida, Michigan, North Carolina, Pennsylvania, and Wisconsin] also overwhelmingly blame the president for the second wave of coronavirus infections across the country."

Milligan would have been more accurate had she stated that a majority of the voters surveyed who *agreed* that it was "accurate to say the country is now experiencing another wave of coronavirus infections" (Priorities.org)—those in such agreement comprising 56 to 68 percent of voters surveyed in the key states—blamed Trump for the new wave. There was no misinterpretation, however, when Milligan added, "The survey found that majorities of voters [in the key battleground states] saw Trump 'much less' or 'somewhat less' favorably because of his practice of holding in-person rallies, with people standing shoulder to shoulder and not wearing masks" (Milligan, "Trump's Rallies...").

It's unclear whether such sentiments played heavily into Trump's losing four of those six key battleground states—all of which he'd won when lightning struck in 2016. Apparently intent on doing everything possible to coax lightning into striking again, Republicans proceeded to launch numerous legal challenges in Arizona, Michigan, Pennsylvania, and Wisconsin. For his part, Trump seemed intent, along with his backers or enablers, on viewing impending deadlines for vote count certifications or Electoral College tabulations in a far different manner than Gore had done in 2000. While Gore was committed to avoiding any action that would disrupt the electoral process beyond established deadlines relating to the peaceful transfer of power, Trump and other Republicans seemed committed to *causing* disruption and preventing solutions from materializing in time to facilitate the peaceful transfer of power from the incumbent to the president-elect. Clearly, the intent was to maintain a state of disarray and keep up the agitation as long as it took until the undesirable election results were overturned.

Trump, who seemed incapable of conceding almost anything—from personal imperfection to his own mortal status—certainly wasn't of any mind to concede the election. Much to the contrary, as reported by Jacob Shamsian and Sonam Sheth in *Business Insider* on January 5, 2021, rather than owning up to "losing the 2020 election to a man he spent months hammering as corrupt, doddering, and mentally deficient, President Donald Trump went on the offense, spreading lies and conspiracy theories about a 'rigged' election marred by 'major fraud' from Democrats."

Nowhere was that "offense" more on display than in Georgia, another key battleground state Trump had won in 2016 and one whose 16 electoral votes he was counting on putting into his win column in 2020 in pursuit of the magic number of 270 that would win him another term as president. From Trump's perspective, things likely seemed well in Georgia on Election Day 2020, as the in-person, Election Day vote count put him solidly ahead of Biden. But the next day, November 4, with the nation's eyes on the battleground races, Los Angeles' ABC7.com reported that "the vote margin had tightened, with Trump now leading by 28,827 votes." Yet "[a]pproximately 91,000 ballots were still outstanding as of 10:15 p.m. ET [Nov. 4]. ... The outstanding ballots included mailed ballots from population-dense counties in the Atlanta metro region that lean Democratic"—a simple fact Trump seemed unable or unwilling to grasp or concede.

Georgia's initial machine counting of the ballots, completed within a few days, declared Biden the winner by a narrow margin—too narrow to confirm a winner without a recount. After the state's presidential votes were audited or recounted by hand, Georgia Secretary of State Brad Raffensperger, a Republican, certified a Biden victory over Trump by a similar narrow margin to what the initial machine count had determined—about 13,000 votes, or 0.25 percent of the total. By Georgia law, Trump, since his vote total was less than 0.5 percent short of Biden's, was entitled to another recount.

After the second recount, Georgia recertified the Biden victory, which in more normal times may have put the issue to rest, resulted in a concession speech, and paved the way for the sort of peaceful transition Gore had put above his own personal interests in 2000.

History will show, however, that Georgia's final certification of the Biden victory on December 6, 2020, only seemed to push the button—or

25. A Sad Ending

motivate a peeved sitting president to push the button—that would put the country into a month-long spin that would culminate in just about the worst way imaginable on January 6, 2021. That date—exactly one month after Georgia's final certification of the Biden victory and two weeks before the president-elect's January 20, 2021, presumed assumption of power— was the scheduled day for a joint session of Congress to count the states' electoral votes and declare Biden's victory. According to precedent, the joint session and declaration were mere formalities to rubber-stamp what the nation had known, in many earlier presidential elections, since Election Day ... and always—even amid the unprecedented uncertainties of 2000—long before the January joint session designated for the final counting of electoral votes.

But what should have been a period of tranquility between Georgia's final certification of Biden's narrow victory in the state and Congress' tally of electoral votes turned out to be anything *but* that, as Trump, his enablers, and many of his supporters wouldn't have had it any other way.

Legal challenges from the Trump camp hardly let up during that theoretical period of calm. Challenges in numerous courts concerning electoral irregularities or accusations that couldn't be proven seemed to bespeak utter narcissism on the one hand and, on the other, the utter desperation people in one extreme political camp felt regarding the prospect of turning over the presidency it had lost to another extreme political camp. And while the desperate efforts of Trump and his allies were sprinkled across several states where they hoped for a miracle or two, by early January Georgia was back on center stage.

On January 3, 2021, a variety of news outlets, led by *The Washington Post*, reported on a telephone call Trump made the previous day to Brad Raffensperger, who apparently wasn't eager to take the call. According to Kristen Holmes, Jim Acosta, and Kaitlan Collins at CNN.com on January 4, 2021, sources indicated that it took 18 attempts on the Trump camp's part before Raffensperger talked to Trump. The January 2 call was recorded and seemed to reveal in undeniable fashion that Trump was willing to go to almost any length to win an election he'd clearly lost. Perhaps figuring the conversation would never reach ears other than his own, Raffensperger's, and a small number of their associates', Trump, after getting nowhere with his stories of dead voters, shredded ballots, mysterious ballot drops, removal of voting machines, and forged signatures, cut right to the chase when, comparing Raffensperger to people directly responsible for the alleged fraud that had cost him a victory in Georgia, he told the Republican secretary of state who'd certified the Biden victory, "It's, it's more illegal for you than it is for them, because you know what they did and you're not reporting it. That's just, you know, that's a criminal, that's a criminal offense. And, you know, you can't let that happen. ... And you are letting it happen. ... All I want to do is this: I just want to find 11,780 votes"—enough to "earn" victory for Trump (Darnell, transcript, 12–13).

The day after Trump's call to Raffensperger was reported—with plenty of comparisons to Trump's July 2020 call to Ukrainian president Zelenskiy—Trump held a large, mostly maskless, rally in Dalton, Georgia, for incumbent Republican U.S. senators David Perdue and Kelly Loeffler, both in heated runoff election campaigns to be decided on January 5. At the rally, overheated attendees wasted little time breaking into a chant of "Fight for Trump!" That same day, Biden didn't seem to draw nearly the same level of reaction at a small rally in Atlanta in support of Democratic senatorial candidates Jon Ossoff and Raphael Warnock.

Yet it was the Democratic challengers who'd win both runoffs by a slim margin. Widely credited with reversing the advantages of incumbency for the Republicans, tilting both runoffs in favor of the Democrats, and handing the balance of power in the U.S. Senate to the Democratic Party were Trump's incessant accusations of rigged elections; Trump's belittling of Georgia's Republican governor and secretary of state, who wouldn't bend to the president's whims, threats, or demands; and Perdue's and Loeffler's association with Trump and their decision to hitch their campaigns to a Trump wagon that seemed to have a wheel or two loose. Despite the fervor still on display at a Trump rally or revival, there appeared to be at least a small, and perhaps growing, number of people committed to the Republican Party who didn't see much hope for the future in Trump's seemingly desperate attempts to stay at the helm of a party he appeared entirely capable of driving into the ground.

Two days after his rally in Dalton, Trump addressed his followers at a Washington, D.C., rally that been in the making for weeks. The January 6, 2021, rally was a last-ditch effort timed to take place just before Congress' official electoral vote tally to confirm Biden would take office on January 20; and Trump, without a prayer of stalling Biden's swearing-in, nonetheless used his pulpit to reiterate his claim of a stolen election and his determination that "We will never give up; we will never concede." He went on to elicit more chants of "Fight for Trump!"; to direct the crowd's attention toward Vice President Mike Pence, who Trump said he hoped "is going to do the right thing" by trying to upend Congress' certification of the Biden victory; and called on his congregation to march with him "over to the Capitol building to peacefully and patriotically make your voices heard" (Rev.com, "Donald Trump Speech 'Save America' Rally Transcript...").

What actually transpired after the rally was, of course, a sad episode in American history, and January 6, 2021, will surely be remembered as a day of infamy that would have been much worse if not for heroic actions by members of the U.S. Capitol Police force—actions in total contrast to those of a president who, in the waning days of his presidency, would be banned from his social media accounts, impeached for a second time, and abandoned by well over a dozen members of his administration and national security officials. Yet Trump—who largely seemed to spend the endgame of his administration hiding in a closet—refused to cede power as numerous observers weighed in on whether he'd try to pardon himself before slipping away to his personal Neverland at Mar-a-Lago in Florida and attempting another run at the presidency, backed by his millions of supporters, in 2024.

Epilogue:
Let It Go

Some saw the obvious crack in the Republican Party—illustrated by the willingness of some elected Republicans to declare Biden the president-elect and to blame the Capitol insurrection on Trump—as a hopeful sign; and, at least for a very brief time, that seemed entirely reasonable. Unfortunately, the myth was dispelled in short order when comments made by some key Republicans on or shortly after January 6, 2021, were soon reworded in the light of obvious political considerations even when Trump was relatively voiceless and out of sight in Florida. Seven Republican senators, meanwhile, voted to convict Trump during the ex-president's second Senate trial on February 13, 2021, bringing the vote count to 57–43—but that was 10 votes shy of what was needed for a guilty verdict ... and it seemed certain that stalwart "Trumpublicans," hoping to do nothing to rattle their shaky leader-in-exile, would seek ways to make those seven Republican senators who voted for conviction pay for their impudence. As for the House of Representatives, the Republican reaction was strong and seemingly devoid of any nonpolitical principle when Wyoming's Liz Cheney publicly held to her view that the presidency hadn't been stolen from Trump and that the Republican Party—which Cheney had no intention of leaving—needed to untangle itself from the ex-president.

As far as the Democratic Party in the early Biden era is concerned, it seems to have signaled to its millions of adherents that it considers many key issues closed for debate as the party focuses on pushing forward an agenda, often seen as radical, while the party has control of the White House and the upper hand in both houses of Congress.

One result of that thinking, of course, is more of the party-line voting and standstills that have impeded real progress in American political and social life for so long. While 2021 saw a few developments that many Americans across the board viewed as positive—a guilty verdict in the

Derek Chauvin trial, renewed commitment to environmental issues, and a reopening of much of the country due to an effective rollout of Covid-19 vaccines—there seem to be no clear signs suggesting real steps have been taken to begin closing the political divide.

Despite serious concerns over the course of 2021 about Biden administration decisions and actions in Afghanistan and along the U.S. southern border, many observers seem to view the transition to a president who at least seems familiar with the "rules" of Washington, coupled with apparent movement—albeit inconsistent—toward national recovery from the pandemic, as a sign that life will, at least fairly soon, return to normal for Americans. It shouldn't be overlooked, however, that any picture of "normal" that materializes post-pandemic will be dominated at every level of government and society by two unduly powerful political entities that disagree on just about everything other than their "right" to share power and, in effect, exclude all other voices from having a say in decisions that impact all Americans. Whatever becomes of the Republican Party in coming years, whether post–Trump or *with* Trump, every reasonable indication is that the party will keep its seat on the seesaw that represents American politics—and when a majority of American voters get tired of seeing a Democratic majority up on the high seat, the Republican Party will get its turn on top again.

Many everyday Americans, partisan journalists, and politicians readily admit that the American two-party system—evident from the early years of nationhood but never more dysfunctional than it is now—is in need of repair. It seems more convincing to argue, though, that a highly undemocratic, duopolistic system that has stifled good reason and divided a beacon of democracy into two warring camps shouldn't or *can't* be repaired. Clearly, the American two-party system has been off the rails for some time; and, given events of recent times, the most merciful and sensible path for Americans to follow, it seems evident, is to get out of our bubbles, let the two-party system go straight off a cliff, and adopt a new outlook and standard based on true principles of democracy.

Bibliography

ABC7.com (WABC Los Angeles). "2020 Georgia Election Results by County, GA Electoral College Votes" (4 November 2020), https://abc7.com/2020-georgia-election-results-ga-electoral-votes-presidential-race-trump-biden/7560678/. Last accessed 6 June 2021.

Abramowitz, Alan I., and Steven Webster. "The Only Thing We Have to Fear Is the Other Party." University of Virginia Center for Politics (4 June 2015), http://www.centerforpolitics.org/crystalball/articles/the-only-thing-we-have-to-fear-is-the-other-party/. Last accessed 25 August 2019.

Acosta, Allen. In-person interview. 18 November 2019.

Amash, Justin. "Our Politics Is in a Partisan Death Spiral. That's Why I'm Leaving the GOP." *Washington Post* (4 July 2019), https://www.washingtonpost.com/opinions/justin-amash-our-politics-is-in-a-partisan-death-spiral-thats-why-im-leaving-the-gop/2019/07/04/afbe0480-9e3d-11e9-b27f-ed2942f73d70_story.html. Last accessed 25 April 2021.

American Constitution Society. "Stark Contrasts Between the Mueller Report and Attorney General Barr's Summary," https://www.acslaw.org/projects/the-presidential-investigation-education-project/other-resources/stark-contrasts-between-the-mueller-report-and-attorney-general-barrs-summary/. Last accessed 23 May 2021.

Applewhite, Jarratt. Campaign website for Applewhite's 2018 independent run for the New Mexico state legislature, https://applewhite4nm.com/. Last accessed 14 August 2019.

Arnold, Sky. "Third Party Ballot Rules in Tennessee." WZTV Fox 17 Nashville report (10 August 2016), https://fox17.com/news/local/third-party-ballot-rules-in-tennessee. Last accessed 11 September 2021.

Associated Press. "Text of Letter Announcing AG Barr Received Mueller Report" (22 March 2019), https://apnews.com/article/719fb6dc299f43339ead6af26626459d. Last accessed 23 May 2021.

Axios. "Read Christine Blasey Ford's Initial Letter to Diane Feinstein" (23 September 2018), axios.com/brett-kavanaugh-christine-blasey-ford-feinstein-letter-9337f417-1078-4334-8a81-c2b4fc051f99.html. Last accessed 3 September 2019.

Ballotpedia. Information pertaining to large city "nonpartisan" municipal elections and mayoral candidates in 2016 and 2017, https://ballotpedia.org/Partisanship_in_United_States_mayoral_elections_(2016); https://ballotpedia.org/Partisanship_in_United_States_municipal_elections,_2017; https://ballotpedia.org/Largest_cities_in_the_United_States_by_population. Last accessed 25 August 2021.

Balz, Dan. "George H.W. Bush Was the Accidental Catalyst That Built the New Republican Party." *Washington Post* (2 December 2018), https://www.washingtonpost.com/politics/george-hw-bush-was-the-accidental-catalyst-that-built-the-new-republican-party/2018/12/02/2a4adaf8-f659-11e8-8c9a-860ce2a8148f_story.html. Last accessed 25 April 2021.

Baumgarten, April. "Al Jaeger Won't Run for Re-election After 25-year Career as North Dakota Secretary of State." *West Fargo Pioneer* (8 April 2018), https://www.westfargo

pioneer.com/news/4428749-al-jaeger-wont-run-re-election-after-25-year-career-north. Last accessed 27 August 2019.

BBC. "Justin Amash: U.S. Congressman Quits the Republican Party" (4 July 2019), https://www.bbc.com/news/world-us-canada-48794498. Includes Donald Trump's "total Loser!" tweet in response to Amash's decision. Last accessed 8 April 2021.

Beavers, Olivia. "Schiff: Trump's Ukraine Call 'a Classic Mafia-like Shakedown.'" *The Hill* (25 September 2019), https://thehill.com/policy/national-security/463008-schiff-trumps-ukraine-call-a-classic-mafia-like-shakedown. Last accessed 25 April 2021.

Becker, Jo, Matt Apuzzo, and Adam Goldman. "Trump Team Met with Lawyer Linked to Kremlin During Campaign." *New York Times* (8 July 2017), https://www.nytimes.com/2017/07/08/us/politics/trump-russia-kushner-manafort.html. Last accessed 25 April 2021.

Beekman, Daniel, and Jim Brunner. "Jenny Durkan, Former U.S. Attorney, to Run for Seattle Mayor." *Seattle Times* (11 May 2017), https://www.seattletimes.com/seattle-news/politics/jenny-durkan-former-us-attorney-to-run-for-seattle-mayor/. Last accessed 9 October 2019.

Benen, Steve. "The Immigration Deal Trump Should've Taken, but Didn't." MSNBC (12 December 2018), https://www.msnbc.com/rachel-maddow-show/the-immigration-deal-trump-shouldve-taken-didnt-msna1174156. Last accessed 22 May 2016.

Bergengruen, Vera, Alana Abramson, and Abby Vesoulis. "Ex-Ukraine Ambassador Marie Yovanovitch Testifies to 'Intimidating' Trump Tweet in Impeachment Hearing: The Biggest Moments." *Time* (15 November 2019; updated 19 November 2019), https://time.com/5729145/impeachment-hearing-live/. Last accessed 4 May 2021.

Berman, Russell. "The Real Reasons Why the Government Shut Down." *The Atlantic* (20 January 2018), https://www.theatlantic.com/politics/archive/2018/01/the-real-reasons-why-the-government-shut-down/551027/. Last accessed 22 May 2021.

Bierschbach, Briana. "Pot Party Candidate Said GOP Recruited Him to 'Pull Votes' from Minnesota Democrat." Minneapolis *Star Tribune* (28 October 2020), https://www.startribune.com/gop-recruited-pot-party-candidate-to-pull-votes-from-dfler-he-said/572888651/. Last accessed 16 May 2021.

Bishop, Greg. "Election Reform Group: Illinois Unique in Voters Publicly Declaring Party Affiliation at Polling Place on Primary Day." Macomb News Now (March 2018), macombnewsnow.com/macomb-news/353271. Last accessed 12 August 2019.

Blitzer, Ron. "McCarthy Dismisses Amash Impeachment Comments: 'He Wants to Have Attention.'" Fox News (19 May 2019), https://www.foxnews.com/politics/mccarthy-dismisses-amash-impeachment-comments-he-wants-to-have-attention. Last accessed 25 April 2021.

Bohrer, Becky. "Alaska's Independent Governor Suspends Reelection Bid Days After Lieutenant Governor Quit." Associated Press article in the *Chicago Tribune* (19 October 2018), https://www.chicagotribune.com/nation-world/ct-alaska-governor-suspends-re-election-bid-20181019-story.html. Last accessed 11 August 2019.

Brawner, Steve. "The Legislator Without a Party Label." Independent Arkansas (28 September 2018), http://independentarkansas.com/mark-mcelroy/. Last accessed 23 August 2019.

Brennan Center for Justice. "Who Draws the Maps? Legislative and Congressional Redistricting" (30 January 2019), https://www.brennancenter.org/analysis/who-draws-maps-states-redrawing-congressional-and-state-district-lines. Last accessed 24 September 2019.

Breuninger, Kevin. "Critics Warn Ex-GOP Rep. Justin Amash: A Third-party White House Bid Helps Trump in 2020." CNBC (29 April 2020), https://www.cnbc.com/2020/04/29/critics-to-justin-amash-third-party-white-house-bid-helps-trump-in-2020.html. Last accessed 9 June 2021.

———. "New Jersey Rep. Jeff Van Drew, Anti-impeachment Democrat, Flips to Republican Party." CNBC (19 December 2019), https://www.cnbc.com/2019/12/19/jeff-van-drew-anti-impeachment-democrat-flips-to-republican-party.html. Last accessed 7 May 2021.

Brown, Emma. "California Professor, Writer of Confidential Brett Kavanaugh Letter,

Speaks Out About Her Allegation of Sexual Assault." *Washington Post* (16 September 2018), https://www.washingtonpost.com/investigations/california-professor-writer-of-confidential-brett-kavanaugh-letter-speaks-out-about-her-allegation-of-sexual-assault/2018/09/16/46982194-b846-11e8-94eb-3bd52dfe917b_story.html. Last accessed 2 September 2019.

Brunner, Jim. "Poll: There's a Path for Independent Legislative Candidates in Washington, If They Can Get Past Primary." *Seattle Times* (3 May 2018), www.seattletimes.com/seattle-news/politics/poll-theres-a-path-for-independent-legislative-candidates-in-washington-if-they-can-get-past-primary/. Last accessed 15 June 2021.

Bryan, Bob. "The Government Shutdown Is Now the Longest on Record and the Fight Between Trump and Democrats Is Only Getting Uglier. Here's Everything You Missed." *Business Insider* (21 January 2019), https://www.businessinsider.com/government-shutdown-timeline-deadline-trump-democrats-2019-1. Last accessed 22 May 2021.

Burke, Melissa Nann. "Trump Calls Amash Loser, Questions Loyalties After Impeachment Tweet." *The Detroit News* (19 May 2019), https://www.detroitnews.com/story/news/local/michigan/2019/05/19/trump-amash-impeachment-tweets/3731883002. Last accessed 8 June 2021.

C-SPAN. "Representative Schiff Says He's Reserving Judgment on Impeachment of President Trump" (3 December 2019), https://www.c-span.org/video/?c4834964/representative-schiff-reserving-judgment-impeachment-president-trump. Last accessed 5 September 2021.

_____. Video and Transcript of Proceedings during the House Intelligence Committee's Impeachment Inquiry (26 September 2019), https://www.c-span.org/video/?464509-1/acting-director-national-intelligence-maguire-testifies-whistleblower-complaint. Last accessed 28 April 2021.

_____. Video and Transcript of Testimony by Marie Yovanovitch during the House Impeachment Inquiry (15 November 2019), https://www.c-span.org/video/?466135-1/impeachment-hearing-ukraine-ambassador-marie-yovanovitch. Last accessed 4 May 2021.

Canon, Gabrielle, Ben Jacobs, and Erin Durkin. "Congress Passes Deal to Avert Shutdown as Trump Passes Emergency Declaration to Build Wall—As It Happened." *The Guardian* (14 February 2021), https://www.theguardian.com/us-news/live/2019/feb/14/trump-news-live-government-shutdown-deal-latest-updates-democrats-republicans-us-politics-today. Last accessed 22 May 2021.

CBS Minnesota. "City of Minneapolis Releases Transcript of 911 Call on George Floyd" (28 May 2020), https://minnesota.cbslocal.com/2020/05/28/city-of-minneapolis-releases-transcript-of-911-call-on-george-floyd-released/. Last accessed 4 July 2021.

CBS News. "A Timeline Surrounding Donald Trump, Jr.'s Meeting with the Russian Lawyer" (11 July 2017). https://www.cbsnews.com/news/a-timeline-surrounding-donald-trump-jr-s-meeting-with-the-russian-lawyer/. Last accessed 8 June 2021.

Choi, David. "Lt. Col. Vindman's Former Army Commander Pushes Back on Trump's Decision to Dismiss Officer from National Security Council Staff." *Military Times* (10 February 2020), https://www.militarytimes.com/news/your-army/2020/02/10/lt-col-vindmans-former-army-commander-pushes-back-on-trumps-decision-to-dismiss-officer-from-national-security-council-staff/. Last accessed 8 May 2021.

CNN. "Read Trump's Phone Conversation with Volodymyr Zelensky." Transcript of the call (26 September 2019), https://www.cnn.com/2019/09/25/politics/donald-trump-ukraine-transcript-call. Last accessed 6 September 2021.

_____. "Read: Whistleblower Complaint Regarding President Trump and Ukraine." The whistleblower's letter to Sen. Burr and Rep. Schiff (published 26 September 2019), https://www.cnn.com/2019/09/26/politics/read-whistleblower-complaint-trump-ukraine/index.html. Last accessed 29 April 2021.

_____. "State of the Union 2019: Read the Full Transcript" (6 February 2019), https://www.cnn.com/2019/02/05/politics/donald-trump-state-of-the-union-2019-transcript. Last accessed 22 May 2021.

Coaston, Jane. "Why Third Parties Likely Won't Be a Big Deal This Year." Vox (3 November

2020), https://www.vox.com/2020/11/3/21535058/third-party-vote-2020-trump. Last accessed 5 July 2021.

Collin, Dorothy. "It's Reagan vs. Congress in Standoff." *Chicago Tribune* (2 August 1987), https://www.chicagotribune.com/news/ct-xpm-1987-08-02-8702260219-story.html. Last accessed 25 August 2019.

Collins, Sean, and Alex Ward. "The Timeline of Trump's Decision to Withhold Aid to Ukraine Is Increasingly Suspicious." Vox report (27 September 2019), https://www.vox.com/policy-and-politics/2019/9/24/20881505/donald-trump-withhold-aid-ukraine-timeline-whistleblower. Last accessed 25 April 2021.

Commission on Presidential Debates. Debates.org. Last accessed 5 September 2021.

Cook Political Report. 2020 National Popular Vote Tracker, https://cookpolitical.com/2020-national-popular-vote-tracker. Last accessed 16 May 2021.

Coppins, McKay. "The Man Who Broke Politics." *The Atlantic* (November 2018). https://www.theatlantic.com/magazine/archive/2018/11/newt-gingrich-says-youre-welcome/570832/. Last accessed 25 August 2019.

Corn, David, and Tim Murphy. "Newt in His Own Words: 33 Years of Bomb-Throwing." *Mother Jones* (7 April 2011), https://www.motherjones.com/politics/2011/04/newt-gingrich-greatest-rhetorical-hits/. Last accessed 25 August 2019.

———. "A Very Long List of Dumb and Awful Things Newt Gingrich Has Said and Done." *Mother Jones* (15 November 2016), https://www.motherjones.com/politics/2016/11/very-long-list-dumb-and-awful-things-newt-gingrich-has-said-and-done/. Last accessed 24 September 2019.

Cottier, Cody. "Roscoe Defies History to Win as Independent." *Jackson Hole Daily* (7 November 2018), https://www.jhnewsandguide.com/jackson_hole_daily/local/article_01f5ce40-ebff-5227-99c1-a0ffd0d1891f.html. Last accessed 21 August 2019.

Cullison, Alan, Rebecca Ballhaus, and Dustin Volz. "Trump Repeatedly Pressed Ukraine President to Investigate Biden's Son." *Wall Street Journal* (21 September 2019), https://www.wsj.com/articles/trump-defends-conversation-with-ukraine-leader-11568993176. Last accessed 26 April 2021.

Cummings, William. "Read the Full Text of Brett Kavanaugh's Opening Remarks to the Judiciary Committee." *USA Today* (27 September 2018), https://www.usatoday.com/story/news/politics/onpolitics/2018/09/27/brett-kavanaugh-testimony-opening-statement/1440896002/. Last accessed 3 September 2019.

Darnell, Tim. "READ: Transcript of Trump's Phone Call to Georgia Secretary of State." *Atlanta Journal-Constitution* (4 January 2021), https://www.ajc.com/news/nation-world/read-transcript-of-trumps-phone-call-to-georgia-secretary-of-state/IRLR3EXOMVFJFJIVYYUQ2C6QTM/. Last accessed 6 June 2021.

DC Statehood Green Party. http://dcstatehoodgreen.org/. Last accessed 21 August 2019.

Diamond, Ann. Phone interview. 6 November 2019.

Diamond, Jeremy. "Donald Trump, Jr., Releases Email Chain on His Russian Meeting." CNN (11 July 2017), https://www.cnn.com/2017/07/11/politics/trump-jr-russia-lawyer-emails/index.html. Last accessed 25 May 2021.

Doherty, Brian. "Libertarian Bethany Baldes Gets Within 60 Votes of Victory in Wyoming State House Race Against Incumbent GOP Minority Leader." Reason.com (7 November 2018), https://reason.com/2018/11/07/libertarian-bethany-baldes-in-wyoming-st/. Last accessed 21 August 2019.

Dragu, Paul. "The Retired Cowboy vs. the Promising Newcomer: Who Are Sivertsen & Bachmeier?" *Havre* [Montana] *Herald* (17 July 2018), https://www.havreherald.com/2018/07/17/the-retired-cowboy-vs-the-promising-newcomer-personal-looks-into-sivertsen-bachmeier/. Last accessed 7 November 2020.

Drutman, Lee. *Breaking the Two-Party Doom Loop: The Case for Multiparty Democracy in America*. New York: Oxford University Press, 2020.

———. "Let a Thousand Parties Bloom." Foreignpolicy.com (19 October 2019), https://foreignpolicy.com/2019/10/19/us-democracy-two-party-system-replace-multiparty-republican-democrat/. Last accessed 9 June 2021.

Duffy, Michael. "George H.W. Bush Accomplished Much More as President Than He Ever

Got Credit For." *Time* (1 December 2018), https://time.com/4754901/president-george-hw-bush-accomplishments/. Last accessed 5 September 2021.

Dugyala, Rishika. "Trump Singles Out Mitt Romney in Post-acquittal Twitter-Rant." Politico (9 February 2020), https://www.politico.com/news/2020/02/09/trump-singles-romney-twitter-rant-112893. Last accessed 4 July 2021.

Dulio, David A., and James A. Thurber. "America's Two-Party System: Friend or Foe?" *Administrative Law Review*, Vol. 52, No. 2 (Spring 2000), 769–792. Last accessed 9 June 2021.

Dwyer, Dustin. "Who Is Justin Amash and Why Is He Willing to Go Against His Own Party?" NPR article (15 June 2019), https://www.npr.org/2019/06/15/732511971/who-is-justin-amash-and-why-is-he-willing-to-go-against-his-own-party. Last accessed 9 June 2021.

Edwards, Mickey. *The Parties Versus the People: How to Turn Republicans and Democrats Into Americans*. Kindle ed. New Haven: Yale University Press, 2012.

Egan, Paul. "Michigan Election 2018: Here Are Your Third-party Options." *Detroit Free Press* (23 October 2018), https://www.freep.com/story/news/politics/elections/2018/10/23/independent-third-party-candidates-michigan-election/1672449002/. Last accessed 23 August 2019.

Eilperin, Juliet, and Spencer S. Hsu. "Va.'s Goode Leaves Democrats to Be an Independent." *Washington Post* (25 January 2000), https://www.washingtonpost.com/archive/politics/2000/01/25/vas-goode-leaves-democrats-to-be-an-independent/c1d3f8d9-07e1-467c-9222-5b8e44941eed/?utm_term=.b5a562ca2d20. Last accessed 5 September 2021.

Eligon, John. "Lawmaking Maverick Resumes Course in Nebraska." *New York Times* (9 January 2013), https://www.nytimes.com/2013/01/10/us/ernie-chambers-nebraska-senator-returns-to-capitol.html. Last accessed 8 June 2021.

Enten, Harry. "These Are the Republicans Who Are Against Trump and for Impeachment." CNN (1 October 2019), https://www.cnn.com/2019/10/01/politics/impeachment-polling-analysis/index.html. Last accessed 2 May 2021.

Fair.org. "Language: A Key Mechanism of Control" (1 February 1995), https://fair.org/home/language-a-key-mechanism-of-control/. Last accessed 25 August 2019.

Fandos, Nicholas, and Michael S. Schmidt. "Letter Claims Attempted Assault by Teenage Brett Kavanaugh." *New York Times* (14 September 2018), https://www.nytimes.com/2018/09/14/us/politics/kavanaugh-assault-allegation-letter.html. Last accessed 2 September 2019.

Farias, Christian. "How a Lone Republican Set an Example for Democrats on the Mueller Report." *New York Times* (20 May 2019), https://www.nytimes.com/2019/05/20/opinion/how-a-lone-republican-set-an-example-for-democrats-on-the-mueller-report.html. Last accessed 19 May 2020.

Farrow, Ronan, and Jane Mayer. "Senate Democrats Investigate a New Allegation of Sexual Misconduct, from Brett Kavanaugh's College Years." *The New Yorker* (23 September 2018), https://www.newyorker.com/news/news-desk/senate-democrats-investigate-a-new-allegation-of-sexual-misconduct-from-the-supreme-court-nominee-brett-kavanaughs-college-years-deborah-ramirez. Last accessed 4 September 2019.

Federal Election Commission. Mission statement, https://www.fec.gov/about/mission-and-history/. Last accessed 5 September 2019.

———. Comprehensive 2016 Federal Election Results (December 2017), https://www.fec.gov/resources/cms-content/documents/federalelections2016.pdf. Last accessed 5 September 2019.

Flaherty, Joseph. "Meet the New Mayor: Thelda Williams to Serve in Interim Before Special Election." *Phoenix New Times* (11 June 2018), https://www.phoenixnewtimes.com/news/thelda-williams-phoenix-mayor-special-election-stanton-10510277. Last Accessed 11 August 2019.

Flake, Jeff. *Conscience of a Conservative: A Rejection of Destructive Politics and a Return to Principle*. New York: Random House, 2017.

Forgey, Quint. "Trump Attacks 'Failed Presidential Candidate' Romney After Impeachment Vote." Politico (6 February 2020), https://www.politico.com/news/2020/02/06/

trump-attacks-mitt-romney-after-impeachment-vote-111344. Last accessed 30 May 2020.
Fox News. "Transcript: 'Fox News Sunday' Interview with President Trump" (19 July 2020), https://www.foxnews.com/politics/transcript-fox-news-sunday-interview-with-president-trump. Last accessed 5 July 2021.
Fuller, Matt. "The One House Republican Who Can't Stop Criticizing Donald Trump." *Huffington Post* (1 December 2016), https://www.huffpost.com/entry/justin-amash-donald-trump_n_58406d7ae4b017f37fe35a9e?guccounter=1. Last accessed 22 May 2020.
Galen, Reed. "How Republicans and Democrats Prevent Independent Candidates from Getting on the Ballot." NBC (17 April 2018), https://www.nbcnews.com/think/opinion/how-republicans-democrats-prevent-independent-candidates-getting-ballot-ncna866466. Last accessed 8 June 2021.
Gallup. Major Political Party Affiliation and Non-Affiliation, 2004–2021, https://news.gallup.com/poll/15370/party-affiliation.aspx. Last accessed 8 May 2021.
Gambino, Lauren. "Peter Strzok Hearing Revealed One Thing—Washington's Partisan Dysfunction." *The Guardian* (13 July 2018), https://www.theguardian.com/us-news/2018/jul/13/peter-strzok-hearing-congress-fbi-trump-russia-partisan-dysfunction. Last accessed 15 July 2019.
Gehl, Katherine M., and Michael E. Porter. "Why Competition in the Politics Industry Is Failing America: A Strategy for Reinvigorating Our Democracy." Harvard Business School Report, https://www.hbs.edu/competitiveness/Documents/why-competition-in-the-politics-industry-is-failing-america.pdf. Last accessed 10 June 2021.
Gentzkow, Matthew, Jesse M. Shapiro, and Matt Taddy. "Measuring Group Differences in High-Dimensional Choices: Method and Application to Congressional Speech." National Bureau of Economic Research (July 2016; revised March 2019), https://www.nber.org/papers/w22423. Cited in Thompson's "Why Democrats and Republicans Literally Speak Different Languages." Last accessed 24 September 2019.
Gerzon, Mark. *The Reunited States of America: How We Can Bridge the Partisan Divide*. Kindle ed. Oakland: Berrett-Koehler, 2016.
Gillespie, J. David. *Challengers to Duopoly: Why Third Parties Matter in Two-Party American Politics*. Kindle ed. Columbia, South Carolina: University of South Carolina Press, 2012.
———. *Politics at the Periphery: Third Parties in Two-Party America*. Columbia, South Carolina: University of South Carolina Press, 1993.
GOPAC. Gopac.org. Last accessed 8 September 2021.
Gore, D'Angelo. "Sen. Manchin Often Votes with Trump." Factcheck.org (24 August 2018), https://www.factcheck.org/2018/08/sen-manchin-often-votes-with-trump/. Last accessed 5 September 2019.
Gormley, Michael. "Miner, Sharpe Survive Challenges to Get on Ballot for Governor." *Newsday* (4 September 2018), https://www.newsday.com/news/region-state/independent-governor-candidates-1.20835779. Last accessed 16 September 2019.
Graham, David A. "Barr Misled the Public—And It Worked." *The Atlantic* (1 May 2019), https://www.theatlantic.com/ideas/archive/2019/05/barr-misled-the-publicand-it-worked/588463/. Last accessed 8 June 2021.
Greenblatt, Alan. "America's One and Only City Council Run by Libertarians." Governing.com (January 2017), https://www.governing.com/archive/gov-crystal-minnesota-libertarians.html. Last accessed 8 June 2021.
Grenoble, Ryan. "Trump Allies Smear Decorated Veteran Testifying in Impeachment Inquiry." *Huffington Post* (29 October 2019), https://www.huffpost.com/entry/alexander-vindman-trump-smear-impeachment_n_5db84a27e4b02aee7d36c12b. Last accessed 5 May 2021.
Griffin, Robert. "Party Hoppers: Understanding Voters Who Switched Partisan Affiliation." Voter Study Group (December 2017), https://www.voterstudygroup.org/publication/party-hoppers. Last accessed 26 August 2019.
Grim, Ryan. "Diane Feinstein Withholding Brett Kavanaugh Document from Fellow Judiciary Committee Democrats." *The Intercept* (12 September 2018), https://theintercept.

com/2018/09/12/brett-kavanaugh-confirmation-dianne-feinstein/. Last accessed 26 September 2019.

Gunderson, Dan. "Collin Peterson Defeat Brings 30 Years as a Self-styled Congressional Maverick to a Close." *Minnesota Public Radio* (5 November 2020), https://www.mprnews.org/story/2020/11/05/collin-peterson-defeat-brings-30-years-as-a-selfstyled-maverick-to-a-close. Last accessed 7 May 2021.

Gutman, David. "'We Were Wrong': Washington PAC Supporting Independents Sees No Future for Centrist Third Party." *Seattle Times* (28 May 2019), https://www.seattletimes.com/seattle-news/politics/we-were-wrong-washington-pac-supporting-independents-sees-no-future-for-centrist-third-party/. Last accessed 8 June 2021.

Hageman, John. "Jaeger Submits Signatures for Independent North Dakota Secretary of State Bid." *West Fargo Pioneer* (9 August 2018), https://www.westfargopioneer.com/news/government-and-politics/4483503-jaeger-submits-signatures-independent-north-dakota-secretary. Last accessed 27 August 2019.

Hair, Steve. "Dr. Ann Diamond Discusses Her Campaign to Replace Rep. Condotta." NCWLIFE.com (9 May 2018), https://www.ncwlife.com/24061-2/. Last accessed 20 November 2019.

_____. "12th District House Candidate Ann Diamond Speaks." NCWLIFE.com (30 January 2018), https://www.ncwlife.com/12th-district-house-candidate-ann-diamond-speaks/. Last accessed 20 November 2019.

Hasen, Richard L. "Entrenching the Duopoly: Why the Supreme Court Should Not Allow the States to Protect the Democrats and Republicans from Political Competition." *Supreme Court Review*, Vol. 1997 (1997), 331–371. Last accessed 9 June 2021.

Hayes, Terry, and Greg Orman. "Independents Can Unite America." Real Clear Politics (27 February 2018), https://www.realclearpolitics.com/articles/2018/02/27/independents_can_unite_america__136378.html. Last accessed 28 August 2019.

Hertel, Nora G. "'All from a Counterfeit Bill': What We Know About Fake Currency and George Floyd's Death." *USA Today* report published in the *St. Cloud Times* (3 June 2020), https://www.sctimes.com/story/news/2020/06/03/what-we-know-fake-currency-and-george-floyds-death-minneapolis-counterfeit-police/5310999002/. Last accessed 1 June 2021.

The Hill staff. "Read: Mueller's Letter to Barr." *The Hill* (1 May 2019), https://thehill.com/policy/national-security/441547-read-muellers-letter-to-barr. Last accessed 8 June 2021.

Hirsch, E.D., Jr. *Cultural Literacy: What Every American Needs to Know*. New York: Vintage, 1988.

Holman, Craig, Lisa Gilbert, and Robert Weissman. "Violation of the Oath of Office by Sen. Mitch McConnell (R-Ky.)." Letter from *Public Citizen* to the Senate Select Committee on Ethics. https://www.citizen.org/article/violation-of-oath-of-office-by-sen-mitch-mcconnell-r-ky/. Last accessed 15 February 2022.

Holmes, Kristen, Jim Acosta, and Kaitlan Collins. "There Were 18 Attempted Calls from the White House to GA Secretary of State's Office, Sources Say." CNN (4 January 2021), https://www.cnn.com/2021/01/04/politics/trump-brad-raffensperger-calls-georgia/index.html. Last accessed 19 May 2021.

Horsley, Scott. "Kavanaugh Supreme Court Confirmation Hearings Off to a Raucous Start." National Public Radio (4 September 2018), https://www.npr.org/2018/09/04/643707613/kavanaugh-supreme-court-confirmation-hearings-begin. Last accessed 2 September 2019.

Hurley, Lawrence. "Ruth Bader Ginsburg Hopes 'Cooler Heads' Prevail on Supreme Court Vacancy." *Business Insider* (7 September 2016), https://www.businessinsider.com/ruth-bader-ginsburg-hopes-cooler-heads-prevail-on-supreme-court-vacancy-2016-9. Last accessed 15 May 2021.

Indyreader.org. "Poverty Don't Know Color, Interview with Annie Chambers." *Indypendent Reader* Issue 7 (Winter 2008), https://indyreader.org/node/77. Last accessed 23 August 2019.

Ipsos.com. "Ipsos/538 Impeachment Tracker" (December 2019–Jan 2020), https://www.ipsos.com/en-us/news-polls/538-impeachment-tracker-2019. Last accessed 7 May 2021.

Ismail, Aymann. "The Store That Called the Cops on George Floyd." Slate (6 October 2020), https://slate.com/human-interest/2020/10/cup-foods-george-floyd-store-911-history.html. Last accessed 8 May 2021.

Jacoby, Jeff. "George Washington Was Right About 'Baneful' Two-party Politics." *Boston Globe* (12 July 2019), https://www.bostonglobe.com/opinion/2019/07/12/george-washington-was-right-about-baneful-two-party-politics/2eLxM2oXRtMvDG7VjWP5eM/story.html. Last accessed 6 April 2021.

Jamison, Dennis. "George Washington's View on Political Parties in America." *Washington Times* (31 December 2014), https://www.washingtontimes.com/news/2014/dec/31/george-washingtons-views-political-parties-america/. Last accessed 24 August 2019.

Jeter, Jon. "Spending Limits Helped Ventura Win." *Washington Post* (5 November 1998), https://www.washingtonpost.com/wp-srv/politics/campaigns/keyraces98/stories/ventura110598.htm. Last accessed 8 June 2021.

Johnson, Kirk. "Bill Walker, Governor of Alaska, Suspends Campaign Amid Sinking Polls." *New York Times* (19 October 2018), https://www.nytimes.com/2018/10/19/us/alaska-governor-bill-walker-suspends-campaign.html. Last accessed 11 August 2019.

———. "Bill Walker, Next Governor of Alaska, Traversed Unlikely Path." *New York Times* (24 November 2014), https://www.nytimes.com/2014/11/25/us/politics/next-governor-for-alaska-traversed-unlikely-path.html. Last accessed 11 August 2019.

Johnson, Ryan. "ND Secretary of State Candidate Drops Out, Raising Questions About GOP's Next Steps." Inforum.com, in association with WDAY Fargo (21 May 2018), https://www.inforum.com/news/4448876-nd-secretary-state-candidate-drops-out-raising-questions-about. Last accessed 27 August 2019.

Jones, Jeffrey M. "War Through Partisan Lenses." Gallup News (15 November 2005), https://news.gallup.com/poll/19924/war-through-partisan-lenses.aspx. Last accessed 25 August 2019.

KCPQ-TV (aka Q13 Fox). Introductory piece on Chris Vance, 2016 Republican candidate for the United States Senate from Washington (on or about 15 September 2016), https://q13fox.com/2016/09/15/voter-guide-u-s-senate-race-chris-vance-republican-challenger/. Last accessed 20 July 2019.

Kercheval, Hoppy. "The Rise of the Independent West Virginia Voter." *West Virginia MetroNews* (18 October 2018), http://wvmetronews.com/2018/10/18/the-rise-of-the-independent-west-virginia-voter/. Last accessed 23 August 2019.

KETV 7 (ABC Omaha). "State Sen. Ernie Chambers Sues God." (19 September 2007), https://www.ketv.com/article/state-sen-ernie-chambers-sues-god/7610332. Last accessed 22 August 2019.

KFSM/KXNW-TV (Fort Smith/Fayetteville, Arkansas). "Elvis Presley is Running for an Arkansas Congressional Seat." Associated Press article (26 February 2018), https://5newsonline.com/2018/02/26/elvis-presley-is-running-for-an-arkansas-congressional-seat/. Last accessed 23 August 2019.

Kiefer, Eric. "Libertarians Standing Tall as Largest Third-Party in New Jersey." Patch (22 August 2018), https://patch.com/new-jersey/belleville/libertarians-standing-tall-largest-third-party-new-jersey. Last accessed 14 August 2019.

Kirby, Jen. "Read Nancy Pelosi's Full Statement on Launching Trump Impeachment Inquiry." Vox (24 September 2019), https://www.vox.com/policy-and-politics/2019/9/24/20882453/impeachment-trump-nancy-pelosi-statement. Last accessed 26 April 2021.

Kitsap Sun editorial board. "Packed Race for District 26, Position 2." *Kitsap Sun* (25 July 2018), https://www.kitsapsun.com/story/opinion/editorials/2018/07/25/our-view-26th-ld-shouldnt-swing-extremes/835859002/. Last accessed 5 September 2021.

Krasselt, Kaitlyn. "Socialist Senate Candidate: Ballot Signatures Wrongly Disqualified." *CTPost* (8 October 1018), https://www.ctpost.com/local/article/Socialist-Senate-candidate-Ballot-signatures-13291201.php. Last accessed 4 July 2021.

Kruse, Michael, and Burgess Everett. "Manchin in the Middle." *Politico Magazine* (March/April 2017), https://www.politico.com/magazine/story/2017/03/joe-manchin-senator-profile-west-virginia-red-state-democrat-bipartisan-214865. Last accessed 6 September 2019.

Kruzel, John. "Read Attorney General William Barr's Summary of Special Counsel Robert

Mueller's Report." Politifact (Poynter Institute) report (24 March 2019), https://www.politifact.com/article/2019/mar/24/read-attorney-general-william-barrs-summary-specia/. Last accessed 23 May 2019.

LadyLiberty1885.com. "Cutting to the Chase: Just the Ford-Mitchell Transcript." (29 September 2018; posted by user A.P. Dillon), https://ladyliberty1885.com/2018/09/29/just-ford-mitchell-transcript/. Last accessed 3 September 2019.

League of Women Voters. History of the League, https://www.lwv.org/about-us/history. Last accessed 30 August 2019.

———. "League Refuses to 'Help Perpetuate a Fraud'" (3 October 1988), https://www.lwv.org/newsroom/press-releases/league-refuses-help-perpetrate-fraud. Last accessed 30 August 2019.

Lee, Michelle Ye Hee. "FEC Commissioner's Departure Leaves Panel with Bare-Minimum Quorum." *Washington Post* (7 February 2018), https://www.washingtonpost.com/politics/fec-commissioners-departure-leaves-panel-with-bare-minimum-quorum/2018/02/07/03fb24a0-0c28-11e8-8890-372e2047c935_story.html. Last accessed 29 August 2019.

Lessmiller, Kevin. "Minor Political Parties Sue Tennessee." Courthouse News (14 October 2013), https://www.courthousenews.com/minor-political-parties-sue-tennessee/. Last accessed 20 August 2019.

Levinthal, Dave. "A Dubious Anniversary for the Federal Election Commission: Commissioners' Terms Expired Long Ago, but Trump and Congress Won't Replace Them." Center for Public Integrity (30 April 2018; updated 7 May 2018), https://publicintegrity.org/federal-politics/a-dubious-anniversary-for-the-federal-election-commission/. Last accessed 25 September 2019.

Levy, Gabrielle. "House Dems File Articles to Impeach Trump." *U.S. News & World Report* (12 July 2017), https://www.usnews.com/news/national-news/articles/2017-07-12/democratic-congressmen-brad-sherman-al-green-file-articles-of-impeachment-against-donald-trump. Last accessed 8 June 2021.

Levy, Spencer. "MD Should Open Primaries to Independent Voters." *Baltimore Sun* (11 April 2018), https://www.baltimoresun.com/opinion/op-ed/bs-ed-op-0412-independent-voter-20180411-story.html. Last accessed 8 June 2021.

Li, Zhou. "Senate Judiciary Committee Votes Along Party Lines to Advance Kavanaugh." Vox (28 September 2018), https://www.vox.com/2018/9/28/17913560/senate-judiciary-committee-brett-kavanaugh. Last accessed 5 September 2019.

Libertarian Party. Bob Johnson's report in the aftermath of the 2020 U.S. elections (November 11, 2020), https://www.lp.org/2020-election/. Last accessed 17 May 2021.

Liptak, Adam. "Ruth Bader Ginsburg, No Fan of Donald Trump, Critiques Latest Term." *New York Times* (10 July 2016), https://www.nytimes.com/2016/07/11/us/politics/ruth-bader-ginsburg-no-fan-of-donald-trump-critiques-latest-term.html. Last accessed 15 May 2021.

Livingston, Abby. "Al Green Pushes Forward with Trump Impeachment." *Texas Tribune* (7 June 2017), https://www.texastribune.org/2017/06/07/al-green-pushes-forward-trump-impeachment/. Last accessed 8 June 2021.

Los Angeles Times editorial board. "The Federal Election Commission is Less Than Useless." *Los Angeles Times* (31 March 2016), https://www.latimes.com/opinion/editorials/la-ed-0331-fec-20160331-story.html. Last accessed 8 June 2021.

Lowi, Theodore J. "Deregulate the Duopoly." *The Nation* (16 November 2000), https://www.thenation.com/article/archive/deregulate-duopoly/. Last accessed 10 June 2021.

Mahoney, Mark. "David Johnson Shares Life Post-Politics." Nwest Iowa (30 May 2020), https://www.nwestiowa.com/news/david-johnson-shares-life-post-politics/article_daa77884-a1f2-11ea-9c49-e7b547551710.html. Last accessed 8 June 2021.

Maisel, L. Sandy. "Ranked Choice Voting: 'As Maine Goes ....'" *The American Interest* (7 August 2018), https://www.the-american-interest.com/2018/08/07/ranked-choice-voting-as-maine-goes/. Last accessed 8 June 2021.

Marist/NPR/PBS NewsHour poll, conducted 3–8 October 2019, surveying 1,123 American adults on topics including their views on the House impeachment inquiry into behavior by President Trump, http://maristpoll.marist.edu/wp-content/uploads/2019/10/NPR_PBS-NewsHour_Marist-Poll_USA-NOS-and-Tables_1910091356.pdf#page=1. Last accessed 3 July 2021.

Markell, Jack. "Reagan's Legacy of Bipartisanship." Politico (5 February 2012), https://www.politico.com/story/2012/02/reagans-legacy-of-constructive-bipartisanship-072468. Last accessed 25 August 2019.

Marks, Rusty. "Democrat-turned-independent Rupie Phillips Goes Republican to Run for Congress." *The State Journal* [Charleston, West Virginia] (11 May 2017), https://www.wvnews.com/statejournal/democrat-turned-independent-rupie-phillips-goes-republican-to-run-for/article_724275ee-935c-5753-b102-59eeeb13b999.html. Last accessed 5 September 2019.

Masket, Seth. "Only One State Legislature Is Now Under Split Party Control." *Pacific Standard* (13 November 2018), https://psmag.com/newgzs/only-one-state-legislature-is-now-under-split-party-control. Last accessed 12 June 2021.

McClennan, David. "NC Voters Are Unhappy. Why Aren't Third-Party Candidates Gaining Ground?" *The News & Observer* [Raleigh, North Carolina] (20 July 2018), https://www.newsobserver.com/opinion/article215122980.html. Last accessed 14 August 2019.

McKinley, Jesse. "Breakaway Democrats in New York Senate Add Another to Their Ranks." *New York Times* (25 January 2017), https://www.nytimes.com/2017/01/25/nyregion/independent-democratic-conference-republicans-state-senate.html. Last accessed 14 August 2019.

Meehan, Mary. "The Federal Election Commission." Cato Institute (1 November 1980), https://www.cato.org/publications/policy-analysis/federal-election-commission. Last accessed 28 August 2019.

Menu, Kathryn G. "Thiele Earns Endorsements from Five Different Political Parties." *Sag Harbor Express* (25 July 2018), https://sagharborexpress.com/thiele-earns-endorsements-five-different-political-parties/. Last accessed 6 October 2019.

Methow Valley News. "Candidate Filing Ends; Diamond Opts Out of 12th District Race" (20 May 2020), https://methowvalleynews.com/2020/05/20/candidate-filing-ends-diamond-opts-out-of-12th-district-race/. Last accessed 4 June 2021.

Michels, Holly K. "Judge Orders Montana Green Party Removed from November Ballot." Helena *Independent Record* (9 July 2018), https://helenair.com/news/state-and-regional/govt-and-politics/judge-orders-montana-green-party-removed-from-november-ballot/article_145ad8f9-8fe7-5891-a2bc-304cdb6ed50d.html. Last accessed 14 August 2019.

Miller, Greg, Ellen Nakashima, and Shane Harris. "Trump's Communications with Foreign Leader Are Part of Whistleblower Complaint That Spurred Standoff Between Spy Chief and Congress, Former Officials Say." *Washington Post* (18 September 2019), https://www.washingtonpost.com/national-security/trumps-communications-with-foreign-leader-are-part-of-whistleblower-complaint-that-spurred-standoff-between-spy-chief-and-congress-former-officials-say/2019/09/18/df651aa2-da60-11e9-bfb1-849887369476_story.html. Last accessed 26 April 2021.

Milligan, Susan. "Spoiler Alert: Third Party Contenders Not a Factor in 2020." *U.S. News & World Report* (15 September 2020), https://www.usnews.com/news/elections/articles/2020-09-15/third-party-contenders-not-a-factor-in-2020-presidential-election. Last accessed 5 July 2021.

_____. "Trump's Rallies Are Turning Voters Against Him." *U.S. News & World Report* (28 October 2020), https://www.usnews.com/news/elections/articles/2020-10-28/trumps-rallies-are-turning-voters-against-him. Last accessed 5 June 2021.

Mitchell, Rachel. Memo to Republican Senators Regarding the 27 September 2018 Testimony of Christine Blasey Ford. Politico (30 September 2018), https://static.politico.com/28/7f/80157df74b96bb352b10f8b7aa66/09-30-18-mitchell-memo-ford-allegations.pdf. Last accessed 3 September 2019.

Mooney, Tom. "Compassion Party Candidates for R.I. Governor, AG Face Drug Charges." *Providence Journal* (4 October 2018), https://www.providencejournal.com/news/20181004/compassion-party-candidates-for-ri-governor-ag-face-drug-charges. Last accessed 20 August 2019.

Murad, Yusra. "As Trump Eyes Restarting Economy, Nearly 3 in 4 Voters Support National Quarantine." *Morning Consult* (25 March 2020), https://morningconsult.com/2020/03/25/coronavirus-national-quarantine-trump/. Last accessed 8 May 2021.
Myers, John. "California Voters Are Joining This Party by Mistake, but Lawmakers Aren't Doing Anything About It." *Los Angeles Times* (30 March 2018), https://www.latimes.com/politics/la-pol-ca-road-map-american-independent-party-20180330-story.html. Last accessed 9 October 2019.
———. "He Once Held the Job as a Republican, but Now Steve Poizner Is Making a No-Party Bid for California Insurance Commissioner." *Los Angeles Times* (12 February 2018), https://www.latimes.com/politics/la-pol-ca-steve-poizner-insurance-commissioner-independent-candidate-20180212-story.html. Last accessed 11 August 2018.
———, Christine Mai-Duc, and Ben Welsh. "Are You an Independent Voter? You Aren't If You Checked This Box." *Los Angeles Times* (17 April 2016), https://static.latimes.com/american-independent-party-california-voters/. Last accessed 1 August 2019.
Nanna, Dustin. "Ohio Libertarians Hit the Ground Running for 2018." *Libertarian Party of Ohio* (9 November 2016), https://lpo.org/732-ohio-libertarians-hit-the-ground-running-for-2018. Last accessed 19 August 2019.
National Archives. George Washington's 26 June 1796 Letter to Alexander Hamilton, https://founders.archives.gov/documents/Hamilton/01-20-02-0151. Last accessed 5 September 2021.
National Governors Association. Biographies of United States Governors, Past and Present, https://www.nga.org/governors/. Last accessed 7 August 2019.
New York Times. "Transcript of Reagan's Remarks to the Convention" (20 August 1976), https://www.nytimes.com/1976/08/20/archives/transcript-of-reagans-remarks-to-the-convention.html. Last accessed 25 August 2019.
News Tribune (Tacoma, Washington). "Editorial endorsements of and comments about Washington legislative candidates" (27 September 2018), https://www.thenewstribune.com/opinion/editorials/article219130045.html. Last accessed 26 July 2019.
Nguyen, Tina. "The Peter Strzok Hearing Was a WWE-Style Bipartisan Beatdown." *Vanity Fair* (12 July 2018), https://www.vanityfair.com/news/2018/07/peter-strzok-hearing-recap. Last accessed 15 July 2019.
Nichols, Ken. In-person interview. 18 March 2019.
Nilsen, Ella. "The House Just Voted to Hold AG William Barr in Contempt of Congress." *Vox* (11 June 2019), https://www.vox.com/2019/6/11/18647093/contempt-of-congress-barr-house-vote. Last accessed 9 June 2021.
NPR. "Alexander Vindman Testimony" (29 October 2019), https://apps.npr.org/documents/document.html?id=6543468-Alexander-Vindman-Testimony. Last accessed 4 May 2021.
———. "How 15 Days Became 45: Trump Extends Guidelines to Slow Coronavirus" (30 March 2020), https://www.npr.org/2020/03/30/822448199/how-15-days-became-45-trump-extends-guidelines-to-slow-coronavirus. Last accessed 8 May 2021.
———. "READ: Christine Blasey Ford's Opening Statement for Senate Hearing" (26 September 2018), https://www.npr.org/2018/09/26/651941113/read-christine-blasey-fords-opening-statement-for-senate-hearing. Last accessed 2 September 2019.
———. "Trump Tells Woodward He Deliberately Downplayed Coronavirus Threat." *Morning Edition* (20 September 2020), https://www.npr.org/2020/09/10/911368698/trump-tells-woodward-he-deliberately-downplayed-coronavirus-threat. Last accessed 8 May 2021.
O'Keefe, Ed. "Angus King to Caucus with Democrats in Senate." *Washington Post* (14 November 2012), https://www.washingtonpost.com/blogs/2chambers/wp/2012/11/14/angus-king-to-caucus-with-democrats-in-senate/. Last accessed 28 August 2019.
Orman, Greg. *A Declaration of Independents: How We Can Break the Two-Party Stranglehold and Restore the American Dream.* Kindle ed. Austin: Greenleaf Press, 2016.
Ortiz, Daniel R. "Duopoly Versus Autonomy: How the Two-Party System Harms the Major Parties." *Columbia Law Review,* Vol. 100, No. 3 (April 2000), 753–774. Last accessed 9 June 2021.

PBS.org. "The History of Presidential Debates: Before Television" (24 September 2004), https://www.pbs.org/now/politics/debatehistory.html. Last accessed 30 August 2019.

———. "The History of Presidential Debates: The Televised Years" (24 September 2004), https://www.pbs.org/now/politics/debatehistory2.html. Last accessed 30 August 2019.

———. "1978 Speech by Gingrich" (1978), https://www.pbs.org/wgbh/pages/frontline/newt/newt78speech.html. Last accessed 12 June 2021.

———. "Watch: Schiff Says Trump Call with Ukrainian President Was a 'Shakedown,'" https://www.pbs.org/newshour/politics/watch-live-rep-schiff-responds-to-whitehouse-notes-of-trump-call-with-ukraine. Last accessed 28 April 2021.

Pecorin, Allison. "From a Controversial Phone Call to Impeachment Calls: A Trump Whistleblower Timeline." *ABC News* (12 November 2019), https://abcnews.go.com/Politics/controversial-phone-call-impeachment-calls-trump-whistleblower-timeline/story?id=65810201. Last accessed 25 April 2021.

Pelzer, Jeremy. "Ohio Libertarians Regain Ballot Access for the First Time in Years." Cleveland.com (12 July 2018), https://www.cleveland.com/open/2018/07/ohio_libertarians_regain_ballo.html. Last accessed 19 August 2019.

Pengelly, Martin. "Clear Majority of Americans Support Trump Impeachment Inquiry, Poll Finds." *The Guardian* (8 October 2019), https://www.theguardian.com/us-news/2019/oct/08/trump-impeachment-inquiry-poll-americans. Last accessed 5 September 2021.

———. "Justin Amash Becomes First Republican to Back Trump Impeachment." *The Guardian* (18 May 2019), https://www.theguardian.com/us-news/2019/may/19/michigans-justin-amash-becomes-first-republican-to-back-trump-impeachment. Last accessed 9 June 2021.

Perticone, Joe. "Republican Patrick Morrisey Is Betting That Bipartisanship Is Dead in His Senate Race Against Democrat Joe Manchin in Deep-Red West Virginia." *Business Insider* (22 October 2018), https://www.businessinsider.com/patrick-morrisey-is-running-on-being-the-anti-joe-manchin-2018-10. Last accessed 6 September 2019.

Peterson, Peter G. *Running on Empty: How the Democratic and Republican Parties Are Bankrupting Our Future and What Americans Can Do About It*. Kindle ed. New York: Farrar, Straus and Giroux, 2004.

Petroski, William. "'Never Trump' Iowa Sen. David Johnson Won't Seek Re-Election." *Des Moines Register* (31 May 2018), https://www.desmoinesregister.com/story/news/politics/2018/05/31/never-trump-iowa-senator-david-johnson-wont-run-again-reelection-indepent-republican-party/660064002/. Last accessed 12 June 2021.

Pew Research Center. "Partisan Antipathy: More Intense, More Personal" (10 October 2019), https://www.pewresearch.org/politics/2019/10/10/partisan-antipathy-more-intense-more-personal/. Last accessed 3 July 2021.

———. "Political Independents: Who They Are, What They Think" (14 March 2019), https://www.pewresearch.org/politics/2019/03/14/political-independents-who-they-are-what-they-think/. Last accessed 9 June 2021.

Pilling, Nathan. "Poulsbo Mayor Betsy Erickson Wants a Second Job in the Legislature. How Would That Work?" *Kitsap Sun* (30 July 2018), https://www.kitsapsun.com/story/news/2018/07/30/how-would-poulsbo-mayor-becky-erickson-handle-second-job-olympia/792764002/. Last accessed 26 July 2019.

Politi, James, Michael Peel, Roman Olearchyk, and Demetri Sevastopulo. "Envoys Pushed to Oust Ukraine Prosecutor Before Biden." *Financial Times* (3 October 2019), https://www.ft.com/content/e1454ace-e61b-11e9-9743-db5a370481bc. Last accessed 28 April 2021.

Pondiscio, Robert. "Let's Set a National Standard for Our Students—a Really Low One." *The Atlantic* (9 April 2013), https://www.theatlantic.com/national/archive/2013/04/lets-set-a-national-standard-for-our-students-a-really-low-one/274808/. Last accessed 25 August 2019.

Portland Tribune editorial board. "Our Opinion: Independent Party Must Prove Viability." *Portland Tribune* (24 July 2018), https://pamplinmedia.com/pt/10-opinion/401538-297572-our-opinion-independent-party-must-prove-viability. Last accessed 20 August 2019.

Bibliography

Pramuk, Jacob, and Tucker Higgins. "Trump Threatened to Keep the Government Closed for 'Months or Even Years' in Meeting with Top Democrats." CNBC (4 January 2019), https://www.cnbc.com/2019/01/04/trump-threatened-to-keep-the-government-closed-for-months-or-even-years-schumer-says.html. Last accessed 22 May 2021.

Priorities.org. "State of the Race" (28 October 2020), https://priorities.org/wp-content/uploads/2020/10/10.28.20-Press-Briefing-1.pdf. Last accessed 18 May 2021.

Providence Journal. "Compassion Party Candidate Says Marijuana Charges Are 'Politically Motivated.'" Associated Press article (5 October 2018), https://www.providencejournal.com/news/20181005/compassion-party-candidate-says-marijuana-charges-are-politically-motivated. Last accessed 20 August 2019.

Public Religion Research Institute. "Fractured Nation: Widening Partisan Polarization and Key Issues in 2020 Presidential Elections" (20 October 2019), https://www.prri.org/research/fractured-nation-widening-partisan-polarization-and-key-issues-in-2020-presidential-elections/. Last accessed 22 May 2020.

Purdue University. "Equal-Time and the Kennedy-Nixon Debates," https://cla.purdue.edu/academic/history/course/debate/kennedynixon/index.html. Last accessed 30 August 2019.

Quinnipiac University. "Poll Examining Voter Reactions to the Kavanaugh Confirmation Hearing and Testimony by Blasey Ford and Kavanaugh" (1 October 2018), https://poll.qu.edu/national/release-detail?ReleaseID=2574. Last accessed 11 November 2020.

Reisman, John P. https://johnreisman.com/. Last accessed 11 November 2020.

Rev.com. "Donald Trump Rally Speech Transcript Dalton, Georgia: Senate Runoff Election" (4 January 2021), https://www.rev.com/blog/transcripts/donald-trump-rally-speech-transcript-dalton-georgia-senate-runoff-election. Last accessed 6 July 2021.

———. "Donald Trump Speech 'Save America' Rally Transcript January 6" (6 January 2021), https://www.rev.com/blog/transcripts/donald-trump-speech-save-america-rally-transcript-january-6. Last accessed 6 July 2021.

———. "Donald Trump Speech Transcript on Vaccine Development for Coronavirus" (15 May 2020), https://www.rev.com/blog/transcripts/donald-trump-speech-transcript-on-vaccine-development-for-coronavirus. Last accessed 4 July 2021.

Rimer, Sara. "Unfettered by Party, He's Set to Govern." *New York Times* (18 November 1994), https://www.nytimes.com/1994/11/18/us/unfettered-by-party-he-s-set-to-govern.html. Last accessed 3 August 2019.

Roberts, Jeannie. "Auditor to Face Libertarian Rival." *Arkansas Democrat Gazette* (31 October 2018), https://www.arkansasonline.com/news/2018/oct/31/auditor-to-face-libertarian-rival-20181-1/. Last accessed 21 June 2021.

Rogers, Joel. "Pull the Plug: A Critical Survey of the Two-Party System." *Administrative Law Review*, Vol. 52, No. 2 (Spring 2000), pp. 743–768. Last accessed 9 June 2021.

Roscoe, Jim. 2018 campaign website, https://www.jimroscoeforwyoming.com. The site has since been updated. Roscoe's statement on why he's an independent is at https://www.jimroscoeforwyoming.com/whyrunindependent. Last accessed 5 September 2021.

Rosenstone, Steven J., Roy L. Behr, and Edward H. Lazarus. *Third Parties in America*. Second ed. Princeton: Princeton University Press, 1996.

Rushford, James W. "My Turn." Cal Matters (3 October 2018), https://calmatters.org/commentary/how-dianne-feinstein-handled-christine-blasey-fords-letter/. Last accessed 9 June 2021.

Salzer, James. "Gingrich's Language Set New Course." *Atlanta Journal-Constitution* (29 January 2012), https://www.ajc.com/news/local-govt—politics/gingrich-language-set-new-course/O5bgK6lY2wQ3KwEZsYTBlO/. Last accessed 24 September 2019.

Samuels, Alex. "The Green Party Needed Nearly 50,000 Signatures to Make It onto the November Ballot in Texas. It Got About 500." *Texas Tribune* (30 May 2018), https://www.texastribune.org/2018/05/30/libertarian-party-green-party-ballot-texas-november-2018/. Last accessed 21 June 2021.

Samuels, Iris. "Montana's Supreme Court Upholds Green Party's Ballot Removal." Associated Press article published in the *Independent Record* [Helena, Montana] (21 August 2018), https://helenair.com/news/state-and-regional/govt-and-politics/

montana-supreme-court-upholds-green-party-s-ballot-removal/article_85a40afc-6a09-54cb-9cb3-449a1b5f3676.html. Last accessed 7 November 2020.

Savage, Charlie. "How Barr's Excerpts Compare to the Mueller Report's Findings." *New York Times* (20 April 2019), https://www.nytimes.com/2019/04/19/us/politics/mueller-report-william-barr-excerpts.html. Last accessed 9 June 2021.

Schallhorn, Kaitlyn. "Kavanaugh Accusers Rocked Confirmation Process: Where Are They Now?" Fox News (31 December 2018), https://www.foxnews.com/politics/kavanaugh-accusers-where-are-they-now. Last accessed 26 September 2019.

Schattschneider, E.E. *Party Government*. London: Routledge, 2003. Originally published by Rinehart & Company, 1942.

Schneider, Gregory S. "Judge Orders Independent Candidate Off the Ballot in Va. Congressional Race, Citing 'Out and Out Fraud.'" *Washington Post* (5 September 2018), https://www.washingtonpost.com/local/virginia-politics/judge-orders-independent-candidate-brown-off-the-ballot-in-va-congressional-race/2018/09/05/222b427c-b11c-11e8-aed9-001309990777_story.html?noredirect=on. Last accessed 11 September 2021.

Seattle Post-Intelligencer. "Cantwell Loans Broke Election Rules, Says FEC" (19 February 2004), https://www.seattlepi.com/local/article/Cantwell-loans-broke-election-rules-says-FEC-1137499.php. Last accessed 22 August 2019.

Seattle Times. "The Times Recommends: Keith Smith for Legislative District 32, House Position 1." Editorial board endorsement (5 July 2018), https://www.seattletimes.com/opinion/editorials/the-times-recommends-keith-smith-for-legislative-district-32-house-position-1/. Last accessed 6 November 2019.

Sessa-Hawkins, Margaret. "Independent Voters Shut Out of MD Primaries." *Maryland Reporter* (11 June 2014), http://marylandreporter.com/2014/06/11/independent-voters-shut-out-of-md-primaries/. Last accessed 9 July 2021.

Shabad, Rebecca. "Barr Defends Himself Amid Calls for Resignation, Slights Mueller's 'Snitty' Letter." NBC (1 May 2019), https://www.nbcnews.com/politics/congress/dems-grill-barr-amid-reports-mueller-s-frustration-n1000546. Last accessed 9 July 2021.

———, and Alex Moe. "Democrats Kill GOP Effort to Censure Rep. Schiff Over Impeachment Inquiry." NBC (21 October 2019), https://www.nbcnews.com/politics/congress/republicans-seek-censure-adam-schiff-n1069376. Last accessed 29 April 2021.

Shamsian, Jacob, and Sonam Sheth. "Trump and His Allies Filed More Than 40 Lawsuits Challenging the 2020 Election Results. All of Them Failed." *Business Insider* (22 February 2021), https://www.businessinsider.com/trump-campaign-lawsuits-election-results-2020-11. Last accessed 5 June 2021.

Sheth, Sonam. "Justin Amash Says 'A Lot of' Republican Lawmakers Agree with Him That Trump Should Be Impeached but Won't Say It Publicly." *Business Insider* (29 May 2019), https://www.businessinsider.com/justin-amash-republicans-agree-impeachment-mueller-report-2019-5. Last accessed 19 May 2020.

Shorman, Jonathan. "Kansas Senator Rejoins Republicans After He Left Party for Orman Campaign." *Wichita Eagle* (29 July 2019), https://www.kansas.com/news/politics-government/article233270452.html. Last accessed 23 August 2019.

Siegel, Benjamin. "Democrat Schiff Compares Trump Call with Ukraine's President to 'Mafia Shakedown.'" ABC News (25 September 2019) https://abcnews.go.com/Politics/democrat-schiff-compares-trump-call-ukraines-president-mafia/story?id=65851441. Last accessed 9 June 2021.

Sifry, Micah. "Why America Is Stuck with Only Two Parties." *The New Republic* (2 February 2018), https://newrepublic.com/article/146884/america-stuck-two-parties. Last accessed 9 June 2021.

Smith, Keith. Phone interview. 5 November 2019.

Smith, Michelle R. "He's an Avid Trump Supporter. His Son, Who Is Not, Is Running Against Him for Office in Rhode Island." Associated Press article published in the *Chicago Tribune* (29 June 2018), https://www.chicagotribune.com/nation-world/ct-father-son-trump-election-20180629-story.html. Last accessed 20 August 2019.

Smith, Samantha. "5 Facts About America's Political Independents." Pew Research Center (5 July 2016), www.pewresearch.org/fatct-tank/2016/07/05/5-facts-about-

Bibliography

americas-political-independents/. Accessed 10 September 2018. (As of 2019, this URL links to a new article, by John Laloggia, titled "6 Facts About U.S. Political Independents.")

Sneve, Joe. "Party Politics Still Play a Role in Nonpartisan Mayoral Races." *Sioux Falls Argus Leader* (9 March 2018), https://www.argusleader.com/story/news/city/2018/03/09/party-politics-still-play-roll-non-partisan-mayoral-races/411096002/. Last accessed 20 August 2019.

Spangler, Todd. "Justin Amash's Rise as Foil to Donald Trump Is No Surprise." *Detroit Free Press* (15 April 2017), https://www.freep.com/story/news/local/michigan/2017/04/15/justin-amash-donald-trump-obamacare/100385722/. Last accessed 9 June 2021.

Stang, John. "A Democrat Won't Win in Central WA, but Can an Independent?" Crosscut article (2 October 2018), https://crosscut.com/2018/10/democrat-wont-win-central-wa-can-independent. Last accessed 24 July 2019.

Stoddard, Martha. "Nebraska Legislative Candidates Spent Combined $2 Million in Primary, Smashed Old Records." *Omaha World-Herald* (22 August 2019), https://www.omaha.com/news/legislature/nebraska-legislative-candidates-spent-combined-million-in-primary-smashed-old/article_026e9e18-6645-5f53-97ae-e99a992120b6.html. Last accessed 22 August 2019.

Stolberg, Sheryl Gay, and Nicholas Fandos. "Christine Blasey Ford Reaches Deal to Testify at Kavanaugh Hearing." *New York Times* (23 September 2018), https://www.nytimes.com/2018/09/23/us/politics/brett-kavanaugh-christine-blasey-ford-testify.html. Last accessed 2 September 2019.

Strand, Ginger. "Among the Gerrymandered." *Pacific Standard* (23 October 2018; updated 22 February 2019), https://psmag.com/magazine/among-the-gerrymandered. Last accessed 24 September 2019.

Strauss, Valerie. "Dark Money Just Keeps Coming on in School Board Races." *Washington Post* (29 October 2017), https://www.washingtonpost.com/news/answer-sheet/wp/2017/10/29/dark-money-just-keeps-on-coming-in-school-board-races/. Last accessed 9 June 2021.

Strider, Dave. Phone interview. 7 November 2019.

Subramanian, Courtney, Nicholas Wu, and Christal Hayes. "Impeachment Hearing: Morrison Says Fellow NSC Staffer Warned About Sondland." *USA Today* (19 November 2019), https://www.usatoday.com/story/news/politics/2019/11/19/impeachment-inquiry-vindman-williams-volker-morrision-testify/4231559002/. Last accessed 5 May 2021.

Sukharev, Nickolai. "Outgoing Delegate Switches to Green Party." *Montgomery County Sentinel* (21 November 2018), https://mont.thesentinel.com/2018/11/21/outgoing-delegate-switches-to-green-party/. Last accessed 23 August 2019.

Supreme Court. "Statement from Justice Ruth Bader Ginsburg" (17 July 2020), https://www.supremecourt.gov/publicinfo/press/pressreleases/pr_07-17-20. Last accessed 15 May 2021.

Tahoe Daily Tribune. "Oscar Goodman Considering Switching Political Affiliation in Bid for Nevada Governor." Associated Press article (15 December 2009), https://www.tahoedailytribune.com/news/oscar-goodman-considering-switching-political-affiliation-in-bid-for-nevada-governor/. Last accessed 6 September 2021.

Thompson, Derek. "Why Democrats and Republicans Literally Speak Different Languages." *The Atlantic* (22 July 2016), https://www.theatlantic.com/politics/archive/2016/07/why-democrats-and-republicans-literally-speak-different-languages/492539/. Last accessed 25 August 2019.

Thomson-DeVeaux, Amelia, and Laura Bronner. "The Impeachment Hearings Just Confirmed Voters' Preexisting Opinions." FiveThirtyEight (4 December 2019), https://fivethirtyeight.com/features/the-impeachment-hearings-just-confirmed-voters-preexisting-opinions/. Article links to Ipsos.com's "Ipsos/538 Impeachment Tracker." Last accessed 3 July 2021.

Totenberg, Nina. "Justice Ruth Bader Ginsburg, Champion of Gender Equality, Dies at 87." NPR (18 September 2020), https://www.npr.org/2020/09/18/100306972/justice-ruth-bader-ginsburg-champion-of-gender-equality-dies-at-87. Last accessed 15 May 2021.

_____. "Senate Confirms Gorsuch to Supreme Court." NPR (7 April 2017), https://www.npr.org/2017/04/07/522902281/senate-confirms-gorsuch-to-supreme-court. Last accessed 2 September 2019.

Tower, Mark. "U.S. Rep. Justin Amash Vows to Remain Vigilant Under Pres. Trump." MLive (15 December 2016; updated 19 January 2019), https://www.mlive.com/news/grand-rapids/2016/12/us_rep_justin_amash_vows_to_re.html. Last accessed 9 June 2021.

Trautwein, Catherine. "Inside the Kavanaugh Hearings: An Oral History." PBS Seattle affiliate KCTS, https://www.pbs.org/wgbh/frontline/article/supreme-court-kavanaugh-collins-flake-heitkamp-blasey-ford/. Last accessed 25 September 2019.

Tribe, Laurence H., and Thomas M. Rollins. "Deadlock: What Happens If Nobody Wins." *The Atlantic,* online edition (October 1980), www.theatlantic.com/past/docs/issues/80oct/deadlock.htm. Last accessed 17 July 2019.

Turley, Jonathan. "Viewpoint: In This Impeachment, People Only Heard What They Wanted To." BBC (6 February 2020), https://www.bbc.com/news/world-us-canada-51389540. Last accessed 8 May 2021.

Unite America, www.uniteamerica.org/. Last accessed 23 June 2021.

United Utah Party, unitedutah.org. Last accessed 20 August 2019.

U.S. Congress. "House Resolution 438: Impeaching Donald John Trump, President of the United States, for High Crimes and Misdemeanors" (12 July 2017), https://www.congress.gov/115/bills/hres438/BILLS-115hres438ih.pdf. Last accessed 9 June 2021.

U.S. Department of Justice. "Report on the Investigation into Russian Interference in the 2016 Presidential Election." Mueller report (March 2019).

U.S. House of Representatives. "The Trump-Ukraine Impeachment Inquiry Report." House Permanent Select Committee on Intelligence (December 2019), https://intelligence.house.gov/uploadedfiles/the_trump-ukraine_impeachment_inquiry_report.pdf. Last accessed 7 May 2021.

Vaillancourt, Cory. "Third Parties in North Carolina Get a Boost in Time for 2018 Elections." Blue Ridge Public Radio, https://www.bpr.org/post/third-parties-north-carolina-get-boost-time-2018-elections#stream/0. Last accessed 14 August 2019.

Vance, Chris. Phone interview. 21 September 2019.

Vermont Progressive Party, progressiveparty.org. Last accessed 20 August 2019.

Virginia Department of Elections. https://www.elections.virginia.gov/. Last accessed 21 August 2019.

Volokh, Eugene. "Joe Biden in 1992: No Supreme Court Nominations 'in the Full Throes of an Election Year.'" *Washington Post* (22 February 2016), https://www.washingtonpost.com/news/volokh-conspiracy/wp/2016/02/22/joe-biden-in-1992-no-supreme-court-nominations-in-the-full-throes-of-an-election-year/. Last accessed 2 September 2019.

Vosler, Christian. "Poulsbo Mayor Betsy Erickson Running for Seat in Legislature." *Kitsap Sun* (18 May 2018), https://www.kitsapsun.com/story/news/local/2018/05/18/poulsbo-mayor-becky-erickson-running-seat-legislature/623925002/. Last accessed 26 July 2019.

Vote Smart, votesmart.org. Last accessed 14 August 2019.

Vote Washington. "2020 Primary Campaign Candidates." https://voter.votewa.gov/CandidateList.aspx?e=865&c=99. Last accessed 9 June 2021.

Washington Courts. "FAQ." https://www.courts.wa.gov/education/campaign_activities/?fa=education_campaign_activities.faqs. Last accessed 29 July 2019.

Washington Post. "Text: Vice President Gore Concedes Election" (13 December 2000), https://www.washingtonpost.com/wp-srv/onpolitics/elections/goretext121300.htm. Last accessed 18 May 2021.

Washington Secretary of State, https://www.pdc.wa.gov/. Last accessed 26 July 2019.

Washington State Legislature. "Members of the Legislature, 1889–2019," http://leg.wa.gov/History/Legislative/Documents/MembersOfLeg2019.pdf. Last accessed 7 September 2019.

Washington State Public Disclosure Commission (PDC), https://www.pdc.wa.gov/. Last accessed 26 July 2019.

WDTV (Clarksburg, West Virginia). "W.Va. Representative Officially Becomes Only

Independent in State Legislature" (27 January 2017), https://www.wdtv.com/content/news/WVa-representative-officially-becomes-only-Independent-in-state-legislature-411882965.html. Last accessed 9 June 2021.

Webley, Kayla. "How the Nixon-Kennedy Debate Changed the World." *Time* (23 September 2010), http://content.time.com/time/nation/article/0,8599,2021078,00.html. Last accessed 30 August 2019.

Weiner, Rachel. "Former Virginia Congressional Candidate Who Got GOP Help Is Convicted of Fraud." *Washington Post* (30 October 2018), https://www.washingtonpost.com/local/public-safety/former-virginia-congressional-candidate-who-got-gop-help-is-convicted-of-fraud/2018/10/30/49d7cef2-dc83-11e8-b732-3c72cbf131f2_story.html. Last accessed 11 September 2021.

Welch, Matt. "Party-Switching N.H. State Rep. Brandon Phinney Gets Slaughtered as a Libertarian." Reason (6 November 2018), https://reason.com/2018/11/06/party-switching-nh-state-rep-brandon-phi. Last accessed 23 August 2019.

Wheaton, Sarah. "Biden in '92: No Election-season Supreme Court Nominees." Politico (22 February 2016), https://www.politico.com/story/2016/02/joe-biden-supreme-court-nominee-1992-219635. Last accessed 2 September 2019.

Wheelan, Charles. *The Centrist Manifesto*. Kindle ed. New York: W.W. Norton, 2013.

———. Phone interview. 1 October 2019.

Wilkie, Christina. "White House Twitter Account Attacks Army Officer Vindman as He Testifies in Trump Impeachment Hearing." CNBC (19 November 2019), https://www.cnbc.com/2019/11/19/white-house-twitter-attacks-vindman-during-trump-impeachment-testimony.html. Last accessed 16 September 2021.

Winger, Richard. "Libertarian Wins Partisan Race for Mayor of McLain, Mississippi." *Ballot Access News* (12 July 2017), http://ballot-access.org/2017/07/12/libertarian-wins-partisan-race-for-mayor-of-mclain-mississippi/. Last accessed 13 August 2019.

Woodward, Bob. *Rage*. Kindle ed. New York: Simon & Schuster, 2020.

Woolverton, Paul. "Man Who Spoiled Georgia U.S. Senate Race for Perdue, Ossoff to Run for Governor in 2022." *Savannah Morning News* (17 December 2020), https://www.savannahnow.com/story/news/2020/12/17/libertarian-announces-run-governor-wont-endorse-ossoff-perdue/3896935001/. Last accessed 16 May 2021.

Yale Law School. "Text of Washington's Farewell Address." *The Avalon Project,* https://avalon.law.yale.edu/18th_century/washing.asp. Last accessed 26 November 2020.

Yuhas, Alan. "Ukraine's President Says Call with Trump Was 'Normal.'" *New York Times* (25 September 2019), https://www.nytimes.com/2019/09/25/world/europe/zelensky-trump.html. Last accessed 28 April 2021.

Zeitlin, Matthew. "Plurality of Americans Don't Want Kavanaugh Confirmed, New Poll Shows." Slate (1 October 2018), https://slate.com/news-and-politics/2018/10/quinnipiac-poll-kavanaugh-popularity-independents-women-democrats.html. Last accessed 3 September 2019.

Zimmerman, Jonathan. "Even George Washington Couldn't Get Along with the Senate." *Los Angeles Times* (8 November 2014), https://www.latimes.com/nation/la-oe-zimmerman-senate-president-20141109-story.html. Last accessed 24 August 2019.

Index

ABC News 157, 168
ABC7.com (Los Angeles) 192
Abramowitz, Alan I. 16
Abrams, Stacey 68
Ackley, Kent 100, 186
Acosta, Allen 35–36, 91–92
Acosta, Jim 193
Adams, John 25–26
Adams, John Quincy 26
Adams, Roy Daryl 106
Agnew, Spiro 9
Agolerov, Aras 155
Alaskan Independence Party 58
The Alliance 187
Amash, Justin 148–153, 183, 185
American Constitution Society (ACS) 145
American Independent Party 24–25, 47–48, 73; voter confusion 47–48
Anderson, John 27, 121–122
Anti-Federalists 4, 57
Anti-Masonic Party 53
Applewhite, Jarratt 78, 98–99
Arkansas Democrat-Gazette 105
Ash, Mark 97
Associated Press 143
Atkinson, Michael 157
The Atlanta Journal-Constitution 14
The Atlantic 14, 17, 27, 139, 146
Ayouaz, Ismaine 74

Bailey, William "Rusty" III 63
Baldes, Bethany 87–88, 95, 186
ballotpedia.org 37, 46, 63–64
Balz, Dan 12
Barr, William 142–146, 148, 151
Barragan, Rodolfo Cortes 93
Barrett, Amy Coney 182
Baumgartner, Michael 46
BBC.com 153, 170
Becker, Jo 155
Beekman, Daniel 40
Benen, Steve 139
Benson, Elmer 61
Bergengruen, Vera 166–167
Berman, Russell 139

Biden, Hunter 157–159, 166–167, 170
Biden, Joe 49, 127, 154, 157–159, 166–167, 170, 180, 182–183, 191–194, 196–197
Bierschbach, Briana 185
Bishop, Greg 69–70
blanket primary 20, 125
Blitzer, Ron 153
Block, Ken 82
Blue Ridge Public Radio 79
Bolton, John 170
Bonds, Anita 104
border wall 47, 138–142
The Boston Globe 150
Boucsieguez, Diodato 36
Brakey, Eric 100
Brandt, Tom 96
Brennan Center for Justice 110
Breuninger, Kevin 169
Brock, Bill 13
Bronner, Laura 168
Brown, Shaun 86
Brown, Terry 71
Brunner, Jim 19–20
Bryan, Bob 139
Buchanan, Pat 61, 189–190
Buckley, James 52
Buckley, William F., Jr. 52
Bull Moose Party 24
Burisma 159, 167, 170
Burr, Aaron 26
Burt, Marshall 186
Bush, George H.W. 11–12, 14, 124, 127; "Chicken Kiev" speech 11
Bush, George W. 16, 118, 128, 189–190
Business Insider 136, 139, 192
"butterfly" ballots 190

C-SPAN 161–162, 166–168
calmatters.org 132
Canon, Gabrielle 142
Cantwell, Maria 45–48, 90
Carter, Jimmy 10, 27, 120–122
Cassidy, Kyle 190
Cato Institute 115
CBS Minnesota 177

CBS News 156
Center for Public Integrity 117
Central Intelligence Agency (CIA) 9
Centrist Manifesto 111–113; *see also* Wheelan, Charles
Centrist Party 36–37, 112–113; voter confusion 36
Chafee, Lincoln 58
Chambers, Annie 104
Chambers, Ernie 76, 186
Chase, Brad 47
Chauvin, Derek 177–178, 197
Cheney, Liz 196
Chicago Tribune 10, 82
Choi, David 171
Cilley, Jonathan 54
Civil Rights movement 9, 55
Civil War period 54–55
Clay, Henry 26
Clinton, Bill 14–16, 124; impeachment 15
Clinton, Hillary 15, 23, 128, 155–156, 184
closed primary system 68–70, 72, 77, 124
CNN 21–22, 140–141, 155, 158, 193
Coaston, Jane 183
Cohen, Jeremy 186
Coleman, Norm 62
Collin, Dorothy 10
Collins, Doug 143
Collins, Kaitlan 193
Collins, Sean 157
Collins, Susan 128, 170
Comey, James 154–155
Commission on Presidential Debates (CPD) 123
Common Sense Independent Party 100
Compassion Party of Rhode Island 82, 102
Condotta, Cary 29–31
A Connecticut Party 58
Conscience of a Conservative 135
Conservative Party (Virginia) 54
Conservative Party of New York 52
Constantine, James Dow 42
Constitution *see* United States Constitution
Constitution Party 56, 69, 74, 78, 81, 83–84, 87
Conway, Steve 34
Cook Political Report 184
Coppins, McKay 14
Corn, David 13–14
Cotton, Tom 185
county politics 42, 62, 71, 76, 80–81, 86, 89, 101, 103, 105–106
Craig, Angie 185
Crawford, William 26
Crist, Charlie 58–59
Crosscut.com 29, 33
Cruz, Ted 84, 98
Cuban, Mark 183
Cullison, Alan 158
Cultural Literacy 17; *see also* Hirsch, E.D.

Daines, Steve 135–136
Daniels, Stormy 117, 143
Daniels, Thurston 44
Darden, Dustin 94
"dark money" 41
Darnell, Tim 194
Davidson, Valerie Nurr'araaluk 65, 93
Davis, David 51
DC Statehood Green Party 88, 104
Deal, Nathan 69
debates, televised 62, 119–123
A Declaration of Independents 7, 108, 125
De Coune, Charles 98
Deferred Action for Childhood Arrivals (DACA) 138–139
Democratic Farmer-Labor Party 73, 79
Democratic Party, establishment of 4; 1860s split 54
Democratic-Republican Party 4, 26, 50, 53, 57, 109
Detroit Free Press 73, 149
Diamond, Ann 29–33, 49, 88–92, 98, 187–188
Diamond, Jeremy 155
Dimond, Chris 94
Dinwiddie, David 105
Doglio, Beth 36
Dole, Bob 121
Doll, John 70, 97
Dorn, Randy 43
Douglas, Stephen 119
Dragu, Paul 75
Dubin, Matthew 36
Duffy, Michael 11
Dugyala, Rishika 170
Dukakis, Michael 11, 63
Dunleavy, Mike 93
Dunn, Reagan 44
Durbin, Dick 128
Durkan, Jenny 40
Durst, Branden 37
Dyer, Caleb Q. 77

Ebke, Laura 96
Education Party 187
Egan, Paul 73
Electoral College 23, 25–26, 28, 111, 123, 151, 183; electoral votes 24–27, 183, 190–194
Employment Party 46
Enten, Harry 164
Erickson, Betsy 92
Everett, Burgess 135

Facebook 17, 31, 101
factcheck.org 135
Fair Vote 69
faithless electors 25
Fandos, Nicholas 129
Farley, Patricia 77, 95
Farmer-Labor Party 55, 60–61, 73
Fauchi, Anthony 174

Index

FDFR Party 47
Federal Bureau of Investigation (FBI) 1, 9, 135, 143–144, 154–155
Federal Communications Commission (FCC) 119, 121
Federal Election Commission (FEC) 90, 115–118, 123, 184
Federalists 3–4, 50, 53, 57
Feinstein, Diane 49, 129–132, 143
Ferguson, Robert 44
filibuster 128
Financial Times 158
fivethirtyeight.com 168
Flaherty, Joseph 66
Flake, Jeff 135
Floyd, George 177–179
Flynn, Michael 154
Ford, Christine Blasey 129–135
Ford, Gerald 9–10, 13, 120, 122
Forgey, Quint 170
Fox News 21–22, 153, 190–191
foxnews.com 135, 153
fox17.com (Nashville) 83
Free Soil Party 50, 54
Freedom Socialist Party 47

Gadell-Newton, Constance 80, 97
Gallego, Ruben 99
Gallup 8, 126, 171–172
Gardner, Will 111
Garland, Merrick 180–181
Gehl, Katherine M. 125
Gentzkow, Matthew 14
Gerry, Elbridge 109
gerrymandering 109–111
Gerzon, Mark 16–17, 110; see also *The Reunited States of America*
Gilded Age 55
Gingrich, Newt 13–15
Ginsburg, Ruth Bader 180–182
Giuliani, Rudy 166
Glover, Don 105
Goehner, Chris 32, 92
Goehner, Keith 30, 32–33
Goldstein-Rose, Solomon Israel 102
Goldwater, Barry 120, 135
Gomes, Ed 67
Goode, Virgil 55–56
Goodman, Carolyn 63
Goodspaceguy 46–47, 187
GOPAC 14
Gore, Al 118, 189–192
Gorsuch, Neil 127–128, 180
Gorton, Slade 46
Goston, Charles 106
government shutdowns 15, 138–142, 166
Graham, David A. 146
Graham, Lindsey 143
Grassley, Charles 132
Graveline, Chris 73, 97

Graves, William 54
Gray, Rick 66, 99
Green, Al 154–155
Green, Angela 99
Green Independent Party (Maine) 100
Green Party 46–47, 49, 66–74, 78–81, 83–88, 93–94, 96–97, 99–106, 112, 118, 183–184, 186, 189
Greenback Party 55, 58
Greening, Jesse "JD" 30–33
Grenn, Jason 66, 94
Grenoble, Ryan 168
Griffin, Robert 109
Grim, Ryan 129
Gross, Al 184
The Guardian 1, 141, 164
Gunderson, Dan 169

Halverson, Marti 88, 94
Hamilton, Alexander 3–4
Hammons, Bill 67
Hannon, Sara 94
Haque, Asim 80, 96
Harrington, Ricky 185
Harris, Kamala 154
Harvard Business School 125
Hathaway, William 52
The Havre Herald 75
Hawkins, Howie 183
Hayes, Teresea "Terry" 72, 100
Hazel, Shane 185
Helker, Scott 67
Hickel, Walley 58
The Hill 145
Hirsch, E.D., Jr. 17; see also *Cultural Literacy*
Hoffer, Doug 85, 101
Holman, Craig 169
Holmes, Kristen 193
Hoover, Herbert 13
Horsley, Scott 128–129
Horton, Willie 11
Hospers, John 25
House Intelligence Committee 157, 159–162, 164, 166–168
House Judiciary Committee 1, 127, 143, 146, 169
House of Representatives, as arbiter of elections 26–27
Human Rights Party 47
Humphrey, Hubert III 62
Hurley, Lawrence 181
Hutchison, Susan 47–48, 90

impeachment 15, 142, 152, 154–156, 158–161, 163–166, 168–173, 195
Independence Party 74, 79, 101
Independence Party of Minnesota 61, 73
Independent American Party 77, 84
"Independent Democrats" 37, 78

Independent Party 47–48; voter confusion 48
Independent Party of Connecticut 67
Independent Party of Louisiana, 71; voter confusion 71
Independent Party of Oregon 81, 93; voter confusion 81
"Independent Republicans" 37–38, 187
"independent" voters 1–2, 7–8, 19–21, 109, 126, 133–134, 136, 165, 171–172
"independents" caucusing with major parties 52, 55, 65–66, 72, 77–78, 94–95, 100, 107, 113, 136, 138, 186
independentarkansas.com 66
The Intercept 129
Ipsos.com 168
Iran-Contra 10, 55
Irvine, Travis 80, 97
Ismail, Aymann 177

Jackson, Andrew 4, 26
Jacoby, Jeff 150–151
Jaeger, Al 110–111
Jahn, Cheri 67, 95
Jamison, Dennis 4
January 6, 2021 194–196
Jarvis, Gilletta 101
Jayapal, Pramila 91
Jefferson, Thomas 25–26, 50
Jenkins, Michael 182
Jenkins, Will 44
Jeter, Jon 61–62
Johnson, Bob 186
Johnson, David 70, 96
Johnson, Gary 78, 98, 184
Johnson, Lyndon B. 120
Jones, John Edward 60
Jones, Paul 95
Jorgensen, Jo 183, 186
Joseph, George W. 60
judicial politics 42–43, 62, 65–66, 97, 104
"jungle" primary *see* top-two primary

Kasich, John 80
Kavanaugh, Brett 127–136, 138, 141, 163, 171
Keiser, Karen 37
Keller, Craig 91
Kemp, Brian 68
Kennedy, Anthony 127–128
Kennedy, John F. 119–120
KFSM/KXNW-TV 105
Kiefer, Eric 77
Kim Jong Un 143, 152
King, Angus 52, 71, 100, 113, 136, 138
Kirby, Jen 158
Kistner, Tyler 185
Knecht, Kathy 66, 99
Know Nothing Party 54
Kruse, Michael 135

Kruzel, John 143–144
Kushner, Jared 155

La Follette, Philip 58
La Follette, Robert 24
"Language: A Key Mechanism of Control" 14
Lara, Richard 93
Larsen, Rick 49, 91
Lea, Andrea 105
League of Women Voters 121–123
Legalize Marijuana Now Party 185
Leahy, Patrick 129
Levinthal, Dave 117
Lewis, John 150
Libertarian Party 24–25, 28, 35–37, 44, 46–47, 49, 65–74, 76–81, 83–89, 91–105, 136, 148, 183–187
Libertarian Party of Arkansas 105, 184
Libertarian Party of Kentucky 71
Libertarian Party of Minnesota 73
Libertarian Party of New Mexico 78
Libertarian Party of North Carolina 104
Linck, Fred 67
Lincoln, Abraham 51, 54, 119
Lindemuth, Jahna 65, 93
Liptak, Adam 181
Loeffler, Kelly 194
Longley, James 58
Los Angeles Times 4, 47–48, 116
Luke, Brian 91
Lutsenko, Yuriy 166

MacBride, Roger 25
Madison, John 50
Maguire, Joseph 157, 161–162
Make It Simple Party 78
Malarsie, Mary 67
Malebranche, Pierre 33–35, 91
Manafort, Paul 155
Manchin, Joe 135–136
Marino, Joseph 71
Marist Poll 165
Martin, Rachel 174
Masket, Seth 107
McCain, John 17, 143
McCarthy, Kevin 153
McCluskey, Steve 74
McConnell, Mitch 169, 180, 182
McCoy, John 38
McElroy, Mark 66, 105
McGavick, Michael 46
McMillan, Jimmy 79
McQueen, Matthew 99
Meehan, Mary 115, 118
Mei, Lily 63
Meier, Julius 60
Mejia, Kenneth 93
Methow Valley News 187
Miller, David 87–88, 95

Miller, Greg 157
Milligan, Susan 184, 191
Mills, Janet 100
Minneapolis *Star Tribune* 185
Mitchell, Rachel 130–134
mlive.com 149
Moderate Party 82
Moe, Alex 164
Monchil, Russ 74
Mondale, Walter 121
Montgomery County Sentinel 103
Moon, Cary 40
Morning Consult 174
Morrisey, Patrick 136
Morrison, Tim 168
Morse, Wayne 52
Mother Jones 13
Mountain Party 86
MSNBC 139
Mueller, Robert 21, 142–146; Mueller report 142–146, 148, 152–154, 156
Murad, Yusra 174
Murkowski, Lisa 135–136
Murray, Ed 40
Murray, Patty 45
Myers, John 48

Nader, Ralph 118–119, 169, 189–190
Nadler, Gerrold 143
Nanna, Dustin 80
National Public Radio (NPR) 128, 165, 167, 174
National Republicans 4–5
Natural Law Party 73
New Day NJ Party 78
The New York Times 10, 52, 129, 145, 155–156, 181
The New Yorker 134
Nguyen, Tina 1
Nineteenth Amendment 121
Nirenberg, Ron 63
Nixon, Richard 8–9, 13, 25, 109, 119–120, 122
Nonpartisan League (North Dakota) 58
nonpartisan offices 2, 39–43, 62, 66, 69, 73–74, 76, 84, 87, 89, 93, 96–97, 102
nonpartisan primaries 68
Norris, George 52
North Carolina Constitution Party 79
North Dakota Democratic-Nonpartisan League Party 79, 111
Nullifier Party 51, 53–54
Nunes, Devin 162

Obama, Barack 16, 40, 127, 138, 170, 180–181
Obamacare 29, 150
Olson, Floyd B. 60–61
Omaha World-Herald 96
open primary system 73–74, 124
Operation Warp Speed 176–177
Opposition Party 54

Orman, Greg 7–8, 70, 97, 108, 116, 118–119, 123, 125; *see also A Declaration of Independents*
O'Rourke, Beto 84, 98
Ortiz, Daniel 66, 94
Ossoff, Jon 185, 194

Pacific Standard 107, 110
Palivos, Anastasia 96
Panama 11
patch.com 77
PBS 13, 121–122, 128, 159, 165
Peace and Freedom Party 67
Pecorin, Allison 157
Pelosi, Nancy 139–140, 142, 153, 158–159, 163, 169
Pence, Mike 194
Pengelly, Martin 164
Penrose, Drew 69–70
Perdue, David 185, 194
Perot, Ross 23–24, 61, 119, 123–124
Persian Gulf 11; First Gulf War 12
Perticone, Joe 136
Petersen, Matthew S. 117
Peterson, Collin 169
Peterson, Peter G. 108–109; *see also Running on Empty*
petitioning 67–68, 73–74, 77, 79–80, 82–84, 86, 97, 111, 125
Pettigrew, Scott 80
Pew Research Institute 19–20, 165
Pham, Savio 37–38
Phillips, Rupert "Rupie" 86
Phinney, Brandon 77, 101
Pinkney, Charles 26
Pirate Party 73
Pizza Party 73
Pluecker, William 186
Poizner, Steve 67, 93
Politi, James 158–159
political action committees (PACs) 29–30, 32, 34–37, 40–43, 63, 86, 115–116
Politico 135, 170, 174
Pondiscio, Robert 17
popular vote 23–26, 57
Populist Party 7–8, 43–44, 51, 55, 58–60
Poroshenko, Petro 159
Porter, Michael E. 125
Portland Tribune 81
Pramuk, Jacob 141
presidential election, 1800 26; 1804 26; 1824 26; 1860 119; 1960 119–120; 1980 10, 27; 1988 11; 2000 118–119
Presley, Elvis 105
Priorities USA 191
Progressive Party 7–8, 24, 55, 58, 63, 81, 187
Prohibition Party 58, 73
Public Citizen 169
Purdue University 119

Quinnipiac University 131–134, 136
Quiroa, David A., Jr. 82, 102
Quiroa, David A., Sr. 82, 102

Raffensperger, Brad 192–194
ranked-choice voting system 72
Rasmussen, Sara 94
Readjuster Party 51
Reagan, Ronald 9–11, 27, 121–122
Reconstruction 51, 54–55, 58–59
Reform Party 24, 46, 61, 73–74, 124, 189–190
Reichert, David 91
Reisman, John P. 36, 112; *see also* Centrist Party
Rent Is Too Damn High Party 79
Republican National Convention 9–10, 24
Republican Party, establishment of 2, 5, 12, 51, 53–54
The Reunited States of America 16, 110; *see also* Gerzon, Mark
Rev.com 176, 194
Reykdal, Chris 43
Richard, Jerome 71
Richards, Janis 84
Ringelstein, Zak 100
Rittereiser, Jason 49
Roberts, Jeannie 105
Roberts, Victoria 73
Robinson, Shane 103
Robinson, William 67
Rogers, John 43
Rollins, Thomas M. 27
Romney, Mitt 95, 170–171
Roosevelt, Theodore 24
Roscoe, Jim 88, 94
Rosenstein, Rod 144
Rossi, Dino 45, 49, 91
Rubio, Marco 58
Running on Empty 108; *see also* Peterson, Peter G.
Rushford, James W. 132
Ryu, Cindy 36

Sadler, Reinhold 60
St. Cloud Times 177
Salzer, James 14
Samuels, Alex 83–84
San Diego Union-Tribune 48
Sanders, Bernie 23, 52, 55, 84, 101, 113, 136, 138, 184
Savage, Charlie 145
Sawyer, David 37
Scalia, Anton 127, 181
Schaefer, Charles 37
Schallhorn, Kaitlyn 135
Schiff, Adam 157–164, 168–169
Schlakman, Ian 104
Schmidt, Michael S. 129
Schneider, Gregory S. 86
school boards 41–42, 66, 69, 74, 98

Schrier, Kim 49, 91
Schumer, Charles (Chuck) 139, 169
Seattle People's Party 187
Seattle politics 40
Seattle Times 19, 36–37, 40
Senate Judiciary Committee 127, 129–135, 143, 145
Seventeenth Amendment 50–51
Shabad, Rebecca 146, 164
Shamsian, Jacob 192
Shapard, Virginia 13
Sherman, Brad 154–155
Sheth, Sonam 192
Shokin, Viktor 158
Shortstop Party 187
Sibilia, Laura 186
Silver Party 58, 60
Silverman, Elissa 88, 104
Sioux Falls *Argus Leader* 83
Sivertsen, Bob 74–75
slate.com 132, 177
Slaughter, Michelle 97
Smith, Harri Anne 65
Smith, Joshua 35
Smith, Keith 36–37
Smith, Michelle R. 82
Smith, Samantha 19–20
Sneve, Joe 83
Snowe, Olympia 52
Socialist Action 67
Socialist Party 73, 187
Soleimani, Qasem 173
Sondland, Gordon 171
Soon-Shiong, Patrick 48
South Dakota Libertarian Party 73
Soviet Union 11, 166–167
Spangler, Todd 149–150
Stallcop, Joseph P. 77
Stand Up America Party 47
Stang, John 29, 33
Stanton, Greg 66
Stein, Jill 184
Stonier, Monica 35
Stop the Insanity Party 78
straight-ticket voting 16
Strand, Ginger 110
Strauss, Valerie 41
Strider, Dave 48
Strzok, Peter 1, 127
Subramanian, Courtney 168
Sukharev, Nickolai 103
Sullivan, Dan 184
Sullivan, John J. 167
Supreme Court *see* United States Supreme Court
Swing, Gary 99

Tacoma *News Tribune* 34
Taft, William Howard 24
Tappan, Levi 99

Index

Tarleton, Gael 36
taxes 7, 8, 10, 12, 15, 34, 37–38, 61, 140
Taylor, Scott 86
Texas Green Party 84
Texas Tribune 83–84
Thiele, Fred 78, 101
Thomas, Nick 67
Thomas, Rick 37
Thompson, Derek 14–15
Thomson-DeVeaux, Amelia 168
Thurmond, Strom 24
Time 11, 120, 166
top-two primary 20, 33, 43–44, 67, 71, 76, 90, 93, 125
Torres, Angel 66, 99
Totenberg, Nina 181
Tower, Mark 149
Trautwein, Catherine 128
Tribe, Lawrence H. 27
Trumbull, Joshua 44
Trump, Donald 1, 14, 47, 70, 91, 96, 98, 117, 127–128, 132, 134–135, 138–146, 148–174, 176–177, 180–184, 187, 189–197
Trump, Donald, Jr. 155–156
Turley, John 170
Twelfth Amendment 25–26
Twitter 150, 153, 155–156, 168, 170–171

Ukraine 1, 156–161, 166–168, 170, 194
Uncle Mover 49, 91
Unionist Party 51, 54
Unite America 19, 66, 72, 78, 95, 98, 100, 111, 113–114
United States Constitution 8, 25–26, 50, 146, 169, 181
United States Supreme Court 51, 127–129, 131–132, 135, 180–182, 189–190
United Utah Party 84
Unity Party of America 67
Unity Restoration Party 187
U.S. News & World Report 184
US Taxpayers Party 73

Vaillancourt, Cory 79
Vance, Chris 29–30, 33, 45, 92, 188
Van Drew, Jefferson 169
Vanity Fair 1
Ventura, Jesse 61–62, 73, 119, 183
Vermont Progressive Party 84–85, 101
Veselnitskaya, Natalia 155–156
Vietnam War 8–9, 55, 61
Vindman, Alexander 167–168, 170–171
Virginia Department of Elections 85–86
Voter Study Group 109
voter.votewa.gov 187
vox.com 135, 157, 183

Waite, Davis Hanson 59–60
Walker, Bill 58, 65, 93
The Wall Street Journal 158
Wallace, Chris 190
Wallace, George 24–25, 47
Walther, Steve 117
Wang, Kun 37
Warnock, Raphael 194
Warren, Elizabeth 49
Washington, George 3–4; Farewell Address 4
Washington Education Association 30, 41
Washington Independents (political action committee) 29, 45, 92, 187–188
The Washington Post 12, 41, 55, 61, 86, 129–131, 151, 157–158, 193
Washington State Legislature 19–21, 28–30, 33–38, 187–188
Washington State Public Disclosure Commission 34, 187
Washington Times 4
Watergate 8–9, 55
wdtv.com 86
Weathers, Tricia 83
Webley, Kayla 120
Webster, Steven 16
Weeks, Adam 185
Weicker, Lowell 58
Weigle, C. Keiki Stacy 31–33
Welch, Matt 101
Wells, Laura 93
West, Kanye 183
Wheaton, Sarah 127
Wheelan, Charles 111–114; *see also* Centrist Manifesto
Whig Party 4–5, 50, 53–54, 57
Whipps, Susannah 102, 186
Wilke, Christina 168
Williams, Thelda 66
Wilson, Woodrow 24
Wisconsin Conservation Congress 87, 96
Woodward, Bob 173–174
Working Class Party 73
Working Families Party 67, 81
write-in candidates 68, 72, 74, 82
Wyman, Kim 29, 48

Yeutter, John 98
Yovanovitch, Marie 166–167
Yuhas, Alan 159

Zeitlin, Matthew 132
Zelenskiy, Volodymyr 156–161, 167–168, 171, 194
Zimmerman, Jonathan 4
Zuckerman, David 85, 101